Rethinking Joseph Conrad's
Concepts of Community

Also available from Bloomsbury

Conrad, Faulkner, and the Problem of NonSense, Maurice Ebileeni
Conrad's Heart of Darkness, Allan Simmons
Conrad's 'Heart of Darkness' and Contemporary Thought, Nidesh Lawtoo

Rethinking Joseph Conrad's Concepts of Community

Strange Fraternity

Kaoru Yamamoto

Bloomsbury Academic
An imprint of Bloomsbury Publishing Plc

B L O O M S B U R Y

LONDON · OXFORD · NEW YORK · NEW DELHI · SYDNEY

Bloomsbury Academic

An imprint of Bloomsbury Publishing Plc

50 Bedford Square	1385 Broadway
London	New York
WC1B 3DP	NY 10018
UK	USA

www.bloomsbury.com

BLOOMSBURY and the Diana logo are trademarks of Bloomsbury Publishing Plc

First published 2017

© Kaoru Yamamoto, 2017

British Library Cataloguing-in-Publication Data
A catalogue record for this book is available from the British Library.

ISBN: HB: 978-1-4742-5002-3
ePDF: 978-1-4742-5004-7
ePub: 978-1-4742-5003-0

Library of Congress Cataloging-in-Publication Data
A catalog record for this book is available from the Library of Congress.

Cover design: Eleanor Rose
Cover image © Private Collection/Bridgeman Images

Typeset by Newgen Knowledge Works (P) Ltd., Chennai, India
Printed and bound in Great Britain

To find out more about our authors and books visit www.bloomsbury.com. Here you will find extracts, author interviews, details of forthcoming events and the option to sign up for our newsletters.

Contents

Acknowledgments

I am grateful to the Ministry of Education, Culture, Sports, Science, and Technology in Japan (Grant No. 24520301) and the University of Shiga Prefecture for providing me with generous financial assistance that allowed me to conduct research and present papers at conferences. My thanks are also due to friends and colleagues who gave invaluable advice and comments on earlier versions of my essays, specifically to Professor Nicholas Royle, without whose initial suggestion this project would not have commenced. Finally, my enduring respect and gratitude go to Minoru Kuriyama, professor emeritus at Osaka City University and the University of Shiga Prefecture.

I would like to express my thanks to the editors and the publishers for permission to reprint, in revised form, material that was first published as follows:

Chapter 1, "Rescuing the Singular Plurality in Joseph Conrad," *Academic Reports of the University Center for Intercultural Education, the University of Shiga Prefecture*, vol. 14 (Hikone: University Center for Intercultural Education, 2009), 91–101.

Chapters 2, 3, and 5 formed chapters in Kaoru Yamamoto, *Jiko no muko e: Konraddo no chutanpen shosestu wo yomu* (*Beyond Self: Readings of Conrad's Novellas and Short Stories*) (Okayama: Daigaku kyouiku shuppan, 2012), 24–37; 38–53; 76–91.

Chapter 4, "Hospitality in 'The Secret Sharer,'" in *Wine in Old and New Bottles: Critical Paradigms for Joseph Conrad*, vol. 23 of Conrad: Eastern and Western Perspectives series, ed. Wiesław Krajka (Boulder, CO: East European Monographs; Lublin: Maria Curie-Skłodowska University Press; New York: Columbia University Press, 2014), 253–268.

Chapter 7, "'The Warrior's Soul' and the Question of Community," *The Conradian: The Journal of the Joseph Conrad Society (UK)* 35. 1 (Spring 2010): 78–91.

Chapter 9, "'Strange Fraternity' in *The Rover*," *L'Epoque Conradienne: Journal of the French Conrad Society*, 38 (2013): 103–117.

Chapter 10, "Toward a Possible Partage of Memory: 'History' and 'Solidarity'" in *Suspense, Solidarity, Memory and Identity* (Newcastle upon Tyne: Cambridge Scholars, 2015), 258–269.

Versions of Chapters 6 and 8 were read as presentations at the annual conferences of Joseph Conrad Society of Japan (Tokyo, 2013) and the Joseph Conrad Society (UK) (London, 2015).

Introduction

This book aims to reevaluate Joseph Conrad's underestimated later works by rethinking his ideas of community as "strange fraternity"—a new friendship that cannot simply be categorized as a nostalgic evocation of a traditional organic community of sailors or warriors. Conrad uses the expression "strange fraternity" in his last completed novel *The Rover* (1923), set in the south of France during the Napoleonic era, referring to the piratical Brothers of the Coast (to which the old rover Peyrol once belonged) as contrasted with the French Revolution idea of Fraternity (from which the protagonist has been away, roving the seas for more than forty years).[1] Conrad's engagement with the strangeness of community, however, can be neither confined to nor even begun with *The Rover*; rather, it runs through the entirety of his works in the manner of "something evermore about to be,"[2] in a constant dialogue with his subjectivist perspective, to the extent that it sometimes makes his art of psychology look "uncongenial." My attempt to trace Conrad's persistent preoccupation with the strangeness of community therefore necessarily entails some preliminary investigation into the neglected vignettes, both in his earlier stories as well as in his canonical works like *Heart of Darkness* and "The Secret Sharer," in order to find out what leads to the notion of "strange fraternity" in his later stories.

Conrad's major works have been marked primarily by their sustained exploration into the nature of the self. But in his later works, Conrad ceases those psychological explorations that characterized his middle works, turning

---

[1] Joseph Conrad, *The Rover* (Oxford: Oxford University Press, 1992), 8. Further references to this edition are given parenthetically in the text.
[2] William Wordsworth, *The Prelude: A Parallel Text*, ed. J. C. Maxwell (Harmondsworth: Penguin, 1971), 238.

instead to human solidarity and the romantic love relationship between men and women, which Thomas Moser famously termed "the uncongenial subject" in his influential book *Joseph Conrad: Achievement and Decline*.[3] Moser thus established the image of Conrad the misogynist and also consolidated his artistic decline with *Chance* (1913), his first commercial success after nearly twenty years as a writer. The idea of Conrad's later deterioration, or the "achievement and decline" paradigm, has been echoed by numerous other critics who identify a radical shift in subject from the private to the public and continue to privilege his art of psychology and thus perpetuate the subject-orientation of the thesis. In *Conrad and Impressionism*, John G. Peters, for example, repeatedly stresses Conrad's affirmation of human individual subjectivity as an impressionist response to ethical anarchy in an irrational and indifferent universe.[4] More recently, Michael Levenson reasserts that the invention of Marlow as a characterized narrator is Conrad's most salient contribution to the ambitious work of modernist subjectivity.[5] Andrea White also lays out how Conrad's prose rendering of an individual consciousness was shaped under the influence of Walter Pater and Henry James in particular, thus firmly locating Conrad in the context of the contemporary Anglo-American literary modernism.[6]

While recent critical approaches, such as gender studies, postcolonialism, and new historicism, have been offering us new readings of Conrad's later work,[7] some critics, even in their challenge against the "tyranny" of the achievement and decline theory,[8] tend to repeat rather than reverse the paradigm by looking for psychological and moral complexity. Robert Hampson, for instance, defends melodrama in *The Arrow of Gold* (1919) as a means of "deeper psychological analysis" of Rita's personality.[9] Likewise, as I shall

---

[3] Thomas Moser, *Joseph Conrad: Achievement and Decline* (Cambridge, MA: Harvard University Press, 1957), 50–130.

[4] John G. Peters, *Conrad and Impressionism* (Cambridge: Cambridge University Press, 2001), 123–158.

[5] Michael Levenson, "Modernism," in *Joseph Conrad in Context*, ed. Allan H. Simmons (Cambridge: Cambridge University Press, 2009), 183.

[6] Andrea White, "Conrad and Modernism," in *A Historical Guide to Joseph Conrad*, ed. John G. Peters (Oxford: Oxford University Press, 2010), 163–196.

[7] To name but a few, Robert Hampson, *Joseph Conrad: Betrayal and Identity* (London: Macmillan, 1992); Susan Jones, *Conrad and Women* (Oxford: Oxford University Press, 1999); Andrew Michael Roberts, *Conrad and Masculinity* (Basingstoke, UK: Macmillan, 2000); and Richard Niland, *Conrad and History* (Oxford: Oxford University Press, 2010).

[8] We borrow the term, the "tyranny" of achievement and decline theory, from John A. Palmer, *Joseph Conrad's Fiction: A Study in Literary Growth* (Ithaca, NY: Cornell University Press, 1968), 265.

[9] Hampson, *Joseph Conrad*, 271.

discuss in Chapters 7 and 9, scholars have tried to find what motivates Peyrol's final commitment to the national cause in *The Rover* and Tomassov's mercy killing of the French officer who saved him from arrest in "The Warrior's Soul" even when Peyrol is, we are told, "a stranger" to "melancholy" as well as "introspection," and the old Russian narrator in "The Warrior's Soul" provides no satisfactory clues to his hero Tomassov's conduct.

If the idea of a unified, stable individual identity of a woman is assumed in Susan Jones's discussion of Conrad's exploration of the construction of "female identity" in fiction, as she puts it, then her otherwise ground-breaking challenge against the image of Conrad as a writer for men might sometimes look, at least to me, almost like a mere inversion of the hierarchy of the "identities" it seeks to subvert.[10] The captain's welcome of the mysterious stranger in "The Secret Sharer," which will be the focus of my discussion in Chapter 4, cannot wholly be explained in terms of a "willed" action issued from an actor's individual consciousness. The young captain welcomes Leggatt before he knows what he is up to, and it is an event that takes place beyond the interests of individual subjects. "The Secret Sharer," while recalling a biblical fratricide—the "brand of Cain" business[11]—surpasses conventional brotherhood in its enactment of an unconditionally welcoming gesture, placing the other's presence above the captain's responsibility to the community to which he belongs. The fellowship between the captain and Leggatt can neither be a simple adding together nor a juxtaposition of the "I" that is assumed to be responsible for "myself" and "my" action. Unconditional hospitality instead "excommunicates," as it were, both the captain and Leggatt, and they can no longer simply be taken as "members" of an organic society. But this departure, this partition or separation, can be regarded as what Jean-Luc Nancy would call "partage," or "sharing-out" in the double sense of the term.[12]

Their "strange fraternity" thus disrupts Conrad's image as a political conservative or reactionary. Conrad's ideas of community have generally been

---

10 Jones, *Conrad and Women*, 2, 223.

11 Joseph Conrad, "The Secret Sharer," *'Twixt Land and Sea* (London: Dent, 1966), 107. Further page references to this edition will be given parenthetically in the text, preceded by *TLS* where it might otherwise be unclear.

12 "Sharing out as parting" in Nancy's use, according to Derrida, first of all means participation, proximity, affinities, crossings, crossovers, and crossbreedings. It is, in Derrida, a sort of community or contempraneity of thinking, language, and discourse. See Jacques Derrida, *On Touching—Jean-Luc Nancy*, trans. Christine Irizarry (Stanford: Stanford University Press, 2005), 218–219.

considered politically conservative for his belief in the organic unity of a nation created by its history and folk tradition.[13] Emphasizing Conrad's awareness of the social unit's priority to the individual self, Avrom Fleishman places Conrad in the organist political tradition of Edmund Burke,[14] whereas Ian Watt sees something of a Nietzschean reactionary equation of altruism, pity, and decadence as the "lamentable historical results of Christianity"[15] in the crew's pity for James Wait and his influence on them in *The Nigger of the "Narcissus"* (1897). According to Watt, the increasing sensitivity to other's sufferings in the novella makes it more and more difficult to maintain the cohesion of the social order.[16] Indeed, Conrad's letters and essays show his critique of contemporary social–democratic ideas and his expectation that England will be "the only barrier to the pressure of infernal doctrines born in continental back-slums."[17] Democracy, he also writes, referring to the 1885 General Election results in Britain, "has elected to pin its faith to the supremacy of material interests."[18] However, just as Zdzisław Najder points to the difficulty of defining Conrad's politics, he is at once traditionalist and revolutionary,[19] conservative and deeply egalitarian and individualist, although not democratic. This conflict, according to Watt,[20] is evident even in *The Nigger of the "Narcissus,"* a story that could be read as a reflection of Conrad's conservatism in its praise of solidarity and collective identity—a novella in which selfishness is apparently subordinated in the end by communal duty. It seems that the individual is not necessarily an antithesis of the collective in Conrad's notion of "community." Rather, being is singularly plural, to borrow Jean-Luc Nancy's phrase,[21] undermining the dichotomy between individuality and collectivity.

---

[13]   Allan H. Simmons, "Politics," in *Joseph Conrad in Context*, 196–197.
[14]   Avrom Fleishman, *Conrad's Politics: Community and Anarchy in the Fiction of Joseph Conrad* (Baltimore: John's Hopkins Press, 1967), 51–77.
[15]   Ian Watt, *Conrad in the Nineteenth Century* (Berkeley and Los Angeles: University of California Press, 1979), 111.
[16]   Watt, *Conrad in the Nineteenth Century*, 109–115.
[17]   Joseph Conrad, *The Collected Letters of Joseph Conrad*, vol. 1, ed. Frederick Karl and Laurence Davies (Cambridge: Cambridge University Press, 1987–2007), 16.
[18]   Joseph Conrad, "Autocracy and War," *Notes on Life and Letters* (London: Dent, 1949), 107.
[19]   Zdzisław Najder, "Conrad and Rousseau: Concepts of Man and Society," in *Joseph Conrad: A Commemoration*, ed. Norman Sherry (London: Macmillan, 1976), 77–90. According to Najder, the dominant trends of nineteenth-century Polish political thought are at the same time traditionalist in their belief in the restoration of national independence and progressive in Polish leadership in international radical movements (ibid., 88–89). Likewise, concerning the nuances of Conrad's politics, see Simmons, "Politics," 195–203.
[20]   Watt, *Conrad in the Nineteenth Century*, 110.
[21]   Cf. Jean-Luc Nancy, *Being Singular Plural*, trans. Robert D. Richardson and Anne E. O'Byrne (Stanford, CA: Stanford University Press, 2000).

At a time when much of the serious fiction being written in England was concerned with social issues while the solipsism was an important part of the cultural atmosphere of the 1890s,[22] the "leap" into an individual consciousness[23] by the author was indeed a unique project[24] that distinguished his writing from that of many of his Edwardian contemporaries.[25] This leap did actually make him a precursor of early modernism or one of the greatest masters of what Ian Watt calls "subjective impressionism."[26] The historical Joseph Conrad (like many of us perhaps) desperately needed the affirmation of human subjectivity and solidarity, believing in man's rootedness in a society. But Conrad's writing, as this little book tries to show, radically undermines the idea of self, gesturing toward the "strange fraternity" that might not be known even to the author himself.[27] Just as the young captain's welcome of Leggatt is an event that goes beyond self-interest, the short story "The Secret Sharer" in itself was a "mysterious arrival" for Conrad amid the agonizing writing process of *Under Western Eyes* (1911), and he accepted it before he was aware of this, just as the young captain did the stranger. Therefore, to reevaluate Conrad's neglected later works not so much through reinstating his later affirmation of communal values, which is inseparably combined with the idea of his creative energy being exhausted, as through going beyond the dichotomy between individuality and collectivity, I would like to read beyond the authorial intention and

---

[22] Watt, *Conrad in the Nineteenth Century*, 172.

[23] Michael Levenson, *A Genealogy of Modernism: A Study of English Literary Doctrine 1908–1922* (Cambridge: Cambridge University Press, 1984), 6.

[24] See Peters's introduction to *A Historical Guide to Joseph Conrad*, 5.

[25] White, "Conrad and Modernism," 167.

[26] As Eloise Knapp Hay and other critics remark, the definition of artistic movements can be arbitrary and sometimes even contradictory, surpassing the scope of this little book. See, Eloise Knapp Hay, "Proust, James, Conrad, and Impressionism," *Style*, vol. 22, no. 3 (Fall 1988): 368–381; Adriaan de Lange, "Conrad and Impressionism: Problems and (Possible) Solutions," in *Conrad's Literary Career*, ed. Keith Carabine, Owen Knowles, and Wiesław Krajka (Boulder, CO: East European Monographs; Lublin, Poland: Maria Curie-Skłodowska University Press; New York: Columbia University Press, 1992), 21–40. Vol. 1 of *Conrad: Eastern and Western Perspectives*, ed. Wiesław Krajka, 23 vols. to date, 1992–. But as long as they refer to the interest in individual psychology and in the foregrounding of subjective consciousness rather than external action, I use the terms impressionism or modernism based on the idea that impressionism, as White succinctly put it drawing on Matz, was "an important chapter in modernism's genealogy," occupying a midpoint between romantic unities and modernist fragmentation. See White, "Conrad and Modernism," 166 and Jesse Matz, *Literary Impressionism and Modernist Aesthetics* (Cambridge: Cambridge University Press, 2001), 2.

[27] For a question of authorial blindness or ignorance, see Jacques Derrida, *Of Grammatology*, trans. Gayatri Chakravorty Spivak (Baltimore and London: Johns Hopkins University Press, 1997), 158; Nicholas Royle, *Jacques Derrida* (London and New York: Routledge, 2003), 18; Andrew Bennett, *The Author* (London and New York: Routledge, 2005), 82–83; Derek Attridge, *Reading and Responsibility: Deconstruction's Traces* (Edinburgh: Edinburgh University Press, 2010, 2011), 113; Derek Attridge, *Singularity of Literature* (London and New York: Routledge, 2004), 23–24. 73.

open a new discussion about Conrad's "community," posing the following question: "Who comes after the subject?"[28]

This book draws on elements of Continental thinkers like Jacques Derrida, Jean-Luc Nancy, and Hannah Arendt, whenever they seem to renew our understanding of the texts in question, believing that Conrad's "strange fraternity" interestingly resonates with their notion of "community" in its calling into question the Western metaphysics of the individual subject—the Western "I"/eye. My concern in this book, with its focus on "strange fraternity," is, nevertheless, not so much simply to argue against the model of Conrad's subjectivist art (which has its own merit and usefulness as mentioned earlier) or even to read Conrad philosophically, as to insist that there are some strange features about his engagement with fraternity that such subject-centered hegemonic theory has prevented from coming into "view," strangeness that interrupts his enterprise of visual impressionism conducted under the Western "I"/eye— by extension, as intellectual historian Martin Jay calls it, "scopic regimes of modernity."[29] Accordingly, my discussion pays more attention to what the "resonant" subject, marked by its property of penetration and ubiquity, hears and what is touched by the "I" in the surrender of the "I" to the other. Conrad's interests in aural and tactile perception that entails the other's presence inevitably gravitate him less toward a straightforwardly referential national history than toward a "history" as responsibility, a sense of "history" that is transcultural, transgenerational. Aurality and plasticity, recalling a "history" across time and space, reverberate in singular plurality, or "strange fraternity."

* * *

To introduce an idea of "who comes after the subject?" in Conrad, I begin Chapter 1 with his struggles in his earlier texts to "rescue" the singular plurality

---

[28]   We borrow the expression from Eduardo Cadava, Peter Connor, and Jean-Luc Nancy, ed. *Who Comes After the Subject?* (New York and London: Routledge, 1991). Andrea White's discussion of Conrad's susceptibility to the influences of "Anglo-American literary modernism" following her concise summary of European thought and literature might imply that Conrad criticism may not be too close to those Continental thinkers. See White, "Conrad and Modernism," 163. Regarding the remoteness of "continental" thought from the philosophy most often practiced in English-speaking countries, see Peter Fenves, "Foreword," *The Experience of Freedom*, by Jean-Luc Nancy, trans. Bridget McDonald (Stanford, CA: Stanford University Press, 1988), xiii. For Continental philosophy as one expression of the cultural divide between the Continental and "the English-speaking world," see Simon Critchley, *Continental Philosophy: A Very Short Introduction* (Oxford: Oxford University Press, 2001).
[29]   Martin Jay, "Scopic Regimes of Modernity," in *Vision and Visuality*, ed. Hal Foster (Seattle: Bay Press, 1988), 3–23.

without the strictures of identity. As Conrad sometimes compares "the creative art of a writer of fiction" with "rescue work," his narrative only occasionally directs us beyond the literal rescue of individual fictional characters in distress, to the rescue of the singular plural being. By considering Conrad's sustained but struggling engagement with strange plurality beyond the classical, preexisting association of individual subjects, this chapter hopes to suggest by way of conclusion that the subjective, impressionistic treatment of experience (framing a subjective experience seen from an individual point of view) might have been more "uncongenial" to Conrad than the love relationship, which can also be rethought as a question of community in Nancy's terms.

In Chapters 2 and 3, I consider the rescue work I undertake in Chapter 1 in terms of a question of voice and hearing. In Chapter 2, I try to show how the deaf Russian sailor, Wamibo, helps the "we" narrator in his shaping impressionist "I" narration toward the story's end by giving the sailor a space that is "safe" from all those "distracting" noises filling the text of *The Nigger of the "Narcissus."* Despite faithfulness to the "visible universe" declared in the preface, this tale of the sea is, as we are made to notice, full of explosive voices and sound, thereby disclosing that the narrator/author is, in fact, more faithful to, or even obsessive about, the audible universe. The text's aural obsession makes the deaf man's presence among the uproarious crew all the more conspicuous even when Wamibo sits beside them staring vacant and dreamy. Wamibo's deafness occupies an important, while minor, part in the perception of the first person plural narrator "we," in facilitating the "we" narrator to concentrate on the visible universe by turning a deaf ear, as it were, to the racket that may sometimes recall the Russian experiences of the author.

In Chapter 3 I demonstrate that Marlow's ear strains toward something singularly plural, by paying particular attention to the resonant nature of the sonorous in *Heart of Darkness*. With his head full of strange voices and sounds from afar, Marlow's "resonant self" (to borrow Nancy's phrase) is spaced, returning to himself not simply as the same but rather as an echo, thereby opening a possible space, inseparably both his and the other's. Thus Marlow's narrative exploration into the heart of darkness, despite his apparent effort to register subjective visual experience, cannot always be subsumed under the terminology of an individual point of view, as his "subject" of listening is hardly objectified, spreading and reverberating through space.

In Chapter 4, by rethinking the captain's welcoming gesture as unconditional hospitality, I propose to read "The Secret Sharer," which has so far been read mainly as the story of "a metaphorical journey towards knowing oneself," less as a story of self-reflection than as that of externally oriented desire to go beyond the self, to speak and give to the other. More than a story "about" hospitality, "The Secret Sharer" is a pivotal work among Conrad's oeuvre in its enactment of welcoming the other—the very condition of community, or strange fraternity.

Chapter 5 supplements Chapter 4's discussion of unconditional hospitality with an examination of the two important but slightly overlooked vignettes of the miserable scorpion and the captain's floppy white hat, in terms of memory premised on the concept of an individual subject. The vignettes of the scorpion drowning in the chief mate's inkwell and the captain's last-minute gift of the hat to Leggatt have to date been discussed separately by mainstream critics, but the forgetfulness in both vignettes curiously synchronizes to undermine the notion of an individual subject as memory's owner. Thus echoing with each other in unconditional hospitality, that is, unexpected events not wholly available to subjective consciousness, these episodes evoke the connection of the question of memory, and by extension, the question of "history" and the singular plurality in Conrad's Napoleonic stories.

Chapter 6 rethinks Conrad's history not in terms of straightforward referentiality but in terms of responsibility, by reading "The Duel" as a story of response to the incessant call of the other. As more and more critics have recently emphasized the eccentricity of the duel between the two officers in Napoleon's Grand Army, their encounter, far from being banal, involving women from time to time, singularly occurs in a "most unsuitable ground" for a duel. One answers to/for the other's perpetual call, but he does so not from "the sympathy of mankind" but, on the contrary, in a fight, laying himself open to a "cut." The duelists' contest without end gestures toward the realm of the impossible and thereby ineluctably presents an aporia, a hole in the text. The "we" narrator, whom this chapter tries to show as deserving more critical attention, implicitly invites readers to draw an analogy between the wounds in the officers' bodies and the gaps in the body of Conrad's "archive" of the Napoleonic era, namely, the short story "The Duel." By way of conclusion, this chapter suggests tentatively linking the textual fissure and a "messianic" opening with the coming of the other to the text: Napoleon and the reader. Such hospitality, a welcome of the other, is what Derrida would think to be the very condition of "history."

"The Warrior's Soul" has been undervalued because of its anachronistic chivalry and apparent indifference to individual psychological tensions, but, in Chapter 7, by examining how self and other are enigmatically together while existing far apart and having little in common, I attempt to reassess "The Warrior's Soul" as a story of "another community." The narrator of this story has been criticized for his "inadequate powers of explanation" about the young hero Tomassov, but the aged Russian warrior, using "we" narration, is less pre-occupied with the protagonist's substantial identity than with the collective suffering of the nameless dead, the stragglers during Napoleon's retreat from Moscow. Far from mere anachronism, this chapter argues, "The Warrior's Soul" displays Conrad's later texts' departure from the traditional understanding of community as a preexisting efficient, organic group of individual subjects, exemplified by the community of soldiers or sailors.

Ever since gender approaches rediscovered *The Arrow of Gold* as an aesthetically self-conscious, modernist text rather than a pseudo-autobiography, there has been an increasing focus on the question of the gaze and Doña Rita's position as the object of male desire. Highlighting points in the text at which plastic imagination interrupts the visual to open a space for another perception of reality, Chapter 8, however, discusses that not only the visual reactions of a detached seer but also the tactile reactions toward Rita, the sensation of palpability felt by the sculptor toward his/her carving, are important in assessing the sense of reality and history in Conrad's later period. Unlike an art object's detached observer, such as the painter Henry Allègre, Monsieur George is often cast as a sculptor who attempts to approach, touch, and identify with Doña Rita. The artist's identification with the object entails not so much the other's appropriation into the self as his surrender of the "I" to the object (the other), an experience of plasticity that develops not through observation but through identification, thus showing, at this phase of Conrad's writing career, how far he is from subjective impressionism in his gesture toward a mode of writing history that aspires to plurality. Far from endorsing a reappropriating movement of self-presence, on the contrary, touch, be it contact, caress, or kiss, can interrupt "the mirror reflection" in its visual dimension.[30] As Nancy insists on the plural singularity at the moment of touching, being in touch with ourselves is what makes us "us";[31] touching is a question of "*contact* of the *with*

---

[30] Derrida, *On Touching—Jean-Luc Nancy*, 290.
[31] Nancy, *Being Singular Plural*, 13.

(*cum* or *co*-) with oneself as well as with the other, the *with* as contact, community as co-tact,"[32] that is, a thinking of an "inoperative community." It is a sharing out without fusion, a community without community, a language without communication, a being-with without confusion.[33] Thus, plastic imagination offers us a glimpse of the ways in which Conrad remembers the past, the ways that can also be linked to his engagement with plurality, a question of community in his later historical novels.

In an attempt to reassess Conrad's last completed novel, *The Rover*, most critics have tended to fill in the ellipses, looking into the motive of the protagonist characterized as a stranger to "melancholy" and "introspection." Instead of reiterating the totalitarian view of an individual self, Chapter 9 rethinks Peyrol's final commitment in terms of Hannah Arendt's political insight into an "action" and its potentialities for plurality. Peyrol's last voyage is more than a belated realization of himself in patriotism, as has been said by most scholars; rather, similar to Arendt's "action" that establishes relationships cutting across all boundaries, it incalculably occurs as a response to the call of the other, evoking the strange fraternity as is contrasted with the French Revolution's *fraternité*.

Lord Jim, for instance, a series of survivors' testimonies to a past traumatic event, can be better understood as a multilayered address to another, demanding a listening, than as a statement of an already given, empirical truth. Thinking thus of Conrad's "history" less as a matter of referentiality than of responsibility, the last chapter aims to show that his texts sometimes permit the possibility of "history" to emerge from the "solidarity" with the others. First, focusing on the traumatic aspects of Conrad's nostalgic recollection, we discuss that his texts are more concerned with the narrators' possession by the past than with the narrators' possession of the past. The subjective nature of Conrad's narrators' remembrance of the past has been highlighted, but they can neither fully represent their experiences nor claim the memories as their own; the experiences only repeat. We go on to link the notion of trauma with a history, drawing on Cathy Caruth who sees the possibility of "history," no longer straightforwardly referential, arising in the very way we are implicated in each other's traumas. The witnessing of the trauma, she asserts, can take place not simply within the individual but rather in cultures and in future generations.

---

[32] Derrida, *On Touching—Jean-Luc Nancy*, 115.
[33] Ibid., 195.

Rescuing the Singular Plurality

"Who Comes After the Subject?"

Joseph Conrad's major works, such as *Heart of Darkness*, are considered to be apocalyptically declaring the end of the human subject in its presentation of Kurtz, who "made that last stride" and "stepped over the edge" of humanity, summing up, "The horror!" in his extremity.[1] While those works have been taken as registering the modernist experience of dissolution of the individual self into a nullity,[2] the question "Who comes after the subject?" has barely been raised, revealing the haunting tenacity of the subject-centered paradigm in Conrad criticism.[3] Under this paradigm, Conrad's middle works presenting the moral agony of an isolated individual have long been more highly rated than his early and later romantic works. The relationship between men and women in his noncanonical works has been alleged to be "uncongenial"[4] to the so-called male-oriented author of nautical tales, but by employing this love relationship along with other relationships, as we shall see in what follows, Conrad, in those less studied works, explored the possibility of community that is not, as Nancy's, predicated on the idea of an individual subject. According to Nancy, community is

---

[1] Joseph Conrad, *Youth / Heart of Darkness / The End of the Tether* (London: Dent, 1967), 151. Further page references to *Heart of Darkness* and *Youth* will be given parenthetically in the text, preceded by *HD* and *Y* where it might otherwise be unclear.

[2] Seamus Dean, "Imperialism/Nationalism," in *Critical Terms for Literary Study*, ed. Frank Lentricchia and Thomas McLaughlin, 2nd ed. (1990: Chicago and London: University of Chicago Press, 1995), 355.

[3] For a discussion of the idea of the subject in Conrad from Derridean and gender approaches, see, for example, *Conrad in the Twenty-First Century: Contemporary Approaches and Perspectives*, ed. Carola M. Kaplan, Peter Lancelot, and Andrea White (New York and London: Routledge, 2005), 241–279. The primal concern, however, in a group of the essays in the section titled "Conrad and Subjectivity" is Conrad's complex construction of subjectivity.

[4] Moser, *Joseph Conrad*, 50–130.

not "the space of the *egos*" but of "the *I*'s that are not *egos*." It is not "a communion that fuses the *egos* into an *Ego* or a higher *We*."[5] A community, for
Nancy, is "not a project of fusion, or in some general way a productive or
operative project—nor is it a *project* at all."[6] A community in Nancy is thus
"inoperative," singularly plural, as we shall see again later in our discussion
of the Escampobar farm in *The Rover* in Chapter 9. In contrast to a classical
model of community, in which unity opposes plurality, Conrad's "we," like
Nancy's, is neither the adding together nor the juxtaposition of the "I"'s.[7]
Rather, his "community," in which unity is not necessarily opposed to plurality, anticipates Nancy's notion of the singularly plural.[8] This chapter will
trace Conrad's attempts in his earlier texts to "rescue" the singular plurality
without strictures of identity.

The rescue was a popular contemporary theme during the Victorian and
Edwardian eras, as is shown in Jefferson Hunter's reading of the Edwardian
canonical works of Henry James and E. M. Forster, in particular, as rescue
novels. Although there is no allusion to Conrad's work as a "rescue novel"
in Hunter's *Edwardian Fiction*,[9] the Polish author frequently turns to this
Victorian and Edwardian favorite theme in his earlier Malay novels and in

---

[5] Jean-Luc Nancy, *The Inoperative Community*, ed. Peter Connor, trans. Peter Connor, Lisa Garbus, Michael Holland, and Simona Sawhney (1991: Minneapolis and London: University of Minnesota Press, 2006), 15, in particular, and also see his *Being Singular Plural*.

[6] Nancy, *The Inoperative Community*, 15.

[7] Brian Richardson argues the radical dimension of Conrad's collective narration in his "Conrad and Posthumanist Narration: Fabricating Class and Consciousness Onboard the *Narcissus*," in *Conrad in the Twenty-First Century*, ed. Kaplan, Mallios, and White, 213–222, and also in his *Unnatural Voices: Extreme Narration in Modern and Contemporary Fiction* (Columbus: Ohio State University Press, 2006), 37–60. Unlike Nancy, however, Richardson regards Conrad's collectivity more as some-thing intersubjective than as something beyond the idea of an individual subject.

[8] J. Hillis Miller refers to Nancy's idea of "inoperative community" in his analysis of Conrad's fictional republic Sulaco as "noncommunity." Giving, however, "a somewhat different meaning from his [Nancy's] own" (as he says), Miller looks for the "villains" in the disastrous dislocation of commu-nity in *Nostromo* in his "'Material Interests': Conrad's *Nostromo* as a Critique of Global Capitalism," in *Joseph Conrad: Voice, Sequence, History, Genre*, ed. Jakob Lothe, Jeremy Hawthorn, and James Phelan (Columbus: Ohio State University, 2008), 160–177.

[9] For a discussion of the rescue as a contemporary popular theme, see for example, Jefferson Hunter, *Edwardian Fiction* (Cambridge, MA: Harvard University Press, 1982), 173–188. Hunter reads the Edwardian canonical works of Henry James and E. M. Forster as rescue novels in Chapter 12, "Continental Rescues and Autumnal Affairs," in which, however, he never mentions Conrad while he focuses on his adventure fiction primarily in Chapter 10, "Conrad and Adventure" (ibid., 124–152). For a postcolonial approach to the rescue theme, see Christopher GoGwilt, *The Invention of the West: Joseph Conrad and the Double-Mapping of Europe and Empire* (Stanford, CA: Stanford University Press, 1995), 67–87. Gary Geddes also approaches Conrad's later works in terms of imaginative rescue. See Gary Geddes, *Conrad's Later Novels* (Montreal: McGill-Queen's University Press, 1980), 11–40. But he highlights the romance pattern of the "rescue of the individual in dis-tress" (ibid., 5).

his later work, such as *Chance*. Yet, his narrative only occasionally directs us beyond the literal rescue of individual fictional characters in distress, to the rescue of the singular plural being. The prolonged composition process of *The Rescue: A Romance of the Shallows* (1920), which went on through almost his entire literary career, shows that the rescue theme is, in fact, his lifelong interest and he sometimes likens "the creative art of a writer of fiction" to "rescue work."[10] In considering his continued engagement with plurality beyond the classical, preexisting association of individual subjects, this chapter will suggest by way of conclusion that the subjective, impressionistic treatment of experience may be more "uncongenial" to Conrad than the love relationship, which is also a question of "community" in Nancy's terms.

* * *

Conrad's early novels, *Almayer's Folly* (1895), *An Outcast of the Islands* (1896), and *The Rescue*, which form a Malay trilogy, all feature a "rescuer," Captain Tom Lingard, an English trader. In *An Outcast of the Islands*, he twice rescues Peter Willems, a Dutch sailor. When Willems runs away as a boy from a Dutch ship, Lingard places him with a merchant as a clerk. Willems does well until he is sacked for stealing his employer's money to pay off gambling debts and is turned out of his house by his Malay wife. Just before Lingard fortuitously arrives to offer him a new post, Lingard's protégé Willems, with nowhere to go, feeling "as if he was the outcast of all humankind,"[11] contemplates suicide at the end of the jetty, as is symbolically presented in the following passage. This story has been read as a description of the extreme isolation of a white man, Willems. Yet what is to be rescued, as is shown in the quotation below, seems to be something more than a solitary subject:

> The end of the jetty; and here in one step more the end of life; the end of everything. Better so. What else could he [Willems] do? Nothing ever comes back. He saw it clearly. The respect and admiration of them all, the old habits and old affections finished abruptly in the clear perception of the cause of his disgrace. He saw all this; and for a time he came out of himself, out of his selfishness—out of the constant preoccupation of his interests and

[10] Joseph Conrad, "Henry James," in *Notes on Life and Letters* (London: Dent, 1949), 13.
[11] Joseph Conrad, *An Outcast of the Islands* (Oxford: Oxford University Press, 1992), 30. Further references to this edition are given in the text.

his desires—out of the temple of self and the concentration of personal thought. (30)

It is customary to see despair in this abysmal alienation from which Lingard is trying to rescue Willems as an individual soul; however, in this passage, Willems is not himself any more—with his being thrown out of himself. He is, in fact, in the very exteriority in which his being can hardly relate to itself. Indeed, the repetition of the possessive "his" all the more underscores that Willems is "miserable," dispossessed of everything he had, literally at "the end of his tether." But this is not as utterly hopeless as has been thought, because the repetition of the phrase "out of" might invite us to open up and come out of ourselves to reach toward something relational. In fact, this "self-outside-itself" is the location of what Nancy calls "the singular being," which is "the modern experience of community" with its lack of the characteristics or the structure of individuality.[12] We may then be allowed to read *An Outcast of the Islands* as opening the possibility of "community" rather than as a story of isolation of the self-deluded white man.

This aspect is further developed in Conrad's next published novella, which presents "a group of men held together by a common loyalty and a common perplexity in a struggle not with human enemies, but with the hostile conditions."[13] *The Nigger of the "Narcissus,"* begun as an escape from writing *The Rescue*, tells of the symbolic rescue of the only black sailor on board, James Wait. From the moment he first arrives late for a roll call, Wait provokes dissent and gradually infects the crew's spirit. He persistently malingers, predicting his imminent death, so that eventually the captain orders him to be confined to a deckhouse cabin. When the *Narcissus* is caught in a fierce storm, the crew desperately attempts to rescue him from his confinement. It is commonplace to see rescue in *The Nigger of the "Narcissus"* as one of the tests the crew "heroically" undergo during the journey from Bombay to England in the process of building solidarity and overcoming their selfishness.[14] The assumption here is the opposition of individuality against collectivity,[15] but a closer

---

[12] Nancy, *The Inoperative Community*, 18–19.
[13] Joseph Conrad, "Stephen Crane," *Tales of Hearsay and Last Essays* (London: Dent, 1963), 94.
[14] See, for example, Allan H. Simmons, *Joseph Conrad* (London: Macmillan, 2006), 55.
[15] See, in particular, Watt, *Conrad in the Nineteenth Century*, 94–125. This binary opposition is still taken for granted even in the Bakhtinian, postmodernist analysis by Bruce Henricksen, *Nomadic Voices: Conrad and the Subject of Narrative* (Urbana and Chicago: University of Illinois Press, 1992), 30–46. While invoking on the one hand the dichotomy of *Gemeinschaft* and *Gesellschaft*—traditional, face-to-face community with its emphasis on social cohesion versus modern mass

examination of the rescue scene reveals disruption of the binary opposition. What we see happening instead in the furious gale is, in effect, the indissociability of singularity from plurality:

> We staggered away from the door [of the deckhouse cabin], and, alarmed by a sudden roll, fell down in a bunch. It appeared to us that the side of the house was more smooth than glass and more slippery than ice. There was nothing to hang on to but a long brass hook used sometimes to keep back an open door. Wamibo [a Russian Finn sailor] held on to it and we held on to Wamibo, clutching our Jimmy. He had completely collapsed now. He did not seem to have the strength to close his hand. We stuck to him blindly in our fear.... We stood up surrounding Jimmy. We begged him to hold up, to hold on, at least. He glared with his bulging eyes, mute as a fish, and with all the stiffening knocked out of him. He wouldn't stand; he wouldn't even as much as clutch at our necks; he was only a cold black skin loosely stuffed with soft cotton wool; his arms and legs swung jointless and pliable; his head rolled about; the lower lip hung down, enormous and heavy. We pressed round him, bothered and dismayed; sheltering him we swung here and there in a body; and on the very brink of eternity we tottered all together with concealing and absurd gestures, like a lot of drunken men embarrassed with a stolen corpse.[16]

In the narrative attempt to present a bunch of sailors and their efforts to rescue the collapsed sailor, their togetherness seems to be highlighted here, but the way the crew "blindly" hold on to Jimmy, on the contrary, only reveals their inefficiency and even hollowness as a group rather than the bond between men. Indeed, they are "together" as "a body" of men surrounding and sheltering

---

society with its emphasis on individual rights, Deresiewicz on the other hand believes that Victor Turner's dichotomy, which sets "structure" against *communitas*, is more relevant in explaining the situation depicted in the text. Especially during the storm, the ship's condition leaves the hierarchy temporarily powerless to do anything but watch and wait. *Communitas*, as Turner understands it, is a form of community that cuts across all boundaries of cultural difference and socioeconomic development, a state of marginality or transition marked by an intense experience of comradeship, equality, and communion, a disappearance of social hierarchies and differentiations and the coming to the fore of "an essential and generic social bond." Deresiewicz thus claims that the storm produces two acts of singular moral beauty, the rescue of Wait and the cook's "miraculous" making of coffee. Both are irrelevant to the sailing of the ship, thus outside of the hierarchy's purview, and the actions bespeak a feeling of common fellowship. See, William Deresiewicz, "Conrad's Impasse: *The Nigger of the 'Narcissus'* and the Invention of Marlow," *Conradiana*, vol. 38, no. 3 (Fall 2006): 209–210.

[16] Joseph Conrad, *The Nigger of the "Narcissus"* (Oxford: Oxford University Press, 1984), 71. Further page references to this edition will be given parenthetically in the text, preceded by *NN* where it might otherwise be unclear. Roman numeral references are to Conrad's Preface.

Jimmy, but they can do nothing but "blindly" stick to him, begging him to hold up. Hollow at its core, a group of men swing and totter around the black man like a shabby, "loosely stuffed" doll with "absurd gestures." One might wonder whether the "we" is rescuing Jimmy or Jimmy is rescuing the "we" in this stormy confusion. Fittingly compared to a group of "drunken" tomb robbers, crowding round its "stolen," hollow center, they are more like what Nancy calls an "inoperative community" than some preexisting heroic sailor's group as has long been understood. Jimmy and the crew, on the verge of separation, form a strange group, or "singular plurality" in Nancy's terms.

Furthermore, the act of hanging on to a hook in the passage above, reminiscent of Conrad's comparison of writing to rescue work "carried out in darkness against cross gusts of wind swaying the action of a great multitude,"[17] draws our attention to the author's (and the "we" narrator's) precarious hold on the narrative's subject. In a letter to Edward Garnett when he was struggling with "The Rescuer" (later revised as *The Rescue*), Conrad bemoans "the chaos of [his] sensations" that disrupts the story's progressive episodes, while his contemporary British writers have something to begin with, "something to catch hold of":

> I feel nothing clearly. And I am frightened when I remember that I have to drag it all out of myself. Other writers have some starting point. Something to catch hold of. They start from an anecdote—from a newspaper paragraph .... They lean on dialect—or on tradition—or history—or on the prejudice or fad of the hour; they trade upon some tie or some conviction of their time—or upon the absence of these things—which they can abuse or praise. But at any rate they know something to begin with—while I don't.[18]

Having nothing to begin with or even to anchor itself to, the narrative viewpoint floats and fluctuates. However hard the narrative tries to focus on the plural "we," Jimmy's singular existence always rises from beyond the symbolic cabin door; or the other way around, however hard it tries to focus on the singular Jimmy, the plural "we" "pressed round" the sailor in the passage just cited. Individuality in Conrad seems to be indissociably bound up with

---

17   Conrad, "Henry James," 13.
18   Conrad, letter to Edward Garnett, June 19, 1896, in *The Collected Letters of Joseph Conrad*, vol. 1, 288.

collectivity. Conrad's understanding of human existence seems never easily subsumed under such a clear dualism between singularity and plurality.

Critics often explain the relationship between the crew and the black sailor in terms of the dialectic of the self and the other. Bruce Henricksen, for instance, asserts that *The Nigger of the "Narcissus"* emphasizes "the bonding of the crew, which must purge itself of disruptive individualism" and of "the black 'other.'"[19] The narrative, indeed, connects the crew's narcissistic search for an identity of "we" with Jimmy's identity; they cannot think about themselves without thinking about the black sailor. The crew, as well as readers, are always made to wonder who the black sailor is and doubt if he is, as he claims, really sick and going to die. The self-evidence of "we" is always threatened by this mysterious black man amongst them. Every time they look into "the mirror of the sea," they see this lazy, malingering black "other," a reflection of themselves, instead of their idealized, heroic, image.[20] Appropriate to the story's title, the black seaman's existence always stands in the way of their narcissistic love of self. In addition to "weight" as a burden, the word "wait" can be a noun meaning "a delay," as Cedric Watts explains, and the ship appropriately makes slow progress until Jimmy's death.[21] The crew is ever delayed in their narcissistic search for themselves.

However, Jimmy is not simply an appropriable other, which is, a projection of the crew's negative characteristics, first repressed then pathologized, later rescued and recovered from repression, and then effectively wiped out. Possibly for Conrad as well as for Nancy, who suggests that we think of being as community, being is not the other; being is always "with."[22] What is taking place when "the crowd stepped forward like one man" (*NN*, 160) during Jimmy's burial at sea just before they arrive home is not the achievement of an ideal "we" through the expulsion of the black other; but rather, the burial, or this "exposure to death," is the very basis of "friendship," the "community"

---

[19] Henricksen, *Nomadic Voices*, 25.
[20] For Wait's role as a mirror, see Donald T. Torchiana, "Myth, Mirror, and Metropolis," rpt. in Joseph Conrad, *The Nigger of the "Narcissus,"* ed. Robert Kimbrough (New York and London: W. W. Norton, 1979), 275–287. See 276–278 in particular. Gerard Morgan also interprets the title after the fashion of Thomas Moser as signifying "a progression of the soul, an explorer's journey into the interior," into "the reflective self-awareness of Narcissus afloat on an immense mirror in the darkness" in his "Narcissus Afloat" in Conrad, *The Nigger of the "Narcissus,"* ed. Robert Kimbrough, 265.
[21] For the Wait/weight homophone, see Cedric Watts, *A Preface to Conrad*, 2nd ed. (1982; London and New York: Longman, 1993), 196–197; Simmons, *Joseph Conrad*, 57.
[22] Nancy, *Being Singular Plural*, 4, 19, 38.

which is revealed through death, according to Nancy and Maurice Blanchot.[23] Blanchot's description of the friendship in *The Unavowable Community*, which was inspired by Nancy's *The Inoperative Community*, can be read as an illustration of Jimmy's "uncanny presence/absence" and "our" "relation without relation" with him:

> "The basis of communication" is not necessarily speech, or even the silence that is its foundation and punctuation but the exposure to death, no longer my own exposure, but someone else's, whose living and closest presence is already the eternal and unbearable absence, an absence that the travail of deepest mourning does not diminish. And it is in life itself that that absence of someone else has to be met. It is with that absence—its uncanny presence, always under the prior threat of a disappearance—that friendship is brought into play and lost at each moment, relation without relation or without relation other than the incommensurable .... Such is, such would be the friendship that discovers the unknown we ourselves are, and the meeting of our own solitude which, precisely, we cannot be alone to experience ... .[24]

After struggling with the unavowable relationship, *The Nigger of the "Narcissus"* allows the "I" narrator suddenly to emerge from the disbanding crew in the closing scene. This sudden appearance of the "I" narrator has been taken as a typically modernist phenomenon. For example, Michael Levenson, who established Conrad as the representative early modernist, states that "with his [the 'I' narrator's] appearance, the text struggles towards self-consciousness."[25] Unable to find such a safe landing place, as it were, either at the story's beginning or end, the characters (as well as the author) in *The Rescue* might have felt stranded. The very inappropriable nature of what Conrad attempts to rescue makes it all the more difficult to complete *The Rescue*. And yet, it is not, as Moser once contended, the misogynist author's inability to deal with the

---

[23] Nancy, *The Inoperative Community*, 14–15.

[24] Maurice Blanchot, *The Unavowable Community*, trans. Pierre Joris (New York: Station Hill, 1988), 25.

[25] Levenson, *A Genealogy of Modernism*, 9. Simmons follows this trend in his essay, "*The Nigger of the 'Narcissus'*: History, Narrative, and Nationalism" in *Joseph Conrad*, eds. Jakob Lothe, Jeremy Hawthorn, and James Phelan, 148. Henricksen, on the other hand, regards the appearance of the "I" narrator as the postmodernist resolution of the contradiction (between the individual / the collective), asserting that *The Nigger of the "Narcissus"* lays bare the process in which an "I" emerges as a subject from the ideological text, with the communal narrative voice giving way to an individual "I." See, Henricksen, *Nomadic Voices*, 37–46. I would suggest, however, that the emergence of the "I" can be read as the enactment of what Nancy elaborates as follows: "the plural liberates (or shares) the singular, the singular liberates (or shares) the plural in a community *without subject*" in *Who Comes After the Subject?* ed. Eduardo Cadava, Peter Connor, and Jean-Luc Nancy, 8.

uncongenial subject of love that delayed the completion.[26] Nor, as GoGwilt argues, is Lingard's failure to rescue the Malay people a proof of his or the author's limitation in understanding Malay culture.[27] *The Rescue*, a recount of the competing claims for Lingard's rescue, addresses a far more complicated nature of friendship between different cultures and genders.

The words "friend" or "friendship" occur quite frequently in *The Rescue*, challenging our efforts to trace who belongs to which group in a tangled web of political intrigues woven by both local tribes and European traders. The friendship between the colonizer and the colonized singularly begins through "the exposure to death" in the extract just cited. After a fight following Lingard's reckless intrusion into the local tribes' territory, which European traders have not penetrated, the English trader and a Malay prince establish a bond by exchanging their first handshake "over the prostrate body," "on the very spot where the Malay seaman had lost his life."[28] Here "the price of a death" (72) is referred to as what fate exacts as "the gift of friendship" (73). This unique bond plunges the English adventurer further into the ongoing uncertainty of local politics. When the prince becomes a fugitive during a civil war after the death of the old king, Lingard promises to restore his exiled friend and his princess sister to their kingdom. But his plan is thwarted by the arrival of the European yacht people who had been stranded. In his effort to save Mr and Mrs Travers and their guest, d'Alcacer, the captain negotiates with the local rival tribes and exposes his "brown friends" (232) to danger and finally to death, thereby breaking his bond with them.

A European lady, Edith Travers and a Malay princess are also called the captain's "friends." Unlike a conventional romance heroine, Edith looks at her lover Lingard from "a strictly human standpoint" even when she has "too much elevation of mind" (166). During the course of long conversation with him, Edith is aware of "something that resembled gratitude and provoked a sort of emotional return as between equals who had secretly recognized each other's value" (283). This may be in part Conrad's attempt to appeal to the increasing number of women readers in the late nineteenth century, but nevertheless a

---

[26] Moser, *Joseph Conrad*, 63–68.
[27] GoGwilt repeatedly stresses *The Rescue*'s "inability either to rescue a concept of Malay culture or to give a cultural coherence to 'the western race'" in his *The Invention of the West*, 74–75.
[28] Joseph Conrad, *The Rescue: A Romance of the Shallows* (London: Dent, 1949), 72. Further page references will be to this edition, preceded by *R* where necessary. Roman numeral references are to Conrad's "Author's Note."

moment of "ecstasy" between Lingard and Edith offers us a glimpse of the possibility of community. According to Nancy, the singular being is not properly
the subject of ecstasy, for ecstasy has no "subject," but ecstasy (community)
"happens to" the singular being, which does not have the nature or structure of
individuality.[29] This is what happens between the lovers when Lingard sees her
throwing back her hood under the brig's swing-lamp, which lights the cabin
with an extraordinary brilliance:

> The radiant brightness of the little place enfolded her so close, clung to
> her with such force that it might have been part of her very essence. There
> were no shadows on her face; it was fiercely lighted, hermetically closed, of
> impenetrable fairness.
>
> Lingard looked in unconscious ecstasy at this vision, so amazing that it
> seemed to have strayed into his existence from beyond the limits of the con-
> ceivable. It was impossible to guess her thoughts, to know her feelings, to
> understand her grief or her joy. But she knew all that was at the bottom of
> his heart. He had told her himself, impelled by a sudden thought, going to
> her in darkness, in desperation, in absurd hope, in incredible trust. He had
> told her what he had told no one on earth, except perhaps, at times, himself,
> but without words—less clearly. He had told her and she had listened in
> silence. She had listened leaning over the rail till at last her breath was on his
> forehead. (214)

What is going on here appears to be an amorous union between a man and
a woman, the self and the other, yet Mrs Travers is more than the appropriable other or an object of male desire.[30] Lingard's "unconscious" gaze seems
to be almost devouring her, but it cannot make her completely his own,
revealing his ignorance of her thoughts and feelings—"her very essence."
In this excessive brightness, the boundary between her supposedly inner
"essence" and the outer radiance of so enclosed a place cannot be distinguished. Her face is "fiercely lighted" with no shadows on it, but her
fairness is nonetheless "impenetrable." Mrs Travers seems to know everything about him, but her apparently profound knowledge cannot fall into

---

[29] Nancy, *The Inoperative Community*, 6–7.
[30] Thinking of the relationship between Mrs Travers and Lingard in terms of heterosexual desire,
Robert Hampson states that it is through the encounter with Mrs Travers that Lingard confronts
woman as Other. See Robert Hampson, *Cross-Cultural Encounters in Joseph Conrad's Malay
Fiction* (New York: Palgrave, 2000), 164.

epistemological categories. Aptly named, she "traverses" the limits of her identity, "straying into his existence from beyond the limits of the conceivable." She is also traversed by him but in a "sudden," "absurd" and "incredible" way that exceeds expectation and rational explanation. Their ecstatic love is thus an unheard-of traversal beyond words and cannot constitute a pure collective totality.

Conrad's narrative engagement with plurality in *The Nigger of the "Narcissus,"* in particular, has, until quite recently, notoriously been misunderstood and often regarded as a failure in its violation of mimesis. However, a more enlightened view is that of Brian Richardson, for example, who reevaluates the fluctuating "we" narrative voice in *The Nigger of the "Narcissus"* as anticipating many subsequent nonrealistic voice and narration used, for example, by postcolonial African writers, such as Zakes Mda, Ayi Kwei Armah, and Ngũgĩ wa Thiong'o.[31] Although Conrad's philosophical principles have often been taken as plain, they are, in fact, far in advance of his time. It is no wonder that he complained of losing "all sense of form" in a letter while *The Rescue* was being written. This blindness, so to speak, cannot, as has often been done, be easily attributed to Conrad's inability to maintain mastery over his material, because he went on to affirm in the same letter, "what to write I know."[32] The "what to write" that he thought he knew, which is, what is to be rescued, is also in advance of identification; it is in its very nature always to come. Unsurprisingly, therefore, Lingard failed in his rescue act, and *The Rescue* had to "wait" for about twenty years before the last words finally came in 1919.[33] If the long drawn-out process of *The Rescue* might indicate the impossibility of Conrad's artistic enterprise, which is, his persistent search for a possible form for his concept of the singular plurality, then we may be allowed to surmise that a technique that postulates a single perceiving subject must have been uncongenial to a Polish author with his non-Western eyes, just as the Western metaphysics of the subject are to Nancy in their exclusion of the notions of community.[34] Of course, Conrad may have been acutely aware, as is Nancy, that meaning exists only by virtue of a "self." As John Peters rightly

[31] Richardson, *Unnatural Voices*, 48–55.
[32] Conrad, letter to Edward Garnett, June 7, 1898, in Conrad, *The Collected Letters*, vol. 2, 66.
[33] Conrad writes in "Author's Note" to *The Rescue* that he did not return to the novel after he finished *The Nigger of the "Narcissus"* because he said to himself, "That thing [*The Rescue*] can wait" (ix).
[34] The question of community, Nancy writes, is "so markedly absent from the metaphysics of the subject." See his *The Inoperative Community*, 4.

asserts in his discussion of Conrad's impressionism, Conrad surely rejected moral nihilism by focusing on his belief in human subjectivity.[35] In a similar vein, underscoring the importance of self-generated morality in Conrad, Michael Levenson states that Conrad tried to articulate "an ethics that could be generated from within subjectivity, consciousness turning back on itself in an act of primal restraint."[36] But while producing his so-called impressionistic masterpieces like *Heart of Darkness* and *Lord Jim*, meanwhile setting aside *The Rescue*, he all the more firmly showed his belief that there is no "self" except by virtue of a "with."[37] Not surprisingly, he eventually outgrew the art of seeing things under Western eyes, shifting in his later period to the seemingly chivalric romance, a genre originally not solely concerned with the behavior of the self but a polite, unselfish behavior, especially of men toward women.[38] We could probably argue then that Conrad's later shift is predicted in his preface to *The Nigger of the "Narcissus,"* although it has been known primarily as his impressionistic manifesto with its much celebrated passage, "My task which I am trying to achieve is, by the power of the written word to make you hear, to make you feel—it is, before all, to make you *see!*" (*NN* xlii). Indeed, the artist, as Conrad puts it, "descends within himself, and in that lonely region of stress and strife" (xl), to find the terms of his appeal. More importantly, however, what Conrad repeatedly emphasizes throughout this preface is, that "one temperament" of the artist is not disengaged from "all the other innumerable temperaments" (xli): the artist speaks to "the latent feeling of fellowship with *all* creation" and to "the solidarity in dreams, in joy, in sorrow, in aspiration, in illusions, in hope, in fear, which binds men to each other, which binds together, *all* humanity—the dead to the living and the living to the unborn" (xl) (italics added). Comparing this manifesto to Wordsworthian "democratic formulation of the role of the artist in civilization," Watt raises a question of the very existential status of Conrad's solidarity in our time.[39] Nevertheless, as we have

---

[35]   Peters, *Conrad and Impressionism*, especially, Chapter 5, "Radical relativism, epistemological certainty, and ethical absolutes: Conrad's impressionist response to solipsism and anarchy" (ibid., 123–158).

[36]   Levenson, "Modernism," 185.

[37]   Nancy, *Being Singular Plural*, 94.

[38]   If we are to understand the romance method, according to Gillian Beer, we have to abandon the critical metaphors of perspective (with its suggestion of far and near) or depth (with its suggestion that what is deepest is most significant). See Gillian Beer, *The Romance* (London: Methuen, 1970), 20–21.

[39]   Watt, *Conrad in the Nineteenth Century*, 80, 81.

seen earlier, Conrad's solidarity did happen at the space his texts open in their rescue operations. In the sense that his solidarity always occurs differently at each new reading, it actually "binds together, all humanity—the dead to the living and the living to the unborn," opening the possibility of sharing of humanity.

2

The Deaf Russian Finn's Secret Agency in *The Nigger of the "Narcissus"*

Amongst the clamorous, international crew of the *Narcissus*, there is an enigmatic Russian Finnish shipmate named Wamibo, who can barely hear and simply stares upward, dreamy-eyed. The presence of a deaf man in the midst of "a stormy chaos of speech" (128) aboard the ship in such an aurally oriented text as *The Nigger of the "Narcissus"* in itself raises some interesting questions. However, the repeated emphasis on the international composition of the crew, by increasing the reader's illusion that he or she is looking at a "'microcosm', illustrative not of one or two nationalities but of human nature generally,"[1] has caused most critics to focus primarily on the organic community of the crew as a whole[2] rather than on a specific nationality of an individual sailor. Strangely enough, the Bakhtinian approach that conceives of a text as a composite of voices does not pay due attention to the sailor who cannot hear any of those voices.[3] Thus, the Russian Finn has been overlooked in most discussions of this novella, except by Ernest J. Moyne, who explains his presence in terms of the Finn's age-old reputation as a wizard with an uncanny power over the weather,[4] and by Albert

---

[1] Cedric Watts, *The Deceptive Text: An Introduction to Covert Plots* (Brighton, UK: Harvester, 1984), 67–68.

[2] Elio Di Piazza argues, "Nationalities integrate and reinforce the organized ranks of the ship, exemplifying the international composition of Conrad's ideal community." See Elio Di Piazza, "Conrad's Narrative Polyphony in *The Nigger of the 'Narcissus,'*" in *Beyond the Roots: The Evolution of Conrad's Ideology and Art*, ed. with an introduction by Wiesław Krajka (Boulder, CO: East European Monographs; Lublin, Poland: Maria Curie-Skłodowska University Press; New York: Columbia University Press, 2005), 31. Vol. 14 of *Conrad: Eastern and Western Perspectives*, ed. Wiesław Krajka, 23 vols. to date, 1992–.

[3] Michael S. Macovski, *Dialogue and Literature: Apostrophe, Auditors, and the Collapse of Romantic Discourse* (New York and Oxford: Oxford University Press, 1994), 3.

[4] Ernest J. Moyne, "Wamibo in Conrad's *The Nigger of the 'Narcissus,'*" *Conradiana* vol. 10, no. 1 (1978): 55–61. Singleton supposes that Jimmy is the cause of the head winds, "aided by Wamibo's (he was a Finn—wasn't he? Very well!) by Wamibo's spells delayed the ship in the open sea" (142).

Guerard, who makes a passing mention of Wamibo's primitive savageness in the text's psychic geography.[5]

Wamibo's significance, however, should not be ignored, given that this deaf Russian Finn, as Ian Watt indicates, was an addition to the international composition of the crew.[6] There seem to have been some Finns and a Norwegian aboard the ships on which Conrad sailed, but there was no one identifiable as a Russian Finn on the real *Narcissus*, which Conrad joined as second mate for its journey home from June 5 to October 16, 1884, and Wamibo is in fact very different from the two Finns whom Conrad mentions as shipmates elsewhere.[7] We are left wondering, then, what induced the author to put the Russian Finn on board the *Narcissus* in his first fictional engagement with Englishness.[8]

In the text of *The Nigger of the "Narcissus,"* which is, as we realize from the outset, full of explosive sounds and voices, hearing and seeing are, as a Bakhtinian critic puts it, "in conflict for priority."[9] Despite the manifested faithfulness to the visible universe in the famous "Preface" (xlii), the narrator/ author appears to be more faithful (indeed even obsessive about) the audible universe than the ocular one. The novella's preoccupation with the auditory presents an interesting contrast with the silence, which the narrative sometimes creates around Wamibo. The Russian Finn is unable to hear the crew's thickly accented cries and curses; Jimmy's "fine baritone voice" (119) and his violent cough, "metallic, hollow, and tremendously loud" (18), "a fit of roaring, rattling cough" (24); the howl of gales; and "the clamour of ringing metal spread round the ship" (126). Peripheral to the "we" group of sailors, the deaf

---

[5] Focusing on the scene in which James Wait is rescued from the flooded deckhouse during the gale, Guerard describes Wamibo as the "savage *super ego*" in the Freudian triad that "would convert Wait into the *id* and the whole area (carpenter's shop and cabin) into all that lies below full consciousness." Admitting however that "such literalism of reading of psychic geography" is "not very rewarding," Guerard goes on to compare Wamibo to still more primitive, half-savage figures such as Sam Fathers in Faulkner's *The Bear* and Lions in *Go Down, Moses*. See Albert Guerard, *Conrad the Novelist* (Cambridge, MA: Harvard University Press, 1969), 112–113. Ian Watt makes a cursory allusion to the Russian Finn's "inarticulate frenzies of participation" in the rescue of Jimmy in his *Essays on Conrad* (Cambridge: Cambridge University Press, 2000), 80.

[6] Watt, *Conrad in the Nineteenth Century*, 92.

[7] Ibid. Gerard Morgan thinks that the solitary Finn was Lofstedt, aboard since Penarth. The Finn of *Narcissus*, he supposes, somehow gives way to the "Russian Finn," Wamibo, whose name compounds Wamibo, the Norwegian of *Loch Etive*'s outward voyage to Sydney, with Waraboi, the Finn of the same ship's homeward voyage. Gerald Morgan, "The Book of the Ship *Narcissus*," in Conrad, *The Nigger of the "Narcissus,"* ed. Robert Kimbrough, 205, 210.

[8] Simmons, *Joseph Conrad*, 56.

[9] Aaron Fogel, *Coercion to Speak: Conrad's Poetics of Dialogue* (Cambridge, MA: Harvard University Press, 1985), 49. For another Bakhtinian reading of *The Nigger of the "Narcissus,"* see Henricksen, *Nomadic Voices*, 23–46.

man can hardly comprehend what is taking place around him. The narrator nevertheless describes the unobtrusive man as "safe" because he "never spoke intelligibly … [and] seemed to know much less about it all [Jimmy's case] than the cat" (141). I would suggest that, amid the tempest of curses, Wamibo's inability to listen provides a site, which is "safe" from all the "distracting noise" (4) filling the text, thereby helping the "we" narrator to concentrate on the surface reality, or the visible universe as stated in the author's artistic manifesto, in his attempt to give an "impressionistic" description of the *Narcissus*'s journey from Bombay to London. Therefore, this chapter will discuss the previously neglected, deaf minor character's secret agency in shaping an "impressionistic" narration, which culminates in the birth of the "I" narrator.

* * *

The narrative begins in Bombay harbor as the crew of the *Narcissus* gather in the forecastle on the evening of her homeward voyage to London. Most suitably, these obscure newcomers board in the shadows of the night, as "silhouettes of moving men [who] appear[s] for a moment, very black, without relief, like figures cut out of sheet tin" (3). Unidentified and invisible, with any bond of sea still unformed between them, they nonetheless "make us hear" their presence in the dark aft of the main deck through a hum of voices. The narrative's preoccupation with the audible is a way of presenting "an unrestful episode in the obscure lives of a few individuals out of all the disregarded multitude of the bewildered, the simple and the voiceless" (xl). There continues an inquiry into the auditory, which is also an inquiry into the invisible:[10] "Soon after dark the few liberty-men and the new hands began to arrive in shore-boats rowed by white-clad Asiatics, who clamored fiercely for payment before coming alongside the gangway-ladder. The feverish and shrill babble of Eastern language struggled against the masterful tones of tipsy seamen, who argued against brazen claims and dishonest hopes by profane shouts" (4). Similarly, "[t]he resplendent and bestarred peace of the East" is torn into "squalid tatters by howls of rage and shrieks of lament raised over

---

[10]   Regarding an inquiry into the auditory as an inquiry into the invisible, see Don Ihde, *Listening and Voice: Phenomenologies of Sound* (Albany: State University of New York Press, 2007), 51. Ihde remarks that listening makes the invisible "present" in a way that is similar to the presence of the inaudible in vision.

sums ranging from five annas to half a rupee" (4).[11] As "the distracting noise"
(4) gradually subsides, the narrator, as if straining his eyes into the shadowed
forecastle, begins to depict the newcomers making friends with the old hands.
Then, under the two forecastle lamps, which are turned up high and shedding
"an intense hard glare" (5), we are told of hats pushed far on the backs of heads,
"white collars, undone, stuck out on each side of red faces" and "big arms in
white sleeves" (5) gesticulating; after that, we are made to hear "the growling
voices hum[ming] steady amongst bursts of laughter and hoarse calls" (5). In
the ongoing conflict between the audible and the visible, the deaf Russian Finn
makes his first, quite indistinct appearance:

> A little fellow, called Craik and nicknamed Belfast, abused the ship violently,
> romancing on principle, just to give the new hands something to think over.
> Archie, sitting aslant on his sea-chest, kept his knees out of the way, and
> pushed the needle steadily through a white patch in a pair of blue trousers.
> Men in black jackets and stand-up collars, mixed with men bare-footed,
> bare-armed, with coloured shirts open on hairy chests, pushed against one
> another in the middle of the forecastle. The group swayed, reeled, turning
> upon itself with the motion of a scrimmage, in a haze of tobacco smoke. All
> were speaking together, swearing at every second word. A Russian Finn,
> wearing a yellow shirt with pink stripes, stared upwards, dreamy-eyed, from
> under a mop of tumbled hair. Two young giants with smooth, baby faces—
> two Scandinavians—helped each other to spread their bedding, silent,
> and smiling placidly at the tempest of good-humoured and meaningless
> curses. (5–6)

Conrad, who expressed his "desire to do for seamen what Millet ... has done
for peasants" in a letter of December 23, 1897,[12] follows the French painter
in many ways, as Simmons points out, in his romanticization of the sailors'
manual work in this novella.[13] But the portrait quoted above looks more
impressionist than Barbizon in its attention to the colors and the atmospheric haze of tobacco smoke.[14] Here our attention may be drawn more to

---

[11] I shall return to the bubbling "Asiatic" noises later in this chapter in relation to Conrad's Russian
     experience.
[12] Conrad, *The Collected Letters*, vol. 1, 430–431.
[13] On the iconography of labor in Millet's paintings and Conrad's recourse to pictorialism and the
     formal demands of symmetry and balance, see Simmons, *Joseph Conrad*, 54.
[14] Regarding typical impressionist images of haze, fog, mist, and blurred contours, see Maria Elizabeth
     Kronegger, *Literary Impressionism* (New Haven, CT: College and University Press, 1973), 46,

the jumbled, patchwork nature of the group portrait than to the orderly, dig-
nifying image of sailors' labor. The narrator seems to be somewhere inside
or near the group, as is surmised from the way in which his visual focus
shifts from one crew member to another. Although Deresiewicz discerns a
tone of comradely affection drawn from Conrad's personal experience in this
passage,[15] the narrator's visual perception turns less to the typically masculine aspects of the sailors than to their somewhat effeminate or queer traits:
Archie at his needlework, "sitting aslant on his sea-chest, with his knees out
of the way"; men in black jackets and collars pushing against "bare-footed"
and "bare-armed" men with "coloured shirts open on hairy chests"; the two
giant Scandinavians "with smooth, baby faces" helping each other to "spread
their bedding." In keeping with their hybridity, the group is presented as hazy,
elusive, and amorphous. The narrator apparently intends to portray the group
as hybrid, placing them "in a haze of tobacco smoke," swaying, reeling, and
turning upon itself, rather than reducing its members into homogeneity. The
"hazy" impression through the eyes of the narrator, one is tempted to suggest,
might not be very different from, or may even overlap in part, the vision of
the "dreamy-eyed" Wamibo.

   As Uri Margolin's close examination indicates, the relation between the
"we" utterer and the class of persons denoted by this use of "we" is not unique,
but rather it allows for a whole range of possibilities.[16] One must not, therefore, take the "we" as a simple multiplication or extension of the "I," but still,
if we assume that the "we" in the text refers to most of the crew, that is, to
the men on the forecastle as opposed to the officers, then it should include
the "dreamy-eyed" (6), "uncomprehending" (132) Wamibo as well. In other
words, Wamibo's perspective and inability to listen occupy an important,
though minor, place in the perception of the first-person plural narrator "we."
When the "we" speaker takes refuge, as it were, in Wamibo's lack of auditory

---

47. On persistent images of mist or haze in Conrad and Impressionism, see Watt, *Conrad in the Nineteenth Century*, 169–180. On an elusive atmosphere, see Lange, 21.

[15] Deresiewicz, "Conrad's Impasse," 211.

[16] Uri Margolin, "Collective Perspective, Individual Perspective, and the Speaker in Between: On 'We' Literary Narratives," in *New Perspectives on Narrative Perspective*, ed. Willie Van Peer and Seymour Chatman (Albany: State University of New York Press, 2001), 241–245. See also Richardson, *Unnatural Voices*, 37–60. As Richardson points out, the narrator is simultaneously homodiegetic and heterodiegetic. "If the narrator is a character on the ship," Richardson writes, "he cannot enter the minds of others or report conversations he has not observed; if he is omniscient, he can't break fingernails onboard, but only pare them silently, from a distant vantage point far above his creation" (ibid., 42).

perception, then he may be able to cut off the tempestuous, "distracting noise" surrounding him (4), while we readers are left with only a hazy and smoky vision, or a foggy "impression" of the group of sailors seen in the dreamy eyes of the "muddleheaded" Russian Finn (66). Thus, Wamibo's "dreamy" vision, I would propose, anticipates the oft-quoted "dream-sensation" of Conrad's impressionist narrator Marlow in *Heart of Darkness*. Trying to make his listeners "see" the story of Kurtz waiting to be saved in the depths of Africa, Marlow reflects:

> It seems to me I am trying to tell you a dream—making a vain attempt, because no relation of a dream can convey the dream-sensation, that commingling of absurdity, surprise, and bewilderment in a tremor of struggling revolt, that notion of being captured by the incredible which is of the very essence of dreams ....
>
> ... No, it is impossible; it is impossible to convey the life-sensation of any given epoch of one's existence—that which makes its truth, its meaning—its subtle and penetrating essence. It is impossible. We live, as we dream—alone .... (*HD* 82)

We may also remember here that Marlow's yarn, which is untypical of seamen, is likened by the frame narrator to a misty halo (48) in the beginning of the tale.

The *Narcissus* crew jeer at "half-witted" Wamibo and sometimes treat him as a nuisance ("Wamibo, held back by shouts—'Don't jump! ... Don't come in here, muddle-head!'—remained glaring above us" [66]), whereas the narrator finds in his muddle-headedness a certain sense of security: "Wamibo never spoke intelligibly, but he was as smileless as an animal—seemed to know much less about it all [Jimmy's case] than the cat—and consequently was safe" (140–141).[17] Moreover, the narrator presents the deaf Russian as reliable when he is most needed. When a sea is about to sweep over them in a furious gale, Jimmy collapses and does not have the strength to close his hand, yet the crew (the "we") are more afraid of the hook giving way than of Wamibo letting go the hook to which they hang on, because "the brute" is "stronger than any three men in the ship" (71).

---

[17]   Marlow in *Heart of Darkness* also says that "a fool ... is always safe" (*HD* 97).

Wamibo's dreamy unintelligence, which is recurrently called to our attention,[18] may not squarely contravene the author's statement in the preface that
"the artist appeals to that part of our being which is not dependent on wis-
dom" (xl), allowing instead for a link to impressionist presentation of phenomena in the order of their perception before they have been "distorted"
into intelligibility.[19] The universe in Wamibo's vision is neither intelligible
nor well organized but rather shadowy and hazy: his "dreamy and puzzled
stare" can hardly "distinguish the still men from their restless shadows" (97).
Thus we might say that the Russian Finn's dreamy deafness, as it were, in the
"we" perception, opens for the narrator a site, which is "safe" from all those
"distracting" noises. Seeking shelter in vagueness, or the safe space, the "we"
narrator can leave his impressions of people and events as hazy as they are
without reducing them to a certain understandable picture. In his discussion of the shift from the merely visible to the valuable, Michael Levenson
points out a dual movement in modernist fiction, that is, the combination
of an initial commitment to life's surface and the subsequent enhancement
provided by subjectivity. Levenson's "psychologistic" theory of literary meaning insists on the primacy of consciousness and the "muteness" of the mere
event,[20] a word choice that bears an interesting similarity to the silence
made possible through Wamibo's lack of auditory sensation. In other words,
Wamibo is there among the "we" to help the "we" narrator achieve a visual,
impressionist commitment to surface reality without being distracted by the
surrounding noises.

* * *

Wamibo almost invariably comes on the scene when the crew (the "we"), "distracted" by a certain type of noise, desperately longs to "get out of [its] hearing"
(67). The words of Donkin, an orator who knows "how to conquer the naïve
instincts of that crowd" (12), elicit compassion in the crew, who provide him

---

[18] "The Finn emitted at last an uncouth grunt, and, stepping out, passed through the patch of light,
weird and gaudy, with the face of a man marching through a dream" (16); "Wamibo dreamed"
(159); "Wamibo, still in his working clothes, dreamed, upright and burly in the middle of the
room" (133).

[19] Kronegger, *Literary Impressionism*, 37. Watt coined the term "delayed decoding" to describe the
narrative device used to bridge the gap between impression and understanding. See Watt, *Conrad
in the Nineteenth Century*, 175–180.

[20] Levenson, *A Genealogy of Modernism*, 21.

with a blanket, a pair of shoes, and trousers. As Donkin is about to withdraw
with these gifts to the bunk, following Belfast's advice, he notices Wamibo in
his way:

> "Take that bunk by the door there—it's pretty fair," suggested Belfast. So
> advised, he [Donkin] gathered the gifts at his feet, pressed them in a bundle
> against his breast, then looked cautiously at the Russian Finn, who stood on
> one side with an unconscious gaze, contemplating, perhaps, one of those
> weird visions that haunt the men of his race.—"Get out of my road, Dutchy,"
> said the victim of Yankee brutality. The Finn did not move—did not hear.
> "Get out, blast ye," shouted the other, shoving him aside with his elbow. "Get
> out, you blanked deaf and dumb fool. Get out." The man staggered, recov-
> ered himself, and gazed at the speaker in silence.—"Those damned furriners
> should be kept under," opined the amiable Donkin to the forecastle. "If you
> don't teach 'em their place they put on you like anythink." He flung all his
> worldly possessions into the empty bed-place, gauged with another shrewd
> look the risks of the proceeding, then leaped up to the Finn, who stood pen-
> sive and dull.—"I'll teach you to swell around," he yelled. "I'll plug your eyes
> for you, you blooming square-head." Most of the men were now in their
> bunks and the two had the forecastle clear to themselves. The development
> of the destitute Donkin aroused interest. He danced all in tatters before the
> amazed Finn, squaring from a distance at the heavy, unmoved face. (13)

The Russian Finn's dense immobility in the face of the "startling visitor from
a world of nightmares" (10) stands out here. Unable to hear Donkin, Wamibo
simply stands in his way with "an unconscious gaze." Even though shoved
aside, the deaf man soon recovers and returns to a silent gaze. Firm as a wall
facing Donkin, Wamibo looks as if attempting to block his "filthy loquacity
flow[ing] like a troubled stream from a poisoned source" (101). Also, the
Russian Finn hangs his head over his breast beside "all that crowd of cold and
hungry men" who are "waiting wearily for a violent death" in suspense during
the gale: "not a voice was heard; they were mute, and in somber thoughtful-
ness listened to the horrible imprecations of the gale" (61). Jimmy unceas-
ingly keeps up "a distracting row" (67) in the deckhouse after the gale, whereas
Wamibo plays a key role, the narrator recounts, in rescuing Jimmy while "[t]he
agony of his [Jimmy's] fear [wrings their] hearts so terribly that [they long] to
abandon him, to get out of that place ... to get out of his hearing" (67). The
more complacent and rebellious the crew become as the weather settles down,

the more persuasive they find Donkin's words even though they dislike him. They conveniently forget their recent scare and decry their officers as useless, but they listen to "the fascinating Donkin" (100). Their contempt for him is "unbounded—and [they] [can] not but listen with interest to that consummate artist" (100) whose "care for [their] rights ... [and] ... disinterested concern for [their] dignity, [are] not discouraged ... by the disdain of [their] looks" (100). Donkin protests against injustice, shouting, "Who thanked us? Who took any notice of our wrongs? Didn't we lead a 'dorg's loife for two poun' ten a month?" (100) In doing so, he causes the crew to wonder if their "miserable pay" is enough to compensate them for the risk to their lives and for the loss of their clothes. "We've lost every rag!" the orator cries, making them "forget that he, at any rate, had lost nothing of his own" (100). They listen as Donkin speaks "with ardour, despised and irrefutable" (101): "His picturesque and filthy loquacity flowed like a troubled stream from a poisoned source" (101); they "abominated the creature and could not deny the luminous truth of his contentions" (101). The narrator, though apparently fascinated and overwhelmed by Donkin's speech along with the other sailors, never fails to remind us (and perhaps himself) of the presence of "uncomprehending" Wamibo beside the group: "The younger men listened, thinking—this 'ere Donkin's a long-headed chap, though no kind of man, anyhow. The Scandinavians were frightened at his audacities; Wamibo did not understand ..." (100–101). It is almost as if the narrator flees into Wamibo's silent "dreaminess," shielding himself from the orator's "filthy loquacity" by summoning and conjuring up the deaf sailor.

Now we begin to see that the sound and voice filling the universe of *The Nigger of the "Narcissus"* is "distracting" not only because it is loud but, more importantly, because it is charged with a certain meaning less to the "we" narrator than to the author behind him. Allan H. Simmons discerns in the clamor and vernacular of the sailors' voices Conrad's attempt to "render phonetically British vocal inflections and dialects."[21] The task of the artist advocated in the "Preface" is, according to Simmons, to "articulate and make sense of" their hubbub,[22] giving voice to the voiceless. Simmons thus highlights the novel's attempt to "represent the character of his [Conrad's] adopted nation"[23] as his

---

[21] Simmons, *Joseph Conrad*, 56.

[22] Allan H. Simmons, "Representing 'the simple and the voiceless': Story-Telling in *The Nigger of the 'Narcissus,'*" *The Conradian*, vol. 24, no. 1 (Spring 1999): 47–48.

[23] Ibid., 46.

first fictional engagement with Englishness and his developing sense of himself as an English writer, thinking subversive and revolutionary thoughts in a British context.[24] Perhaps most of Conrad's contemporary "friends of the sea,"[25] along with the baby-faced Scandinavians cited earlier, could have smiled "placidly" at the "tempest" of curses of seamen, curses which sound simply "good-humoured" or "meaningless" (6) to them. But the clamorous vernacular of sailors' voices, on the contrary, might have conveyed a certain meaning for Conrad—a meaning that remains in excess of the contemporary British society, his adopted homeland, of which the *"Narcissus"* is presented as a microcosm, mirroring the social structure of England.[26]

"[G]rievously disappointed" by the result of the general election in Britain, Conrad famously showed his concern with "the rush of social-democratic ideas" from a broader, European perspective in a letter to Spiridon Kliszcewski on December 19, 1885:

> The newly enfranchised idiots have satisfied the yearnings of Mr. Chamberlain's herd by cooking the national goose according to his recipe. The next culinary operation will be a pretty kettle of fish of an international character. Joy reigns in St. Petersburg, no doubt, and profound disgust in Berlin: the International Socialist Association are triumphant, and every disreputable ragamuffin in Europe feels that the day of universal brotherhood, despoliation and disorder is coming apace, and nurses day-dreams of well-plenished pockets amongst the ruin of all that is respectable, venerable and holy. The great British Empire went over the edge, and yet on to the inclined plane of social progress and radical reform. The downward movement is hardly perceptible yet, and the clever men who started it may flatter themselves with the progress; but they will soon find that the fate of the nation is out of their hands now! The Alpine avalanche rolls quicker and quicker as it nears the abyss—its ultimate destination! Where's the man to stop the crashing avalanche?
>
> Where's the man to stop the rush of social-democratic ideas? The opportunity and the day have come and are gone! Believe me: gone forever! For the sun is set and the last barrier removed. England was the only barrier to the pressure of infernal doctrines born in continental back-slums. Now,

---

[24] Simmons, *Joseph Conrad*, 56.

[25] Conrad dedicated *The Nigger of the "Narcissus,"* "this tale about my friends of the sea," to Edward Garnett.

[26] Watt, *Conrad in the Nineteenth Century*, 110; Jeremy Hawthorn, *Joseph Conrad: Narrative Technique and Ideological Commitment* (London: Edward Arnold, 1990), 70.

there is nothing! The destiny of this nation and of all gnashing of teeth, to pass through robbery, equality, anarchy and misery under the iron rule of a militarism despotism! Such is the lesson of common sense logic.[27]

We should not be unduly surprised, therefore, when Michael Levenson and Michael North point out Conrad's conservative distrust of the noise of social agitation and his characteristically nineteenth-century association of disquieting sounds with unwanted social reform and discord.[28] However, if the subversive voices evoke another revolutionary activist, Conrad's father Apollo Korzeniowski, then the reaction may imply something more than mere distrust, as we have already seen in the "we" narrator's ambivalent attitude toward Donkin. The narrator cannot but listen with both interest and "unbounded" contempt to that "consummate artist" (100). While Conrad's repulsion at the social revolution in general is amply evidenced both in his essays and novels, he nevertheless seems to listen with much more interest than anyone else in the tale to the revolutionary voice of "the consummate artist," despite his contempt for revolutionary rhetoric.

Donkin's "filthy loquacity" may have brought the author back to his traumatic (Russian) past experience, to his "world of nightmares" (10), which he survived but could not be fully awakened from. The Polish author knew only too well that those revolutionary activities most likely lead to "nightmarish" consequences—in his case, the death of the parents. Non-Western ears in Conrad's works like those of Razumov, "a listener of the kind that hears you out intelligently," have an inclination to listen all too carefully to "forbidden opinions" and end up losing the ability to listen at all.[29] For instance, Razumov's attitude of "an inscrutable listener," in stark contrast to other Russians' "extraordinary love of words" (*UWE* 4), sets in motion a sequence of tragic events. Among a lot of "exuberant talkers, in the habit of exhausting themselves daily by ardent discussion" (6), the reserved young student becomes viewed by revolutionary activists as worthy of being trusted with "forbidden opinions,"

---

[27]   Conrad, *The Collected Letters of Joseph Conrad*, vol. 1. 16.

[28]   Levenson writes, "All through Conrad's novel, the challenge to 'unspoken loyalty' is anarchic speech; through much of the late nineteenth century, the sound of reform seems to have been as disquieting as its political consequences. It is the *noise* of social agitation which is often the great prod to the imagery of reaction." Levenson, *A Genealogy of Modernism*, 32; Michael North, *The Dialect of Modernism* (New York and Oxford: Oxford University Press, 1994), 40.

[29]   Joseph Conrad, *Under Western Eyes* (London: Dent, 1963), 6. Further page references to this edition will be given parenthetically in the text, preceded by *UWE* where it might otherwise be unclear.

but this trustworthiness unexpectedly draws an assassin, Haldin, to his room. Razumov returns to his lodgings to find that Haldin, who has just killed a minister of state with a terrorist bomb, expects Razumov to hide him and help him to escape. Although he barely knows Haldin, Razumov sympathetically listens to him rather than cutting him off and telling him to go away. In fact, he initially agrees to help the terrorist but later betrays him to the authorities. When he confesses his betrayal, the brutal revolutionary Nikita bursts his eardrums, leaving him deaf. Subsequently unable to hear an approaching tram, Razumov is run over by it and severely crippled. *Under Western Eyes* is thus a tragic story of a young man whose problems began when he lent too sympathetic an ear to revolutionary rhetoric.

Likewise, the titular hero of "Prince Roman," the only work in Conrad's corpus to make direct use of Polish historical material, commits himself to the struggle for Polish independence after his wife's death, because "something louder than [his] grief and yet something with a voice very like it calls [him]."[30] After twenty-five years' exile in Siberia, the prince returns home deaf and frail. In this context, we can argue that Wamibo's Russian ears are the first in a long line of Conrad's non-Western ears, yet the revolutionary rhetoric in *The Nigger of the "Narcissus"* falls on deaf ears in this instance. This might be a way of averting (on the author's part) the tragic results that await those who pay too much attention to the revolutionary voices.[31]

Most resounding in *The Nigger of the "Narcissus"* are the sonorous voice and wracking cough of James Wait, who has a cold in his chest. Jimmy's tremendously loud, "metallic" cough, as the narrator often highlights, "resound[s] like two explosions in a vault; the dome of the sky [rings] to it, and the iron plates of the ship's bulwarks [seem] to vibrate in unison" (18–19). Wait has "a fit of roaring, rattling cough, that [shakes] him, [tosses] him like a hurricane, and [flings] him panting with staring eyes headlong on his sea-chest" (24); "the nigger's cough," we are told, is "metallic and explosive like a gong" (39). When the crew, having succeeded in rescuing Jimmy from his deckhouse cabin in severe weather, are recovering with coffee made by Podmore the cook, the

---

[30] Joseph Conrad, "Prince Roman," *Tales of Hearsay and Last Essays* (London: Dent, 1963), 42. Subsequent page references will be to this edition, preceded by *THL* where necessary.
[31] I would think that Stevie's act of "hearing too much" (as his sister Winnie worries) of the conversations of the revolutionists in Verloc's shop in *The Secret Agent* can then be seen as a variation of Wamibo's deafness, but Winnie's mentally disabled brother is killed in the end. See Joseph Conrad, *The Secret Agent* (Oxford: Oxford University Press, 1983), 59.

narrator's perspective particularly fluctuates between the "we" and the "they" as follows:

> As the hours dragged slowly through the darkness Mr. Baker crawled back and forth along the poop several times. Some men fancied they had heard him exchange murmurs with the master, but at that time the memories were incomparably more vivid than anything actual, and they were not certain whether the murmurs were heard now or many years ago. They did not try to find out. A mutter more or less did not matter. It was too cold for curiosity, and almost for hope. They could not spare a moment or a thought from the great mental occupation of wishing to live. And the desire of life kept them alive, apathetic and enduring, under the cruel persistence of wind and cold; while the bestarred black dome of the sky revolved slowly above the ship, that drifted, bearing their patience and their suffering, through the stormy solitude of the sea.
>
> Huddled close to one another, they fancied themselves utterly alone. They heard sustained loud noises, and again bore the pain of existence through long hours of profound silence. In the night they saw sunshine, felt warmth, and suddenly, with a start, thought that the sun would never rise upon a freezing world. (81–82)

One may ask here why the narrator, by using the demonstrative pronoun "they," needs to maintain distance from the now heroically resilient crew in a freezing world. Given the novella's apparent emphasis on selfless acts of heroism, we might expect that the narrator would be happy to proudly identify with the crew who have courageously survived the storm *en masse*. But the narrator's comment that the memories "were incomparably more vivid than anything actual, and they were not certain whether the murmurs were heard now or many years ago" may lead us to wonder if this "cruel persistence of wind and cold" might have brought Conrad back to another "freezing world," the site of the original nightmarish experience of utter solitude in exile deep in Russia. Similarly, these "sustained loud noises" in a freezing world, along with Jimmy's metallic coughs and recurrent "wheezing like a man oppressed in his sleep" (24), could recall a memory of his father Apollo, who was gravely ill with tuberculosis in exile, and also of his own experience of pneumonia while young.[32] In this context, even the aforementioned clamor of the "white-clad Asiatics" and the "feverish and shrill babble of Eastern language" (4) begin

[32] Zdzisław Najder, *Joseph Conrad: A Life* (Rochester, NY: Camden House, 2007), 19–30.

to assume a Russian character. Conrad sometimes uses the adjective "Asiatic" to refer to Russian backwardness; for example, in "The Crime of Partition" he writes that "by the annexation of the greater part of the Polish Republic, Russia approached nearer to the comity of civilized nations and ceased, at least territorially, to be an Asiatic Power."[33] If these noises in the cold darkness, the noises from the nightmarish past, spoke to the Polish author in Russian while he was writing, then they might indeed have been too "distracting" for him to avoid conflating the past and the present, his Russian memories and his contemporary life in England. If the noises distracted him from his visual, impressionist commitment to the surface truth, then it would not be surprising that the narrator should need an earplug, as it were—something that blocks the intrusion of the Russian language—to help him not to repeat the tragedy of Razumov or Prince Roman, who gave a full hearing to the Russian voices.

It is worth remembering here that between 1895 and 1896, a couple of months before Conrad began writing *The Nigger of the "Narcissus,"* his mentor Edward Garnett dissuaded him from working on *The Sisters*, an unfinished story of a young Ruthenian painter from Russia who travelled through Western Europe searching unsuccessfully for a creed to believe in.[34] The voices from the Russian soil most likely lingered in his head while the Polish author was trying to write his first English sea story. Therefore, what matters is not, as Ian Watt casually remarks, that Wamibo "knows no English,"[35] but rather that he does not "hear" Russian, the very noise that presumably "distracted" the Polish author in his struggle to find a place in English literary circles. It might also be relevant that Finland, surrounded by the superpowers, Sweden to the west, Norway to the north, and Russia to the east, had been under persistent threat of invasion, a situation all too familiar for a writer who had spent his early life under Russian oppression. The Grand Duchy of Finland was under the Russian imperial rule from 1809 to 1917. In his Russian subjectivity and in his deafness, Wamibo evokes the violence inflicted upon two other figures in Conrad's stories: Razumov, deafened by Russian conspirators, and the Polish nobleman Prince Roman, who returns home deaf from his Siberian exile. One

---

[33]   Conrad, "The Crime of Partition," *Notes on Life and Letters*, 115.
[34]   Joseph Conrad, *The Sisters: An Unfinished Story* (Milan: U. Mursia, 1968), 33; Joseph Conrad, *Congo Diary and Other Uncollected Pieces*. ed. Zdzisław Najder (New York: Doubleday, 1978), 39, 43.
[35]   Watt, *Conrad in the Nineteenth Century*, 103.

might thus regard Wamibo as the return of the Russian experience, the return of memory of Polish history, and his deafness as the very site of memory.[36] Perhaps it is Conrad himself, through Wamibo's dimmed gaze, who was "contemplating one of those weird visions that haunt the men of his race" (13).

*

Unlike his first two novels set in the East, *Almayer's Folly* and *Outcast of the Islands*, *The Nigger of the "Narcissus"* can be called Conrad's first English novel, with its predominantly English concerns and its celebration of the maritime tradition, which draws on his own sea experience. The novella marks a great step forward in Conrad's literary career, a new departure indeed for him as an English author in its setting and narrative technique. Carefully positioned for the English literary market, it was in fact written under pressure. Conrad was always in debt, but his financial situation became even more desperate after his marriage in 1896. He did not attempt to sell his first two novels to magazines, but he tried with *The Nigger of the "Narcissus"* and W. E. Henley, the influential editor of the pro-imperialist *New Review*, was favorably impressed by the first two chapters.[37] Prompted in part by Edward Garnett's recommendation that he write a sea story,[38] he started to work on a novel about English sailors returning home for that masculine and jingoistic journal. For Conrad, as Tim Middleton observes, writing *The Nigger of the "Narcissus"* was a way of "aligning himself with a particular literary circle with an appetite for tales of men and empire."[39] Turning a deaf ear, as we have seen, to those revolutionary voices from his memory, "with an eye on him [Henley],"[40] and also following his mentor Garnett's advice, Conrad could produce the most English story in his oeuvre with what would become the hallmark of his works: the impressionistic first-person narrator "I," or the modernist narrator on the Victorian sailing ship in Levenson's terms.[41]

---

36 For the return of memory or the site of memory, see Cathy Caruth's reading of Balzac's *Colonel Chabert*, in particular, in *Literature in the Ashes of History* (Baltimore: Johns Hopkins University Press, 2013), 18–35, 54–74.

37 Watt, *Conrad in the Nineteenth Century*, 75–76.

38 Conrad, *The Collected Letters*, vol.1, 268.

39 Tim Middleton, *Joseph Conrad* (London and New York: Routledge, 2006), 32.

40 Conrad, *The Collected Letters*, vol.3, 115. Deresiewicz regards Conrad's first use of the first-person singular as the author's acceptance of his identity as an English writer, aimed at his new literary circle. See Deresiewicz, "Conrad's Impasse," 218–219.

41 Levenson, *A Genealogy of Modernism*, 1–22, especially 9.

The turbulent, tempestuous writing process, often interrupted and intruded upon by voices from the past, would presumably have aroused a desire in the Eastern European sailor-turned-writer not to listen to the "filthy loqua-city flow[ing] like a troubled stream from a poisoned source." He sought instead a "safe" refuge in Wamibo's deafness, vacant staring, and dreamy preoccupation with "weird visions that haunt the men of his race." While the Russian Finn's inability to listen marks the very return of the Russian experience, serving as the site of memory, his "dreamy" vision fortuitously brings about the impressionistic description of the *Narcissus*'s voyage home. The real *Narcissus*, as noted earlier, returned home safely without the aid of a Russian Finn, whereas the fictional *Narcissus* and the novella, or the "we" speaker's narration, might not have reached the end of their journey if not for Wamibo. It is through Wamibo's seeming modest, marginal agency that the author managed to carry his artistic task to completion. In this sense, we may well recognize Wamibo the Russian Finn as a secret agent behind the birth of Conrad the English author and of the impressionist in *The Nigger of the "Narcissus."*

3

Marlow's Ear

Acoustic Penetration into the
Heart of Darkness

Toward the end of *The Nigger of the "Narcissus,"* desperately trying to turn a deaf ear through Wamibo's perception to the nightmarish call of the other(s), the first person plural narrator "we" gives birth to an individual "I." If the "we" narrator of *The Nigger of the "Narcissus,"* in his impressionistic individuation process of the narrative perspective, needs to take refuge in the perception of the dreamy-eyed deaf sailor to shield himself from the "distracting" noises of the other(s), then that might imply that the Polish author finds it somewhat "uncongenial" to adapt himself to a narrative technique premised on subjective consciousness, a technique of "Western eyes," as it were. This chapter, in order to bear witness to Marlow's struggle as a seer, continues the examination of the audible in *Heart of Darkness*, the novella characterized by the narrator's ability to explore and present the problems and experiences of a particular individual filtered through subjective consciousness.[1]

Marlow's exploration into the heart of darkness, as we shall see in what follows, despite his apparent effort to register subjective visual experience, cannot always be subsumed under the terminology of an individual "point of view." Marlow's "subject" of the listening, more often than not, can hardly be objectified, spreading and reverberating through space. With his head full of strange voices and sounds from afar, Marlow's "resonant self" is spaced, returning to himself not as himself but as an echo, thereby opening a possible space inseparably both his and others'. By paying particular attention to the

---

[1] Jakob Lothe, *Conrad's Narrative Method* (Oxford: Oxford University Press, 1989), 98, 99.

resonant nature of the sonorous that can hardly be objectified as a spatial phe-nomenon, this chapter will argue that Marlow's sense of hearing seemingly goes hand in hand with his "point of view" while straining toward something singularly plural. Thus Marlow's acoustic penetration into the heart of dark-ness opens a possible space of plurality that does not necessarily mean multi-plication or addition of an individual subject but rather a strange community.

* * *

Ian Watt described the narrative method of *Heart of Darkness* as "subjec-tive moral impressionism," observing that the novella, in Marlow's assump-tion that reality is essentially private and individual, accepts and asserts the bounded and ambiguous nature of individual understanding.[2] Emphasizing the function of Conrad's nautical raconteur not merely as "a registering consciousness" but also as a moral commentator and analyst, as Michael Greaney precisely puts it,[3] Watt famously situated Marlow not in the tradi-tion of the captains courageous of Victorian romance but in the tradition of the super-subtle heroes of Henry James's novels of the 1890s. Watt's descrip-tion, Greaney continues, is still the most influential modern discussion of the function of Marlow even in a postmodern critical milieu in which the very assumption of a unified individual is apparently most severely questioned, if not demythologized.[4] John Peters, for example, repeatedly stresses Conrad's affirmation of human individual subjectivity as an impressionist response to ethical anarchy in an irrational and indifferent universe in his *Conrad and Impressionism*.[5] More recently, Andrea White, largely in tune with Greaney's view mentioned above, lays out how Conrad's art of prose-rendering of an individual consciousness was shaped under the influence of Walter Pater and Henry James, in particular, in contemporary Anglo-American literary modernism.[6]

However, if one of Marlow's functions, as Watt has it, is "to represent how much a man cannot know,"[7] then what are we to make of Marlow's occasional

[2]   Watt, *Conrad in the Nineteenth Century*, 174.
[3]   Michael Greaney, *Conrad, Language, and Narrative* (New York: Palgrave, 2002), 60.
[4]   Ibid. For a postmodern discussion of subjectivity, see Nick Mansfield, *Subjectivity: Theories of the Self from Freud to Haraway* (New York: New York University Press, 2000), 13.
[5]   Peters, *Conrad and Impressionism*, 123–158.
[6]   White, "Conrad and Modernism," 163–196.
[7]   Watt, *Conrad in the Nineteenth Century*, 174.

excessive knowledge, or his mysterious power of seeing what is far away in time and space; for example, when Marlow "foresees" his possible encounter with "a flabby, pretending, weak-eyed devil of a rapacious and pitiless folly" (*HD* 65) almost immediately after he arrives in Africa. Marlow's clairvoyance, as it were, has been largely ignored. It is indeed unaccountable in terms of the "bounded" nature of individual understanding, and it is moreover less noticeable beside one of the most often-cited and shocking scenes in *Heart of Darkness*, that of his offering a biscuit to one of those "black shadows of disease and starvation" (66) dying slowly in the shade of a tree. In the following passage, Marlow witnesses skinny black men in chain marching in a file, toiling up the path, but soon his perception is far removed in time and space:

> Instead of going up, I turned and descended to the left. My idea was to let that chain-gang get out of sight before I climbed the hill. ... as I stood on this hillside, I foresaw that in the blinding sunshine of that land I would become acquainted with a flabby, pretending, weak-eyed devil of a rapacious and pitiless folly. How insidious he could be, too, I was only to find out several months later and a thousand miles farther. For a moment I stood appalled, as though by a warning. (65)

Marlow's role as a seer, a witness of colonial atrocities, has been much discussed and cannot be overemphasized. Paying due attention to what he sees here, however, we cannot but notice Marlow's sudden perceptual transition to the thoughts of "several months later and a thousand miles farther." "As though by a warning," Marlow later again "foresees" that Kurtz is already dead when the steamer is attacked in a thick fog and its native helmsman is killed with a spear. Indeed, the sight of the dead body of the helmsman, Watt argues,[8] makes Marlow think of someone else who has also become an immediate part of his mental life and who he fears may have been killed by the same attackers, but we may nevertheless sense something more than that in Marlow's inclusive sense of time and space, something that cannot simply be explained in terms of the narrative technique of an individual perspective. Rather, Marlow's transitive mind is too comprehensive to frame things into a shape from a personal

---

[8] Ibid., 239. Watt on the other hand admits: "The transition in Marlow's mind is certainly evidence that, like much else, his relation to Kurtz is not entirely, not even mainly, rational and conscious: and Kurtz himself is one of Conrad's closest approaches to the portrayal of the unconscious and irrational pole of human behaviour."

viewpoint, as he himself later states, "The mind of man is capable of anything—because everything is in it, all the past as well as all the future" (96). It is little wonder, therefore, that his point of view often wavers in an uncertain way, creating narrative ambiguity. This ambiguity, however, tends to be predominantly taken as one of the key features of the literature of the late nineteenth and early twentieth centuries, and therefore it has reinforced rather than undermined the public image of Conrad as a forerunner of modernism.[9]

By making this point, however, I do not mean to say that Conrad is neither an impressionist nor a modernist.[10] Marlow's relativistic comment, for instance, on the sense of reality—"Your own reality—for yourself, not for others—what no other man can ever know. They can only see the mere show, and never can tell what it really means" (85)—does indeed demonstrate an aspect of Conrad's impressionism, a tendency to view the epistemological process as an individual and not a universal phenomenon.[11] To be sure, one cannot make sense of the external world without an individual perception (however limited it may be), the process whereby the individual sensations of external reality are registered and translated into conceptual terms that can make them understandable to the observer and communicable to other people. Nevertheless, too much emphasis exclusively on the narrative technique of subjective consciousness prevents us from seeing—or, more appropriately for our discussion of aurality and community in this chapter, from hearing—what overflows an individual point of view. Marlow's mysterious anticipation of an encounter with "a flabby, pretending, weak-eyed devil" mentioned above and his obsession with a far-off sound as we shall see in what follows, in fact, hardly subscribe to Peter's account of impressionism, such as, "The object appears as it

---

[9] Allon White, "Conrad and the Rhetoric of Enigma," in *The Uses of Obscurity: The Fiction of Early Modernism* (London, Boston, and Henley, UK: Routledge & Kegan Paul, 1981), 108–129. White, "Conrad and Modernism," 172.

[10] Conrad's impressionism, as has been pointed out, is only one of the many aspects of his art of fiction. See Bruce F. Teets, "Literary Impressionism in Ford Madox Ford, Joseph Conrad and Related Writers," rpt. in vol. IV of *Joseph Conrad: Critical Assessments*, ed. Keith Carabine (Robertsbridge, UK: Helm Information, 1992), 37. Watt also remarks that Conrad certainly knew something about pictorial and literary impressionism, but his tastes in painting, as in music, were distinctly old-fashioned, and he apparently disliked Van Gogh and Cézanne; and that he thought of impressionism as primarily concerned with visual appearances. It is unlikely that Conrad either thought of himself as an impressionist or was significantly influenced by the impressionist movement. Conrad is, in Watt's view, different both from the French Impressionists and from Pater, Crane, or Ford in the sense that he wanted to pay as much attention to the inside as to the outside, to the meaning as to the appearance. Watt, *Conrad in the Nineteenth Century*, 173, 179.

[11] Peters, *Conrad and Impressionism*, 5, 13.

actually appears—at a particular point in space and time and filtered through a particular human consciousness."[12] Rather, Marlow's prediction can better be considered as clairvoyance, or a kind of "telepathy," not in a more generalized sense of sympathetic communication between minds through some unknown channels of the senses but in Nicholas Royle's sense as the question of narrative fiction.

Royle seeks to reconsider the narrator's "unnatural" access to the minds of others, or what he calls "uncanny knowledge," in terms of "telepathy," instead of uncritically relying on the terms of "omniscience" or a "point of view."[13] "Omniscience" assumes complete knowledge of everyone else's thoughts and feelings, while a "point of view" looks into a character's mind and describes what is happening even in the innermost, secret thoughts and feelings. But a narrator in fact inhabits the thoughts, feelings, and perceptions of only one character at a time; what he or she appears to know about is highly circumscribed. The idea of "omniscience," Royle suggests, is inextricably entangled in Christian assumptions, inevitably tending toward totalization, while the notion of "point of view" is reductive if we take account of the force of what is not conscious, of what is not present. Thus Royle describes what is happening in some texts of Charles Dickens and Virginia Woolf not simply as "a matter of light and vision run wild" but rather as a question of voice and thus of "a new readerly ear."[14] In his discussion of "the telepathic," Royle argues that the visual has been privileged since Percy Lubbock's *The Craft of Fiction* (1921) and a "point of view," a visual metaphor, for a hundred years and more has worked to elide or negate the importance of voice. "Point of view," Royle goes further, would in fact be similar to "omniscience" in terms of a sense of unity and to "God." Together with "omniscience," he writes, "point of view" has been a key critical term for "safekeeping of the unitariness" of the figures of "author," "narrator," and "character" alike.[15] Far from being something that presupposes the identity and unity of a subject, what Royle calls telepathy is about "a writing of distant minds, apprehensions of feeling and suffering in and of the distance,

---

[12] Ibid., 21.
[13] Nicholas Royle, *The Uncanny* (Manchester: Manchester University Press, 2003), 256.
[14] Ibid., 262–265.
[15] Ibid., 263; Henricksen also points out that the text of Conrad's preface to *The Nigger of the "Narcissus"* privileges the sense of sight, a privileging that is found in the modernist concept of fictional point of view. See, Henricksen, *Nomadic Voices*, 44.

phantom communications, unconscious, absent or ghostly emotions, without any return to stabilized identities."[16]

It has become customary that Marlow is not only a witness, a seer, of the brutal acts of European colonialism in Africa but is also an avid listener of Kurtz's voice. Whereas much of the discussion of Marlow as a listener pivots on the reciprocity between listeners and speakers, that is, the direct effect of speakers on listeners,[17] my concern here is with Marlow's sensitivity to the far-off drums resounding from the heart of the Dark Continent, the expansive and transitive perception irreducible in terms of the notion of "point of view."

"Listening" as opposed to "seeing," according to Nancy, is marked by its property of penetration and ubiquity. The sonorous present, as it spreads and resonates through space, does not let itself be objectified or projected outward; it can therefore be ungraspable within the logic of presence as "appearing," as phenomenality or as manifestation. Sound in general, Nancy writes, is not exactly a phenomenon; it does not stem from a logic of manifestation. It stems from a different logic, that of evocation. While manifestation brings presence to light, evocation summons presence to itself. As such, sound is not at first intended; on the contrary, sound is what places its subject, which has not preceded it with an aim.[18] In this sense, Marlow's transitive perceiving self can sometimes better be understood as a "resonant" subject than as a phenomenological subject.

Marlow's ears occasionally catch far-off sounds even while his eyes are riveted on the events unfolding in front of him. After he hears that he has got the job, Marlow travels across the English Channel to a city that reminds him of a "whited sepulchre" (55) to sign his employment contract at the Company's office. Marlow takes leave of his aunt and boards the French steamer that is to take him to Africa. The steamer, slipping by the coast, calls at ports to land soldiers and custom-house officers. Indeed, the coast, at once smiling, frowning,

---

[16] Royle, *The Uncanny*, 268.

[17] For Marlow as a listener, see Owen Knowles, "'To Make You Hear ...': Some Aspects of Conrad's Dialogue," *Polish Review*, vol. 20, no. 2–3 (1975): 164–180; Thomas Dilworth, "Listeners and Lies in 'Heart of Darkness,'" *The Review of English Studies*. New Series, vol. 38, no. 152 (Nov., 1987): 510–522; Hans Ulrich Seeber, "Surface as Suggestive Energy: Fascination and Voice in Conrad's 'Heart of Darkness,'" in *Joseph Conrad's Heart of Darkness. Bloom's Modern Critical Interpretations*, ed. Harold Bloom (New York: Infobase, 2008), 79–94.

[18] Jean-Luc Nancy, *Listening*, trans. Charlotte Mandell (New York: Fordham University Press, 2007), 13, 20.

inviting, grand, and savage, appears enigmatic to "intruders" (62) and drowns some in the surf, as if to ward them off, whereas the voice of the dangerous surf along the coast is, to Marlow who feels isolated among those "intruders," "a positive pleasure, like the speech of a brother" (61); it is, for him, "something natural, that [has] its reason, that [has] a meaning" (61). Black fellows shouting and singing in a boat from the shore also, for Marlow, want "no excuse for being there" (61). While what Marlow sees is a series of inanities in the forms of the French man-of-war shelling the bush that hides a camp of what they call "enemies," a boiler wallowing in the grass, an undersized railway truck lying on its back with its wheels in the air, pieces of decaying machinery, and a stack of rusty rails, what he hears is a "continuous noise of the rapids above [that] hover[s] over this scene of inhabited devastation" (63), a noise he later again hears when he sees the misery of natives forced to work in chains and left to die: "The rapids [are] near, and an uninterrupted, uniform, headlong, rushing noise fill[s] the mournful stillness of the grove, where not a breath stir[s], not a leaf move[s], with a mysterious sound—as though the tearing pace of the launched earth . . . suddenly [became] audible" (66). From the Company's chief accountant in immaculate linen in the "great demoralization of the land" (68), Marlow first hears the name of Kurtz as "a first-class agent" (69). Setting out on the 200-mile walk to the Central Station, Marlow hears on a quiet night "the tremor of far-off drums, sinking, swelling, a tremor vast, faint; a sound weird, appealing, suggestive, and wild—and perhaps with as profound a meaning as the sound of bells in a Christian country" (71). He spends three months repairing the damaged steamboat, finally setting off upriver, penetrating deeper and deeper into the heart of darkness to rescue Kurtz who is reported to be ill. When the steamer struggles round a bend, Marlow catches a glimpse of "a whirl of black limbs, a mass of hand clapping, of feet thumping, of bodies swaying, of eyes rolling" (96) under the droop of heavy foliage. Thrilled by the thought of "their humanity" and white men's "remote kinship with this wild and passionate uproar," he responds to "the terrible frankness of that noise, a dim suspicion of there being a meaning in it" (96). "This fiendish row," though incomprehensible to his listeners "so remote from the night of first ages" (96), allows him to look into the depth of his heart and find "truth stripped of its cloak of time" (97) and his own "voice": "What was there after all? . . . An appeal to me in this fiendish row—is there? Very well; I hear; I admit, but I have a voice too, and for good or evil mine is the speech that cannot be silenced" (96–97).

As they approach Kurtz's compound, Marlow's steamer is covered by "the blind whiteness of the fog" (105), from which first comes a muffled rattle and a very loud cry, "as of infinite desolation," and then a "complaining clamour, modulated in savage discords" (101–102). To Marlow it seems "as though the mist itself [screamed], so suddenly, and apparently from all sides at once … this tumultuous and mournful uproar arise[s]" (102). Among "the whites" greatly discomposed and on the alert for a possible attack from the "savages," only Marlow is irresistibly impressed not by their hostility but rather by their sorrow, as he describes here:

> Unexpected, wild, and violent as they [the cries] had been, they had given me an irresistible impression of sorrow. The glimpse of the steamboat had for some reason filled those savages with unrestrained grief. The danger, if any, I expounded, was from our proximity to a great human passion let loose. Even extreme grief may ultimately vent itself in violence. … (107)

Here Marlow's eyes are "of no more use to [him] than if [he was] buried miles deep in a heap of cotton-wool" (107). There seems to be nowhere for him to go and shun this "mournful uproar" that "fills his ears," coming "from all sides at once." Feeling too close to them, Marlow cannot restrain his feeling of compassion; the "impression of sorrow," far from being an impression from a viewpoint at a remove from some object, is "irresistible" and flows over him.

* * *

After the attack in the fog, Marlow finally meets Kurtz at the Inner Station. Broken by illness, "the first-class agent" is reduced to skin and bones, "an animated image of death carved out of old ivory" (134). While he does not seem capable of a whisper, the volume of tone Kurtz emits effortlessly, almost without moving his lips, amazes Marlow: "A voice! a voice! It [is] grave, profound, vibrating" (135). The night the dying Kurtz is brought aboard the steamer, he tries to crawl back to the campfires of his native followers, drawn by "the spell of the wilderness," "the throb of drums," and "the drone of weird incantation" (144) from the jungle. In pursuit of Kurtz, Marlow "confound[s] the beat of the drum with the beating of [his] heart" and is "pleased at its calm regularity" (142). This does not mean that Marlow has lost his senses, for he knows perfectly well what he is doing when he asks Kurtz if he knows what he is doing. Kurtz's response "sound[s] to [Marlow] far off and yet loud, like a hail through a speaking-trumpet" (143). At the very moment when Kurtz, the "wandering and tormented" shadow, seems irretrievably lost, Marlow paradoxically feels that "the foundations of [their] intimacy [is] being laid—to endure—to endure—even to the end—even beyond" (143). Carried back on deck, Kurtz swiftly deteriorates and dies on the journey downriver, leaving his famous last words: "The horror! The horror!" (149). Believing that Kurtz's summing-up, his "judgment upon the adventures of his soul on this earth" (150), is "an affirmation, a moral victory" (151), Marlow remains "loyal to Kurtz to the last, and even beyond," when a long time after he is to hear once more, not his own voice, but "the echo of his [Kurtz's] magnificent eloquence" from his Intended (151–152).

Standing before the door of Kurtz's Intended's house back in the sepulchral city, Marlow has a vision of Kurtz on the stretcher, "opening his mouth voraciously, as if to devour all the earth with all its mankind" (155). Marlow sees Kurtz before him living as much as he has ever lived; but like "a shadow insatiable of splendid appearances, of frightful realities; a shadow darker than the shadow of the night," Kurtz seems "draped nobly in the folds of a gorgeous eloquence" (155). Kurtz's apparition "vengefully" rushes into the house with those sights and sounds that Marlow saw and heard in the heart of Africa: "The vision seem[s] to enter the house with [Marlow]—the stretcher, the phantom-bearers, the wild crowd of obedient worshipers, the gloom of the forests, the glitter of the reach between the murky bends, the beat of the drum, regular and muffled like the beating of a heart—the heart of a conquering darkness" (155–156). In this "moment of triumph for the wilderness," "[t]he memory of what [Marlow] [heard] him [Kurtz] say afar there, with the horned shapes stirring at [Marlow's] back, in the glow of fires, within the patient woods, those broken phrases [come] back to [Marlow], [are] heard again in their ominous and terrifying simplicity" (156). Marlow's "here and now" with Kurtz's fiancé is being invaded and overwhelmed by his "there and then" with Kurtz. Then he shakes hands with the Intended and feels as if Kurtz died "this very minute."

The handshake with her does not necessarily mean direct touch with reality, but rather it carries him beyond time into eternity:

> [W]hile we were still shaking hands, such a look of awful desolation came upon her face that I perceived she was one of those creatures that are not the playthings of Time. For her he [Kurtz] had died only yesterday. And, by Jove! the impression was so powerful that for me too he seemed to have died only yesterday—nay, this very minute. I saw her and him in the same instant of time—his death and her sorrow—I saw her sorrow in the very moment of his death. Do you understand? I saw them together—I heard them together. She had said, with a deep catch of the breath, "I have survived"; while my strained ears seemed to hear distinctly, mingled with her tone of despairing regret, the summing-up whisper of his eternal condemnation. (157)

This can hardly be called a reproduction of an event that occurred at a specific location and at a specific time. Marlow sees and hears Kurtz who died and was buried in a far-off land and his bereaved fiancé in Brussels, together, "in the very moment of his [Kurtz's] death." Marlow's "strained ears," hearing Kurtz's "summing-up whisper of his eternal condemnation" mingled with the fiancé's regretful sigh of survival, thus opening an impossible space that goes beyond time, beyond "the threshold of an eternal darkness," as we see in the extract below. Here the sound of her voice extolling Kurtz's oratorical gift accompanies all the other sounds Marlow heard farther away in the dark Continent:

> "… Who was not his friend who had heard him speak once?" she was saying. "He drew men towards him by what was best in them." She looked at me with intensity. "It is the gift of the great," she went on, and the sound of her low voice seemed to have the accompaniment of all the other sounds, full of mystery, desolation, and sorrow, I had ever heard—the ripple of the river, the soughing of the trees swayed by the wind, the murmurs of wild crowds, the faint ring of incomprehensible words cried from afar, the whisper of a voice speaking from beyond the threshold of an eternal darkness. (159)

Likening the exchange of voices here to Wordsworth's projective address to his sister and Catherine's inclusive cry to Heathcliff, Michael Macovski suggests that such dialogues serve to "disinter the buried voices of a vocative past."[19] It is nevertheless no longer simply "her" voice that Marlow hears, but rather,

---

[19]   Macovski, *Dialogue and Literature*, 167.

incomprehensively, it is at once "hers" and "Kurtz's" that he hears, and therefore it is nobody's, lost and alive, accompanying all the other mysterious sounds Marlow has ever heard far away out there, among which is that violent clamor of "unrestrained grief" (107) behind the white fog. This could be something more than what Macovski calls "a mnemonic exchange with lost voices" or "the echo of dialogue across time";[20] rather, it is an interaction beyond time, "beyond the threshold of an eternal darkness." Her grief over her fiancé's death inexplicably resonates with the "infinite desolation" (102) of those men shouting on the riverbank. This resonance is made possible only in Marlow's auditory perception.[21]

* * *

Since Albert Guerard's influential *Conrad the Novelist*,[22] it has become a critical commonplace to read *Heart of Darkness* not only as the testimony of an eyewitness to the atrocities of European imperialism but also as Marlow's journey into self. The visual aspect of self-exploration in the narrative of *Heart of Darkness* has been thus repeatedly highlighted, thereby reinforcing the impressionistic narrative technique premised on the idea of an individual "point of view" as criteria in the discussion of the novella.

Vincent Pecora's philosophical discussion of voice in *Heart of Darkness* as much more than an aspect of literary technique, that is, as the focus for an investigation of identity and presence, finds in the novella a much earlier Derridean critique of voice (and the spoken word) as the sign of presence, an inviolable human presence in the world that forms the groundwork for a metaphysical and moral order.[23] And yet, despite his Derridean gesture, Pecora's conclusion that Marlow retains some hope in Kurtz's "self-knowledge," the ability to name and thereby conquer the darkness within him, is not so very different from what has been traditionally understood about the novella. For Marlow, as Pecora reads it, it is an affirmation of "the subject," a "self" that in

---

[20] Ibid.

[21] "[T]he whisper of a voice speaking from beyond the threshold of an eternal darkness," (159) remain enigmatic in *Heart of Darkness*, whereas the voices and sounds in *The Nigger of the "Narcissus,"* as we discussed in the previous chapter, have a ring of Russian revolution and revolt. It is interesting to note here that Marlow in *Heart of Darkness* perceives "a vibrating note of revolt" (151) in Kurtz's whisper of "the horror."

[22] Guerard, *Conrad the Novelist*, 1–59. Regarding Marlow's voyage of "self-discovery," see also, Hampson, *Joseph Conrad*, 111, 112, 115; Simmons, *Joseph Conrad*, 88, 97–98.

[23] Vincent Pecora, "Heart of Darkness and *The Phenomenology of Voice*," *ELH*, 52.4 (Winter 1985): 1000–1001.

the end will appear, and will make a "moral" judgment.[24] Marlow's belief in the illusory idea of the self, says Pecora, reflects what Nietzsche called a "metaphysical need" to believe in a neutral independent "subject," prompted by an instinct for self-preservation and self-affirmation in which every lie is sanctified.[25] Pecora's emphasis on human subjectivity in Conrad's art as a filter and shelter from ethical anarchy tempts us to align his reading (contra him) more with the mainstream Conrad criticism[26] than with the tradition of philosophy from Schopenhauer through Nietzsche to Derrida.

A belief in an independent "subject" that creates meaning for human existence is indeed irresistible. Marlow's acoustic exploration into the heart of darkness, as I have described, also appears, or more precisely, "sounds," like a journey into self. Marlow never imagines Kurtz as doing but as "discoursing" (113). To him, Kurtz presents himself as "a voice":

> [O]f all his gifts the one that stood out preeminently, that carries with it a sense of real presence, was his ability to talk, his words—the gift of expression, the bewildering, the illuminating, the most exalted and the most contemptible, the pulsating stream of light, or the deceitful flow from the heart of an impenetrable darkness. (113–114)

He has been looking forward to "a talk with Kurtz" (113). Therefore, what disappoints him most in his conjecture of Kurtz's probable death (evoked by the death of the helmsman) is not the idea that he will never see the man nor shake him by hands but the one that he will never "hear" him, that is, "the idea of having lost the inestimable privilege of listening to the gifted Kurtz" (114). On his way deeper into the heart of darkness, Marlow realizes that he has a voice, too. The appeal of the "fiendish row" on the river-bank just below Kurtz's station somehow leads him to find his own voice "that cannot be silenced" (97).

Thinking literary discourse as "a composite of voices," voices not only of literary characters but also of political, religious, and historical discourses, Bakhtinian approaches seek an analysis of consciousness not in the form of a sole and single *I* but in the form of the interactions of many consciousnesses. As a move away from insularity of the solipsistic Romantic "I," Bakhtin's theory of dialogue stresses what takes places on the threshold, the boundary

---

[24] Ibid., 1009.
[25] Ibid., 1006, 1008–1009. Pecora has lots in common with Peters in his notion of human subjectivity. See Peters, *Conrad and Impressionism*, 60.
[26] See, for instance, Peters, *Conrad and Impressionism*, 60.

between one's own and someone else's consciousness.[27] And yet, for Marlow, who could not defend the Intended nor even himself against the invasion of "a voice speaking from beyond the threshold of an eternal darkness" (159), what happens is the disappearance of the boundary itself. What is at stake, for him, is not simply whether a perceiving self is singular or plural, but rather that it is at once singular and plural. Marlow's sense of hearing opens the impossible space singular and plural alike, in a way that recalls "a resonant subject," in Jean-Luc Nancy's term, that is "an intensive spacing of a rebound that does not end in any return to self without immediately relaunching, as an echo, a call to that same self."[28] The subject who is listening, according to Nancy, does not let itself be objectified or projected outward; it takes place every time it listens:

> To listen is to enter that spatiality by which, *at the same time*, I am penetrated, for it opens up in me as well as around me, and from me as well as toward me: it opens me inside me as well as outside, and it is through such a double, quadruple, or sextuple opening that a "self" can take place.[29]

"While the subject of the target is always given, posed in itself to its *point of view*," Nancy further states, "the subject of listening is always still yet to come, spaced, traversed, and called by itself, *sounded* by itself."[30] If what Marlow's ear is straining toward in his approach to the self is not so dissimilar from the "subject of listening," then his perceptive exploration into the heart of darkness, which is in fact expansive despite its appearance of closing upon himself as a single point of view, is not simply a "metaphor for access to self" but rather "the reality of [the] access."[31] The "mournful uproar" (102) in the white fog and Kurtz's loud voice sounding "far off and yet loud like a hail through a speaking-trumpet" (143) in his nighttime pursuit of Kurtz into the woods, evoke some strange sympathy bordered on, or blended with, abomination, while it confuses on the other hand Marlow's sense of proximity. The thought of "[their] remote kinship with [the] wild and passionate uproar [of black men]"

---

27 Macovski, *Dialogue and Literature*, 3–7.
28 Nancy, *Listening*, 21. Interestingly, in a way strangely "evocative" of the attack in the white fog, an event that, as we have seen above, invites Marlow to find his own voice, Nancy also states: "Visual presence is already there, available, before I see it, whereas sonorous presence *arrives*—it entails an *attack* [italics in the original]" (Ibid., 14).
29 Nancy, *Listening*, 14. "Sonorous time," in Nancy, is not in a point on a line; it is "a time that opens up, that is hollowed out" (ibid., 13).
30 Ibid., 21.
31 Ibid., 12.

thrills Marlow (96); and Kurtz's tenacious adherence, even when he is reduced to a shadow, to his "immense plans" makes Marlow's "blood run cold" (143). And yet, his ears still catch some mournful note in the "savage" clamor of the native people in the forest and also something enduringly intimate in Kurtz's voice. Marlow's "access to self," his access to the heart of darkness, is "the reality of this access, a reality consequently indissociably 'mine' and 'other,' 'singular' and 'plural,' as much as it is 'material' and 'spiritual' and 'signifying' and 'a-signifying.' "[32] Marlow's acoustic penetration into the heart of darkness thus does neither necessarily summon an ambiguous, divided modernist self nor even a Bakhtinian intersubjectivity but rather a being singular and plural alike.

[32]   Ibid.

Hospitality in "The Secret Sharer"

"The Secret Sharer" has long been read as a story of initiation, a story of "a metaphorical journey towards knowing oneself."[1] The narrative indeed presents the "inner drama" of the young captain's psyche,[2] but it also reveals an external gesture of his self, a gesture of going beyond itself: at every move to keep to himself, the young captain, in fact, goes out of his way, out of himself, to meet with the other person, Leggatt. The captain's external orientation has so far received little attention as such, in part because Leggatt has been regarded more as a symbolic manifestation of the captain's unconscious than as the other in flesh and blood. However, Leggatt is, for the captain, more than a symbol of his inner, darker self as has been said.[3] In taking up the stranger on board before asking his name, harboring and helping him to escape, thereby putting lives entrusted to him at risk in the most outrageous way, the captain places the presence of the other above all, above his responsibility to

---

[1] Simmons, *Joseph Conrad*, 169. Regarding the initiation, to name but a few, see Donald C. Yelton, *Mimesis and Metaphor: An Inquiry into the Genesis and Scope of Conrad's Symbolic Imagery* (The Hague and Paris: Mouton, 1967), 272. For the traditional interpretation of "The Secret Sharer," also see John G. Peters, *The Cambridge Introduction to Joseph Conrad* (Cambridge: Cambridge University Press, 2006), 95.

[2] Brian Richardson, "Construing Conrad's 'The Secret Sharer': Suppressed Narratives, Subaltern Reception, and the Act of Interpretation," *Studies in the Novel*, vol. 33, no. 3 (Fall 2001): 317. For other similar readings of "The Secret Sharer" as an inward musing reminiscence, see R. W. Stallman, "Conrad and 'The Secret Sharer,'" rpt. in *Conrad's Secret Sharer and the Critics*, ed. Bruce Harkness (Belmont, CA: Wadsworth, 1962), 97; Daniel R. Schwarz, "'The Secret Sharer' as an Act of Memory," in Joseph Conrad, *"The Secret Sharer": Case Studies in Contemporary Criticism*, ed. Daniel R. Schwarz (Boston: Bedford, 1993), 101.

[3] Concerning Leggatt as a symbol, see, among others, Guerard, *Conrad the Novelist*, 24; and see also Louis H. Leiter, "Echo Structures: Conrad's 'The Secret Sharer,'" rpt. in *Conrad's Secret Sharer and the Critics*, ed. Bruce Harkness (Belmont, CA: Wadsworth, 1962), 145–147, 149; Steve Ressler, *Joseph Conrad: Consciousness and Integrity* (New York and London: New York University Press, 1988), 82; Lothe, *Conrad's Narrative Method*, 71; Schwarz, "'The Secret Sharer' as an Act of Memory," 106, 109–110; Simmons, *Joseph Conrad*, 169.

the community to which he belongs.[4] It is hardly surprising, therefore, that the captain's response to the fugitive, in its apparent "ignorance" of legal and ethical questions, has baffled many critics,[5] but it cannot easily be dismissed as "evasion of justice"[6]; rather, it can be better understood as another justice, that is, an unconditional hospitality surpassing any ethics and any politics, which is what Jacques Derrida and other thinkers argue in the context of the question of the foreigner and immigration laws.[7]

"The Secret Sharer" was written when the author felt perhaps most alienated in his life as an émigré. There was a growing awareness that Conrad held a significant position in English literature, but the contemporary critics, even Edward Garnett, Conrad's early literary mentor and friend, never forgot that he was a Slav and tended to treat him as an oddity as he wrote to Garnett: "I've been so cried up of late as sort of freak, an amazing bloody foreigner writing in English (every blessed reviews of S. A.[*The Secret Agent*] had it so—and even yours) that anything I say will be discounted on that ground by the public, that mysterious beast, takes any notice whatever—which I doubt."[8] Another disappointment for Conrad was Robert Lynd's "brutal" attack of him as "a homeless person" who had abandoned his native country and wrote in an adopted language.[9] This is not to reinstate the idea of authorial intention, but still, we may not be too surprised if the author in his dejection wrote the story that engages with a possible space of "justice" that is unlimitedly open

---

[4]   On the primacy of the presence of the other in hospitality, see René Schérer, *Zeus hospitalier: Élogue de l'hospitalité* (1993; Paris: La Table Ronde, 2005), 148.

[5]   With regard to the "ignorance" of the legal and moral question in "The Secret Sharer," see, for instance, Schwarz, "'The Secret Sharer' as an Act of Memory," 95. Most critics cannot unreservedly accept the captain-narrator's "easy condonation" of Leggatt. See, in particular, H. M. Daleski, *Joseph Conrad: The Way of Dispossession* (London: Faber and Faber, 1977), 173–174; and also see, Lothe, *Conrad's Narrative Method*, 62; Yelton, *Mimesis and Metaphor*, 281; Ressler, *Joseph Conrad*, 85; Daphna Erdinast-Vulcan, *The Strange Short Fiction of Joseph Conrad: Writing, Culture, and Subjectivity* (Oxford: Oxford University Press, 1999), 37.

[6]   Watts, *The Deceptive Text*, 89.

[7]   For the law of hospitality above a "morality" or a certain "ethics," see Jacques Derrida, *Of Hospitality*, trans. Rachel Bowlby (1997; Stanford, CA: Stanford University Press, 2000), 149, 151.

[8]   Conrad, *The Collected Letters*, vol. 3, 488. Garnett stresses Conrad's foreignness in his review on *The Secret Agent* in *The Nation* in 1907: "It is good for us English to have Mr Conrad in our midst visualising for us aspects of life we are constitutionally unable to perceive, for by his astonishing mastery of our tongue he makes clear to his English audience those secret of Slav thought and feeling which seem so strange and inaccessible in their native language." See *Conrad: The Secret Agent. A Casebook*, Ian Watt ed., (London: Macmillan, 1973), 40.

[9]   Najder, *Joseph Conrad*, 390. Conrad responded to Lynd's review in a letter to Garnett: "[T]here is a fellow in *Dly News* who calls me … a man without country and language. It is like abusing a tongue-tied man. For what can one say. The statement is simple and brutal … ." Conrad, *The Collected Letters*, vol.4, 107–108.

to the other(s).[10] Despite its "Hospitality narrative" structure, however, "The Secret Sharer" has not, as Garry Watson points out in his unique essay, been widely read as such.[11] By rethinking the captain's welcoming gesture as an unconditional hospitality, this chapter therefore proposes to read "The Secret Sharer" less as a story of narcissistic self-reflection than as that of an externally oriented desire to go beyond the self to speak and give to the other. The strange relationship between the captain and Leggatt is ever reversible, complicating the dichotomy between the host and the guest, or the same and the other. In doing so, the relationship questions the idea of the interiority of the self, the familiar, and the home.[12]

* * *

Let me first of all quote at length the very important opening passage that depicts the captain-narrator's inner landscape of the mind:

> On my right hand there were lines of fishing stakes resembling a mysterious system of half-submerged bamboo fences, incomprehensible in its division of the domain of tropical fishes, and crazy of aspect as if abandoned forever by some nomad tribe of fishermen now gone to the other end of the ocean; for there was no sign of human habitation as far as the eye could reach. To the left a group of barren islets, suggesting ruins of stone walls, towers, and blockhouses, had its foundations set in a blue sea that itself looked solid, so still and stable did it lie below my feet; even the track of light from the westering sun shone smoothly, without that animated glitter which tells of an imperceptible ripple. And when I turned my head to take a parting glance at the tug which had just left us anchored outside the bar, I saw the straight line of the flat shore joined to the stable sea, edge to edge, with a perfect and unmarked closeness, in one levelled floor half brown, half blue under the enormous dome of the sky. Corresponding in their insignificance to the islets of the sea, two small clumps of trees, one on each side of the only fault in the impeccable joint, marked the mouth of the river Meinam we had just left on the first preparatory stage of our homeward journey; and, far

---

[10] On the "justice, if such a thing exists, outside or beyond law," see Derrida, "Force of the Law: The 'Mystical Foundation of Authority,'" *Deconstruction and the Possibility of Justice*, ed. Drucilla Cornell, Michel Rosenfeld, and David Gray Carlson (New York and London: Routledge, 1992), 15.

[11] We borrow the term the "Hospitality narrative" from Garry Watson, *Opening Doors: Thoughts from (and of) the Outside* (Aurora, CO: The Davies Group, 2008), 158.

[12] The problem of hospitality is "always about answering for a dwelling place, for one's identity, one's space, one's limits, for the *ethos* as abode, habitation, house, hearth, family, home." See Derrida, *Of Hospitality*, 149, 151.

back on the inland level, a larger and loftier mass, the grove surrounding the great Paknam pagoda, was the only thing on which the eye could rest from the vain task of exploring the monotonous sweep of the horizon. Here and there gleams as of a few scattered pieces of silver marked the windings of the great river; and on the nearest of them, just within the bar, the tug steaming right into the land became lost to my sight, hull and funnel and masts, as though the impassive earth had swallowed her up without an effort, without a tremor. My eye followed the light cloud of her smoke, now here, now there, above the plain, according to the devious curves of the stream, but always fainter and farther away, till I lost it at last behind the mitre-shaped hill of the great pagoda. And then I was left alone with my ship, anchored at the head of the Gulf of Siam. (*TLS* 91–92)

It has been traditional to read this passage as mirroring the young captain's anxiety about the loss of his selfhood. As Daphne Erdinast-Vulcan convincingly argues, the narrative moves in a "cinematic" fashion,[13] from the panoramic view of the land to the scenic view of the ship, with the captain's eyes "exploring the monotonous sweep of the horizon." "The whole circle of the horizon," as the captain-narrator reports, within which "theoretically, [he] could do what [he] liked, with no one to say nay to [him]" (113) is the very projection of the inner territory of his selfhood. Alone on her decks the captain, to be sure, tries to retreat to his "psychic laboratory,"[14] "measuring [their] fitness for a long and arduous enterprise, the appointed task of both [their] existences to be carried out, far from all human eyes, with only sky and sea for spectators and for judges" (92), and "wonder[ing] how far [he] should turn out faithful to that ideal conception of one's own personality every man sets up for himself secretly" (94). Despite his emphasis on his strangeness, his feelings of isolation are not simply "narcissistic," as we shall see later in detail, but rather invite him to surpass himself, to encounter with the other.[15] Before going any further, however, in order to understand the significance of the captain's

---

[13] For the projection of the self, see, in particular, Erdinast-Vulcan, *The Strange Short Fiction of Joseph Conrad*, 30–50. Regarding the "cinematic" movement of the narrative vision, see ibid., 38, in particular.

[14] Schwarz, "'The Secret Sharer' as an Act of Memory," 97.

[15] For the "narcissistic" solitude, see Schwarz, "'The Secret Sharer' as an Act of Memory," 96. In contrast, in his discussion of Jean Genet's *Le Funambule*, Schérer states that the solitude is far from being narcissistic; it is, in fact, the primary condition for the meeting with the other. He stresses that hospitality pulls one toward "un surpassement de soi," see Schérer, *Utopies nomads: En attendant 2002* (Paris: Séguier, 2000), 172, 184, 186.

externally oriented gesture, a gesture toward the other, let us pause here for a moment to look at the self-sufficient narrative mode of *Under Western Eyes*.

The apparently introspective nature of the captain in "The Secret Sharer" might enlist him in the rank of those Conradian heroes like Marlow, Kurtz, and Jim in the sense that they all plunge themselves into the endless exploration into the heart of darkness. They are destined to be perpetually tormented by the sense of loss as long as they desire to situate their "I" safely at the center of selfhood. As Marlow discovers the hollow man at the heart of the Dark Continent, so the old English language teacher in *Under Western Eyes* finds the immense blankness in the snow-covered land of Russia. The language teacher embarks on a narrative "enterprise" but in "vain" (*UWE* 25, 126), as is demonstrated in his recurrent disclaimer of his ability to comprehend the Russian character. In a self-enclosed fashion, the old teacher endlessly goes back and forth between himself and the Western readers, thereby becoming more and more out of touch with the object of his narrative, the Russians, or the Eastern other(s). As his narrative unfolds, he gradually effaces the otherness of his Eastern other(s). His narrative failure implies that the other is not a mere object to be subsumed under one of "his" (Western) categories and given a place in "his" (Western) world. The loss of the otherness of the other, in fact, means the loss of the other itself, which is then tantamount to the loss of one's own identity. As long as beings exist in relationship, the absence of the other means the absence of the gaze of the other. One may wonder how a being alone in the world, in the world without the gaze of the other, can have an identity.[16]

Hence it should come as little surprise that the captain-narrator of "The Secret Sharer," which was written as a break from *Under Western Eyes*, is under threat of losing his own inward territory in the opening passages and later; in addition, he is obsessively concerned with the gaze of his crew. Dismissing the captain's belief (that he is constantly scrutinized by his

---

[16] Emmanuel Levinas's argument of the welcoming of the infinity of the other, the face-to-face relation, is especially illuminating in thinking the relationship between the captain and Leggatt. See Emmanuel Levinas, *Totality and Infinity: An Essay on Exteriority*. trans. Alphonso Lingis, (Pittsburgh, PA: Duquesne University Press, 1969), 69, 82–90, 187–219. Note that the welcome in "The Secret Sharer" is also made to Leggatt's "face, a dimly pale oval in the shadow of the ship's side." The captain's first words to Leggatt in his nudity, "What's the matter," are spoken to "the face upturned exactly under [that of the captain]" (*TLS* 98). Regarding the infinitely foreign other in its "nudity," see in particular, ibid., 199–200. For the gaze of the other, see also, Shigeki Yagi, *"Kantai" no Seishinshi (Intellectual History of "Hospitality": From Scandinavian Mythology to Foucault, Levinas and Beyond)* (Tokyo: Kodansha, 2007), 145.

"doubting" subordinates) as "paranoia," critical discussions have tried to "explain" if he really is so "eccentric" as he appears in the eye of the "mistrustful" crew, by searching "alternative," possibly suppressed accounts of the affair.[17] Such arguments, however, inevitably lead to the "epistemological impasse,"[18] since the ultimate truth of the unreliable narrator's statement cannot, by any means, be ascertained. All we can say instead may simply be that the captain does take account of the other(s) and their "criticism" by exposing himself as the other to the gaze of the other(s).[19] He feels that he appears like an irresolute commander to "those people who [are] watching [him] more or less critically" (*TLS* 126), and that the mate's "terrible whiskers flit[s] round [him] in silent criticism" (132) when the captain puts the ship round on the other tack to his chief mate's great surprise. Leggatt also wants to be "seen" by the other (the stranger) as he confesses to the captain, "I didn't mind being looked at. I—I liked it. ... I was glad to talk a little to somebody that didn't belong to the *Sephora*" (110–111). The text's emphasis on the priority of the presence of the other over the knowledge of the other is further strengthened in the captain's lack of desire for knowledge about "the mysterious arrival" (105).[20] Strangely enough, he already "knew well enough ... that [his] double there was no homicidal ruffian"; and he "knew well enough the pestiferous danger of such a character [as the mutinous seaman of the *Sephora*] where there are no means of legal repression" (102). The captain does not think of asking Leggatt for details, which the visitor does not see the necessity of giving either: "... But what's the use telling you? *You* know!" (124).

In her insightful analysis of the opening passages of "The Secret Sharer," Erdinast-Vulcan stresses again and again the short story's "abortive" gesture of self-enclosure, insisting that "The Secret Sharer" is "a last-ditch attempt to shore up the subject position which had crumbled in the writing of the novel

---

[17] Erdinast-Vulcan, *The Strange Short Fiction of Joseph Conrad*, 37; Richardson, "Construing Conrad's 'The Secret Sharer,'" 310; Schwarz, "'The Secret Sharer' as an Act of Memory," 96, 103, 105; James Phelan, "Sharing Secrets," in Conrad, *"The Secret Sharer,"* ed. Schwarz, 130, 134.

[18] Richardson, "Construing Conrad's 'The Secret Sharer,'" 307.

[19] Washida stresses the importance of the self as the other's other occupying some space in someone else's consciousness as the object of love, hatred, or even exclusion. See Kiyokazu Washida, *"Kiku" koto no Chikara (Power of Listening): Essays on Clinical Philosophy* (Tokyo: Hankyu Communications, 1999), 96–97.

[20] It is not surprising that the captain's lack of desire for knowledge leads a critic to label him as "an unintellectual first-person narrator" without "intellectual growth." See Ressler, *Joseph Conrad*, 81, 97.

[*Under Western Eyes*]."[21] Indeed, the captain-narrator's obsession with the borders, such as "fences," "lines," "stakes," "division," and "foundations" in the opening passage cited earlier, can be taken as such. However, what is more important here is, on the contrary, the very crumbling and disappearance of the borders indicative of his weariness of efforts to "stake out a territory of selfhood," to borrow Erdinast-Vulcan's own phrase.[22] For, being more like Marlow in *Chance*, "the expert in the psychological wilderness,"[23] than the old English narrator in *Under Western Eyes* who lost himself as well as the otherness of the other in "a wilderness of words" (*UWE* 3), the captain-narrator in "The Secret Sharer" seems to know already that the sweep of the horizon of his (Western) self is "monotonous," and that he cannot find anything to soothe himself within the reach of his (Western) eye and consciousness. In this respect, therefore, it is no wonder that he should say that the exploration is a "vain task." The horizon of knowledge is eventually interrupted by something unknown. "[T]he only thing on which the eye could rest from the vain task of exploring the monotonous sweep of the horizon" is not something familiar (Western) to him, but rather "the grove surrounding the great Paknam pagoda" (*TLS* 91–92). His roaming eyes, as if they were yearning for something beyond the horizon of his Western self-sameness, make out over the ridges of the islet the mast and light of the unknown ship, the *Sephora*, whose glare disrupts his sight and "the solemnity of perfect solitude" (92) of his self, as it were.

With the horizon of knowledge thus interrupted by the mysterious ship, the captain's solitude, or "strangeness," further prompts a series of "unusual," "unconventional" arrangements (95), whereby he dislocates himself from the center of his selfhood and makes himself appear (as he worries) more and more "eccentric" (97). His dismissal of the officers from the deck in order to be left alone causes yet another "eccentricity," that is, professional deviation, preventing the anchor-watch from being "formally" set and things from "properly" attended to (97), until he encounters with the other at the bottom of the side ladder and welcomes him hospitably.[24] The captain's immediate reaction

---

[21] Erdinast-Vulcan, *The Strange Short Fiction of Joseph Conrad*, 46–47.

[22] Ibid., 38.

[23] Joseph Conrad, *Chance* (London: Dent, 1969), 311. Further page references to this edition will be given parenthetically in the text, preceded by *C* where it might otherwise be unclear.

[24] Stallman makes a passing allusion to the host's welcome of the guest in this story (obviously meaning no more than hospitality in the ordinary sense), the welcome he thinks "stressed" from the start when "[a] mysterious communication was established already" (*TLS* 99) between the captain and Leggatt. See Stallman, "Conrad and 'The Secret Sharer,'" 99.

to "the mysterious arrival" is incomprehensible and unacceptable to most critics and readers, but for the captain, conversely, "[i]t was inconceivable that
he[Leggatt] should not attempt to come on board, and even strangely troubling to suspect that perhaps he did not want to" (98). More strikingly, when
the stranger tells him that he killed a man, the captain remarks compassion-
ately and "confidently" that it was in a "[f]it of temper" (101).

* * *

The idea of the willed action is taken for granted when critics say, for example,
that the captain "becomes imprisoned by a nightmare of his own choosing,"[25]
or he "decide[s] to stand by Leggatt."[26] And yet, from the start, the captain's
action is spontaneous, for instance, when he gets the ladder in himself, he
does it "[n]ot from compunction certainly, but, as it were mechanically" (97).
Having seen a series of the captain's "mechanical" reactions to Leggatt, we may
begin to doubt if it is appropriate to use such phrases as his own "choices" or
"decisions" to describe his conducts, on the assumption that they are ascribed
to an individual agent responsible for his or her action. A willed action, issued
from an actor's consciousness, is necessarily bound by his or her egoistic, private, or bodily interests. As René Schérer puts it, the pure, unlimited welcome
of the other, by contrast, cannot be a response to interests, either of the self
or even of the other.[27] Whereas the hospitality in the ordinary sense is offered
to a person identifiable by name, nationality, social position, and so on, the
unconditional hospitality, according to Schérer, can neither simply be a form
of social custom practiced among a group nor indeed a form of experience.[28]
Rather, the unconditional hospitality is an event that takes place beyond the
interests of individual subjects.[29] Once the "I" becomes aware that he or she is
offering a hospitality, then he or she is no longer giving an absolute hospitality but instead, he or she is practicing a hospitality "out of duty."[30] When the

---

[25] Schwarz, "'The Secret Sharer' as an Act of Memory," 101.
[26] Daleski, *Joseph Conrad*, 181. Most critics assume the notion of the captain's "decision." See, for
example, Ressler, *Joseph Conrad*, 85; Phelan, "Sharing Secrets," 129, 130, 134, 141; J. Hillis Miller,
"Sharing Secrets," in Conrad, *"The Secret Sharer,"* ed. Schwarz, 234; Lothe, *Conrad's Narrative
Method*, 61.
[27] Schrérer, *Zeus hospitalier*, 126–7.
[28] Schrérer, *Utopies nomads*, 184.
[29] For disinterestedness and hospitality, see Yagi, *"Kantai" no Seishinshi*, 115–116.
[30] Derrida, *Of Hospitality*, 83.

"I" defines him- or herself as a host (or a master), the "I" sees the arrival as a guest, an object of hospitality from his or her perspective, thereby confining him- or herself into the dichotomy between a host and a guest.[31] As we shall see below, the host and guest relationship between the captain and Leggatt is ever reversible, well in accordance with the ambiguity of the French word "l'hôte," which means at once a host and a guest; both are, in turn, or simultaneously, "l'hôte,"[32] thereby annulling and moving beyond the binary opposition between a host and a guest.

Returning to the opening passages, we notice the repeated emphasis on the departure: "[W]e had just left [the mouth of the river Meinam] on the first preparatory stage of our homeward journey"; "She [the captain's ship] floated at the starting point of a long journey." Standing "at the threshold of a long passage" (92), the captain "wonder[s] how far [he] should turn out faithful to that ideal conception of one's own personality" (94), and thereby imprisons himself in his idealized self-image. The captain spoke to the stranger holding on to the ladder, as Leggatt recalls, "so quietly—as if [the captain] had expected [him]" (110). The captain seemed, to Leggatt, "to have been there [on deck] on purpose" (132). The image of the captain as a prisoner, appearing (to Leggatt) as if he "expected" someone at the threshold, bears a striking similarity to what Derrida describes as "the master of the house who 'waits anxiously on the threshold of his home' for the stranger he will see arising into view on the horizon as a liberator."[33] Derrida elaborates on the "strange logic" of an impatient master (whose subjectivity is hostage) awaiting his guest as a liberator as follows:

> ... the stranger, here the awaited guest, is not only someone to whom you say "come," but "enter," enter without waiting, make a pause in our home without waiting, hurry up and come in, "come inside," "come within me," not only toward me, but within me: occupy me, take place in me, which means, by the same token, also take my place, don't content yourself with coming to meet me or "into my home." Crossing the threshold is entering and not only approaching or coming.[34]

---

[31] On the paradox of hospitality, see Yagi, *"Kantai" no Seishinshi*, 116.
[32] For the ambiguity of the word l'hôte, see, Derrida, *Of Hospitality*, 123–125; Schérer, *Zeus hospitalier*, 147, 148.
[33] Derrida, *Of Hospitality*, 121
[34] Ibid., 123.

Likewise, Leggatt not only comes toward the captain but also "occupies" his mind and his room, eating his food and drinking his "early morning coffee" (127). At the time when Captain Archbold of the *Sephora* visits the still becalmed ship of the narrator in search of his fugitive mate, the narrator (the host) "become[s] so connected in thoughts and impressions with [the guest] that [he] [feels] as if [he], personally, were being given to understand that [he], too, [is] not the sort that would have done for the chief mate of a ship like the *Sephora*" (119).

Moreover, throughout the period of the captain's offering refuge to Leggatt, it is not the guest but the host (the captain) who is overwhelmed by "the strain of stealthiness, by the effort of whispering and the general secrecy of this excitement" (111). Listening to Leggatt's (the guest's) whispered recital of his adventure, the captain (the host) sometimes carelessly raises his voice in excitement and is checked by Leggatt (the guest), while the guest is, by contrast, calm and cautious enough not to be overheard by the crew (109). When Leggatt is nearly discovered by the steward who enters the bathroom unexpectedly, the captain is "even more appalled than before at the closeness of the shave, and marveling at that something unyielding in his [Leggatt's] character which [is] carrying him through so finely" (131). The captain (the host) thinks he "come[s] creeping quietly as near insanity as any man who has not actually gone over the border" (130), whereas Leggatt (the guest) preserves his sanity, with no agitation in his whisper: "Whoever [is] being driven distracted, it [is] not he [Leggatt] (the guest). He (the guest) [is] sane" (131).

When the captain (the master) "shave[s] the land as close as possible" (139), "something unyielding" in his character, in turn, "carries him through so finely," thereby calling to our mind the guest's previous "closeness of the shave" in the bathroom. Additionally, in the Koh-ring venture, the captain (the host) seizes the blubbering chief mate and goes on shaking him, thus duplicating Leggatt's (the guest's) murderous attack on the mutinous seaman on the *Sephora*: "I hadn't let go the mate's arm and went on shaking it. 'Ready about, do you hear? You go forward'—shake—'and stop there'—shake—'and hold your noise'—shake—'and see these head-sheets properly overhauled'—shake, shake—shake" (141).[35] When the host and the guest slip out of the room

---

[35]   Many critics note the captain's doubling of Leggatt's murderous attack on the mutinous seaman. See Leiter, "Echo Structures," 142; Ressler, *Joseph Conrad*, 90; Phelan, "Sharing Secrets," 142; Miller, "Sharing Secrets," 240.

through a tiny dark passage to the sail-locker, the guest is referred to as "the double captain." Struck by "[a] sudden thought," the host imagines himself as the guest, "wandering barefooted, bareheaded, the sun beating on [his] dark poll," and "snatch[es] off his floppy hat and tri[es] hurriedly in the dark to ram it on his other self [the guest]" (138).

Some critics have remarked that Leggatt's steady self-control and confidence makes him better fitted to command.[36] But the very exchangeability of the captain and Leggatt, complicating the clear-cut opposition between the ideal and the real, undermines the image of Leggatt as the captain's ideal. Their relationship instead corresponds to the ambiguity of the French word "l'hôte," which means both a host and a guest, alternately, as we have seen above, or simultaneously as follows: during their forced whispering, the captain feels that they both are the guests, "the two strangers in the ship, faced each other in identical attitudes" (110); later, when Leggatt asks the captain to "maroon" him amongst the islands off the Cambodian shore, the captain feels "as if the ship had two captains to plan her course for her" (134).

The captain more than once says, "this sort of thing [can]not go on very long" (112, 123). It cannot last, to be sure, less because murder will become public sooner or later than because a pure hospitality is an impossible and contradictory event, in which the master of the house who is at home comes to enter his home "from the inside *as if* he came from outside," through the guest who comes from outside.[37] Perfectly contradictorily indeed, the captain and Leggatt are no more united than ever at the very moment of their separation: "Our hands met gropingly," says the captain, "lingered united in a steady, motionless clasp for a second. ... No word was breathed by either of us when they separated" (138). Meanwhile, on the deck, all hands stand waiting for the captain's order, and when the ship is drawing ahead he achieves "the perfect communion" with the ship and his first command: "And I was alone with her. Nothing! no one in the world should stand now between us, throwing a shadow on the way of silent knowledge and mute affection, the perfect communion of a seaman with his first command" (143). This triumphant and neat

---

[36] For the "ideal conception of himself made manifest in Leggatt," see, among others, Daniel Curley, "Legate of the Ideal," in *Conrad's Secret Sharer and the Critics*, ed. Bruce Harkness (Belmont, CA: Wadsworth), 75–82. See also Schwarz, "'The Secret Sharer' as an Act of Memory," 105; Ressler, *Joseph Conrad*, 83, 84.

[37] Derrida, *Of Hospitality*, 125, 127.

ending may tempt us to believe that the inexperienced young captain finally overcomes his strangeness to gain full knowledge of himself and his ship.[38] But one may also wonder if he really ceases to be a stranger at the end. For the captain is intimately welcomed by Leggatt in their separation; after he leaves, the captain is accepted both by the crew among whom (as he repeats) he earlier felt strange and by the ship he found "very inviting" at first (96). It is the captain, the host himself, who is invited by the ones whom he invites. If the captain is thus offered a hospitality by the other(s), then the captain, the host, is the very guest, the stranger. The captain, the host who receives the guest is here received "*in* his own home ... *from* his own home .... The *hôte* as host is a guest."[39]

If the captain is the stranger who is welcomed in his home, from his home, then it further suggests that his own home, his ship, "does not belong to him." What he thinks his ship (his home) is not, in fact, his own: "The one who welcomes is first welcomed in his own home." This "originary dispossession" of "what is most his own ... mak[es] of one's home a place or location one is simply passing through."[40] Perhaps in this sense (rather than in the sense of an autonomous self's narcissistic feeling of isolation, his/her nostalgia toward the lost self, as we have seen earlier), the captain feels that he is a stranger to himself and the ship at the starting point of his journey. Feeling dispossessed of his own ship, his own initiative, the captain cannot help but wait without waiting for "*who or what turns up*";[41] he waits until Leggatt arrives and "[t]he dwelling opens itself to itself ... as a 'land of asylum or refuge.'"[42] According to Schérer, the exile (the stranger) is welcomed by the host, because the person who welcomes him recognizes in him the image of himself as an exile; but hospitality can assure the visitor not so much of a permanent residence as simply of his/her survival.[43] The captain (the host) simply "made [Leggatt] (the visitor) hold on a little longer," as Leggatt says (*TLS* 110). Arguably, the text's affirmation lies

---

[38] For the dominant view that the captain recovers his integrity, ceasing to be a stranger to himself, see Daleski, *Joseph Conrad*, 171, 182; Schwarz, "'The Secret Sharer' as an Act of Memory," 109; Miller, "Sharing Secrets," 246; Erdinast-Vulcan, *The Strange Short Fiction of Joseph Conrad*, 45.

[39] Jacques Derrida, *Adieu to Emmanuel Levinas*, trans. Pascale-Anne Brault and Michael Naas (Stanford, CA: Stanford University Press, 1999), 41.

[40] Ibid., 42.

[41] Regarding unconditionally hospitable "saying yes *to who or what turns up*," see Derrida, *Of Hospitality*, 77.

[42] For the idea that the master of the house is already "*a received hôte*," see Derrida, *Adieu to Emmanuel Levinas*, 41–42.

[43] See Schrérer, *Zeus hospitalier*, 40, and regarding the survival of a voyager, see 126–127, in particular.

more in the captain's and Leggatt's strangeness, their being an exile, "a fugitive and a vagabond on the earth" (142),[44] than its "self-affirming action" for which it has been praised.[45] The last statement of the story, "[A] free man, a proud swimmer striking out for a new destiny" (143), has sometimes been taken as "deliberately ambiguous" in its reference to either Leggatt or the captain.[46] We may then argue that thus liberated from the the same/other opposition they both strike out for a new destiny as strangers, as free men.[47]

* * *

"The Secret Sharer" was written immediately after a period of serious depression undoubtedly caused by writing *Under Western Eyes*,[48] and Conrad himself maintained in a letter to J. B. Pinker in 1909 that he had written the story for the very purpose of "easing the strain."[49] Unsurprisingly enough, the "therapeutic function" of the story has been pointed out.[50] And yet, an unconditional hospitality is perhaps not simply a gesture of hope but rather a gesture of despair; it happens in the middle of despair.[51] When one is in despair, like Razumov, deprived of his or her own initiative, ruthlessly at the mercy of "the lawlessness of autocracy ... and the lawlessness of revolution" (*UWE* 77), all one can do may be just wait, let things come, as the captain does in the opening of "The Secret Sharer." This is not by all means a mere passivity, however.[52] I would think that without facing up to hopelessness in, or more

---

[44] On the affirmation of exile on the earth, see Schrérer, *Zeus hospitalier*, 40.

[45] Ressler, *Joseph Conrad*, 80; Yelton, *Mimesis and Metaphor*, 282.

[46] Leiter, "Echo Structures," 149. See also Yelton, *Mimesis and Metaphor*, 285 and Stallman, "Conrad and 'The Secret Sharer,'" 97.

[47] I hasten to add here that there is a sense in which Leggatt is both the other and the same. The captain welcomes Leggatt not as a random stranger but as an individual in whom he recognizes himself as an exile. The hospitality is called forth by the perception of the same. I wish to acknowledge the helpful comment of Professor Derek Attridge on this point.

[48] Najder, *Joseph Conrad*, 405.

[49] Conrad, *The Collected Letters*, vol. 4, 303.

[50] Erdinast-Vulcan, *The Strange Short Fiction of Joseph Conrad*, 35. For the concluding note of hope, see also Ressler, *Joseph Conrad*, 81.

[51] Regarding hospitality as a gesture of despair, see Washida, *"Kiku" koto no Chikara*, 257. Also, for waiting and hospitality, see Kiyokazu Washida, *"Matsu" to iu koto* (Tokyo: Kadokawa gakugei shuppan, 2006), 181.

[52] In his discussion of the ethics of reading, Attridge highlights an active dimension of responsibility in Derrida's sense: "Derrida has always stressed that, while one cannot make the other come, one can prepare for its coming. (One name for this activity of preparation is 'deconstruction')." See Attridge, *Reading and Responsibility*, 73. Passivity, Attridge also remarks, is in fact an important aspect of the coming into being of the new. See Attridge, *Singularity of Literature*, 23. Regarding the idea of letting the other come, see Jacques Derrida, *Acts of Literature*, ed. Derek Attridge (London and New York: Routledge, 1992), 340–341.

precisely, through writing *Under Western Eyes*, absolute hospitality in "The Secret Sharer," or more accurately, "The Secret Sharer" as absolute hospitality would not have taken place, as we shall see below.

"The Secret Sharer" is not merely a story about unconditional hospitality, but it is also an enactment of unconditional hospitality at each level of the narrative. After weeks of confinement on board the *Sephora*, Leggatt suddenly jumps into the water "before he [makes] up his mind fairly" (*TLS* 108). Going on swimming "with no place for scrambling out" or going back (109), Leggatt unexpectedly finds the ladder left hanging on the ship's side. The question for him then is "whether [he is] to let go this ladder and go on swimming till [he] sink[s] from exhaustion, or—to come on board [there]." The captain-narrator feels that it is "no mere formula of desperate speech" but "a real alternative in the view of a strong soul" (99). As Leggatt lets things come in this way, the captain also waits until "[t]he dwelling ... opens itself to itself ... as a 'land of asylum or refuge,'" leaving everything up to chance.

To wait without waiting may have also been "a real alternative" in the view of the writer in deadlock. Setting aside *Under Western Eyes*, Conrad would probably have expected, without expectation, that the deadlock be broken through by chance. The short story's "lack of circumstantial accounting for its coming into existence"[53] encourages us to presume that it may unexpectedly have "turned up," as the author writes in his letter to Pinker: "Anyway I started looking for a subject and this one turned up, which could have been made use of in the form of an anecdote, but I hadn't the heart to throw it away. The story ['The Secret Sharer'] you have is the result of that reluctance. We may call it 10,000 words; it is a very characteristic Conrad."[54] According to Conrad, the basic fact of the tale had been in his possession for a good many years ("Author's Note," *TLS* viii); and all of a sudden it came to the author in the shape of a story. He did unconditionally welcome this extraordinary story, the other (text) to his characteristically moralistic major works.

The unspecified narrative occasion of "The Secret Sharer" can also be reconsidered in terms of unconditional hospitality. Unlike *Heart of Darkness* or *Lord Jim*, "The Secret Sharer" does not specify who is narrating and to whom the narrator is addressing his words.[55] The anonymity of the narrator may imply

---

[53]   Miller, "Sharing Secrets," 235; Erdinast-Vulcan, *The Strange Short Fiction of Joseph Conrad*, 46.

[54]   Conrad, *The Collected Letters*, vol. 4, 297–298.

[55]   For readers' response to sharing the "guilty" secrets and the ethical dimensions of the story's lack of specificity, see Phelan, "Sharing Secrets," 128–144, and Miller, "Sharing Secrets," 235. For the idea of the unnamed narrator's incomplete "confession without confession," see Miller, "Sharing Secrets," 234–235.

that after the tortured, drawn-out meditation on the irruption of the other in *Under Western Eyes*, the author becomes ready to address, say yes to himself (to come) not as the self-same but as the other, that is, an unknown, unnamed, and unexpected visitor (a stranger), a guest as a chance.[56] Complaining about the absence of an "embodied other who would dispute or challenge the narrator's interpretation and judgment,"[57] some critics assert that the absence of the narratee as a correcting device puts the reader in "the position of judge or jury."[58] However, thrown out of such a stable position safely separated from the object, the reader might be made aware of him- or herself as the other, an unidentified addressee,[59] an unknown destination, for which the captain and Leggatt strike out at the end of the story. The "very characteristic Conrad" appearance of the story may make it even more challenging for us to offer a reading completely independent from preconceived opinions about it. Still, just as the captain accepts "the mysterious arrival" not in its identity but in its alterity without locking him up into a prison of meaning (as Captain Archbold did to Leggatt) and witnesses every single trace of his escape, so we receive this enigmatic text unconditionally and watch the way its meaning escapes us, leaving a trace of its retreat.[60] We readers are the only witnesses, the secret sharers. This is not to say, however, that the other forever escapes knowing. On the contrary, extending an unconditional welcome to the other, or another justice, is the condition for knowing.[61] Thus, "The Secret Sharer," whether it refers to the text, Leggatt, the narrator, the narratee, the author, or the readers, is neither fully mastered nor possessed but hospitably welcomed, either by its sender (the author/the narrator?) or by its unknown addressee (the author/the narrator/the narratee/the reader?), ever striking out for a new destination, a new reading.

---

[56] Regarding oneself as an unexpected visitor (a stranger), see Satoshi Ukai, *Shuken no Kanata de (Beyond the Horizon of Sovereignty)* (Tokyo: Iwanami Shoten, 2008), 18.

[57] Yelton, *Mimesis and Metaphor*, 281; Lothe, *Conrad's Narrative Method*, 71; Miller, "Sharing Secrets," 234–235; Phelan, "Sharing Secrets," 129; Erdinast-Vulcan, *The Strange Short Fiction of Joseph Conrad*, 37.

[58] Miller, "Sharing Secrets," 237.

[59] On the question of addressee, see Jacques Derrida, "Le facteur de la vérité," *The Post Card: From Socrates to Freud and Beyond*, trans. Alan Bass (Chicago: University of Chicago Press, 1987), 413–496.

[60] On the unconditional welcome of the text, see Tatsuro Umeki, "Text wo Shihai shinai tame ni (Against Appropriation of the Text)," *Gendai Shiso (revue de la pensée d'aujourd'hui): Special Memorial Issue on Jacques Derrida* (Tokyo: Seidosha, 2004), 159–161.

[61] Levinas, *Totality and Infinity*, 89–90.

5

(Dis)owning a Memory in
"The Secret Sharer"

In the previous chapter, I read "The Secret Sharer" not as a story of narcissistic self-reflection but as one of unconditional hospitality, or an externally oriented desire to go beyond the self to speak and give to the other. In an attempt to complement the discussion of unconditional hospitality undertaken in Chapter 4, this chapter examines the two important but slightly overlooked vignettes of the miserable scorpion and of the captain's white floppy hat in terms of ownership of memory premised on the concept of an individual subject. The vignettes of the scorpion drowning in the chief mate's inkwell and of the captain's last-minute gift of the hat to Leggatt have been discussed separately by mainstream critics: one has been interpreted as a Dickensian caricature of the "terrifically" whiskered chief mate and the other as a "deus ex machina" to provide a miraculous solution to the captain's initiation ordeal. However, the captain's and Leggatt's forgetfulness in both vignettes are curiously in concert with each other in undermining the notion of an individual subject as the owner of memory. Thus the amnesia in "The Secret Sharer" inscribes the individual experience as something traumatic that extends beyond the confines of the individual psyche. This chapter will suggest in conclusion that "The Secret Sharer" links the notion of "strange fraternity" and the question of memory, and, by extension, the question of "history," not as straightforward referentiality but as responsibility, which I shall elaborate on in the following chapters.

* * *

In spite of its form of a seaman's reminiscence of his past experience, there has been critical disagreement about the retrospective nature of the captain-narrator's story in "The Secret Sharer." While Daniel Schwarz reads the short story as "a painful act of memory" under the assumption of the "intense reflective process in which the speaker's past comes alive in his memory,"[1] other critics assert that there is no time gap between the original events and their recounting, in contrast to Marlow's narrative in which the effect of the time elapsed between his experience and its recital is important dramatically.[2] In contrast, Albert Guerard goes so far as to remark that "The Secret Sharer" is Conrad's most successful experiment with the method of "nonretrospective first-person narration."[3] More recently, in the eye of Erdinast-Vulcan, for example, the narrator's discourse offers "no hint of retrospective self-doubt."[4] As Conrad acknowledged in the "Author's Note" to *'Twixt Land and Sea*, "The Secret Sharer" is, notwithstanding its autobiographical form, not the record of his personal experience but a tale he has heard and read about, concerning an actual incident that occurred on board the famous tea clipper *Cutty Sark* (*TLS*, viii–ix).

The captain-narrator presents the events without commentary from his vantage point at the time of the narration, from his older, seemingly more mature self. This feature of the narrative technique, James Phelan believes, leads critics to the theory of "nonretrospectiveness," which runs counter to the narrator's remark about the "distance of years" (116).[5] The point Guerard and others make, however, cannot completely be refuted because the narrator does not try to hide his amnesia; he boldly displays his lack of precision, whereby he creates the impression of "nonretrospectiveness," or at least the impression that he is not simply indulging in reminiscences. The narrator's sense of past is notoriously least precise when he admits he is not sure that Archbold was the name of the *Sephora*'s captain:

> The skipper of the *Sephora* had a thin red whisker all round his face, and
> the sort of complexion that goes with hair of that colour; also the particular,

[1]   Schwarz, "'The Secret Sharer' as an Act of Memory," 102.
[2]   Ressler, *Joseph Conrad*, 97.
[3]   Guerard, *Conrad the Novelist*, 27.
[4]   Erdinast-Vulcan, *The Strange Short Fiction of Joseph Conrad*, 37.
[5]   Phelan, "Sharing Secrets," 129.

rather smeary shade of blue in the eyes. He was not exactly a showy figure; his shoulders were high, his stature but middling—one leg slightly more bandy than the other. He shook hands, looking vaguely around. A spiritless tenacity was his [Archbold's] main characteristic, I judged. I behaved with a politeness which seemed to disconcert him. Perhaps he was shy. He mumbled to me as if he were ashamed of what he was saying; gave his name (it was something like Archbold—but at this distance of years I hardly am sure), his ship's name, and a few other particulars of that sort, in the manner of a criminal making a reluctant and doleful confession .... I looked politely at Captain Archbold (if that was his name), but it was the other I saw, in a gray sleeping suit, seated on a low stool, his bare feet close together, his arms folded, and every word said between us falling into the ears of his dark head bowed on his chest. (115–117)

Here the captain-narrator has observed twice that he is unsure about the name of the skipper of the *Sephora* after many years. His forgetfulness about the name of a man, however modest and plain looking he may be as he claims, cannot too readily convince us, especially when the man is Leggatt's captain and one of the key witnesses in his case. On the contrary, his comments on those "particulars" such as Archbold's "thin red whisker," his complexion that "goes with" the color of his hair, "smeary shade of blue" in the eyes, and one of his legs being "slightly more bandy than the other," cannot but attest to a certain level of memory left in him of a man who he calls "not exactly a showy figure." We cannot simply dismiss this trait as a question of poor memory or a tendency of myth-making on the part of the mature narrator,[6] particularly when his loss of memory and his indifference make an interesting contrast with other characters' "tenacious" manner of "sticking to the point" (122). Interestingly, the captain-narrator even goes further to pass a judgement on this unimpressive man that his "main" characteristic is "a spiritless tenacity"; he scornfully labels him as "a tenacious beast" who "[has] thought so much about" the Leggatt case for over two months (117). The narrator as a captain is also under the obligation to surrender Leggatt to the law, but for him it was "pitiless" (119) and Archbold's "tenacity" has in it "something incomprehensible" and "mystical" (118).

---

[6]   Phelan and Schwarz make cursory allusions to the captain's recollection of Archbold. For the narrator's mythmaking, see Schwarz, "'The Secret Sharer' as an Act of Memory,"107. For the narrator's lack of precision, see Phelan, "Sharing Secrets," 129.

Archbold's "guiltily conscientious manner of sticking to the point" (122), along with his whiskers,[7] reminds us of another "tenacious beast" in the story, the chief mate whose "dominant trait" is also "a spiritless tenacity":

> His [The chief mate's] dominant trait was to take all things into earnest consideration. He was of a painstaking turn of mind. As he used to say, he "liked to account to himself" for practically everything that came in his way, down to a miserable scorpion he had found in his cabin a week before. The why and the wherefore of that scorpion—how it got on board and came to select his room rather than the pantry (which was a dark place and more what a scorpion would be partial to), and how on earth it managed to drown itself in the inkwell of his writing desk—had exercised him infinitely. (94)

In tackling what he calls "the facts basic to the why and wherefore of what happens in the story," R. W. Stallman suggests half-jokingly that we readers had better "take all things into earnest consideration" exactly in the manner of the chief mate as described above to evolve a theory about the captain and his secret sharer.[8] After Guerard, critics have kept providing an allegorical interpretation of the scorpion episode,[9] claiming that the details of the scorpion in the inkwell offer us metaphorical or metafictional explanations for the actions and their consequences of another invader in the text, Leggatt.[10] And yet, one might pause for a while to wonder how very different the totalizing desire to explain— or the will to "account [to ourselves] for practically everything that came in [our] way" whereby providing the meanings for the otherwise inexplicable arrival of Leggatt and the following actions—is from the very attitude caricaturized by the captain-narrator in his description of his chief mate. Let me cite here another episode from the earlier part of the story in which the chief mate, overwhelmed with the extent of the second mate's information about another ship,

---

[7]   Wojciech Kozak points out that the excessive growth on his face suggests his belonging to the patriarchal society. See Wojciech Kozak, "Sharing Gender (?) in 'The Secret Sharer,'" in *Beyond the Roots: The Evolution of Conrad's Ideology and Art*, ed. with an Introduction by Wiesław Krajka (Boulder, CO: East European Monographs; Lublin, Poland: Maria Curie-Skłodowska University Press; New York: Colombia University Press, 2005), 330. As for the similarity between Archbold, Leggatt, and the mutinous seaman, see Ressler, *Joseph Conrad*, 90. But Ressler does not go beyond pointing out the similarity.

[8]   Stallman, "Conrad and 'The Secret Sharer,'" 98.

[9]   Leiter, "Echo Structures," 139–140.

[10] In his reading of "The Secret Sharer" as a consistently staging and thematizing narrative interpretation, Richardson argues that the scorpion in the inkwell has "a simply metafictional explanation." See Richardson, "Construing Conrad's 'The Secret Sharer,'" 315. For the rich symbolic connotations of the scorpion episode, such as sexuality, suffering, evil, mothering, suicide, or revenge, see Kozak, "Sharing Gender," 325, 330–331.

the *Sephora* at anchor within the islands, wants to know "what prevented the second mate from telling them all about it at once," and he observes "regretfully that he 'could not account for that young fellow's whims'" (95). The mannerisms at each repetition do enhance a Dickensian atmosphere, yet more significantly, they also serve as a commentary on the reader's response, reminding us of our own desire and tendency to know and explain everything.

What these seemingly trivial Dickensian episodes recurrently evoke is the epistemological questions, the questions of knowledge and understanding as to who the secret sharer is, and why the captain-narrator hides him at the risk of his own ship and crew, around which the main critical discussion of "The Secret Sharer" has so far evolved.[11] In his ridicule of what he calls "'the Bless my soul— you don't say so' type of intellect" (101) of his chief mate, the captain-narrator, I would suggest, poses a question to the dominant Victorian positivist belief in scientific methods through which to arrive at a truth or knowledge. The captain-narrator does not try to know and explain but rather to forget things—the name of the *Sephora*'s captain, in particular—almost as if to say that meticulously "tak[ing] all things into earnest consideration" "in emulation of the chief mate,"[12] to borrow Stallman's words, may drive us to "infinitely" search for an answer, a theory, or a judgment for what has passed without any goal in view. In this respect, those gaps in the narrator's memory about the name of Archbold in his "tenacious" pursuit of Leggatt might be viewed as a form of protest (though modest) in its resistance against our totalizing desire to "account for everything."

What matters for the captain-narrator in welcoming the other, or hospitality, which is a question of urgency, as I have discussed in the previous chapter, is neither the knowledge nor understanding of the guest, but rather, his mere presence. He welcomes the mysterious arrival before knowing "the why and the wherefore" and "how," not to talk of the "who." The narrator repeatedly stresses that he does not need to know more about the Leggatt case; he already "knew well enough the pestiferous danger of such a character [as that of the mutinous seaman strangled by Leggatt] where there are no means of

---

[11]　We could say that gender approaches also have an epistemological tendency in the sense that they attempt to give the homosocial (homosexual) desire between men as an "explanation" for the actions of Leggatt and the captain. For the bond between men, to name but a few, Richard J. Ruppel, *Homosexuality in the Life and Work of Joseph Conrad: Love Between the Lines* (New York and London: Routledge, 2008), 69–81; Jeremy Hawthorn, *Sexuality and the Erotic in the Fiction of Joseph Conrad* (New York and London: Continuum, 2007).

[12]　Stallman, "Conrad and 'The Secret Sharer,'" 98.

legal repression"; again he "knew well enough … that [his] double there was no homicidal ruffian" (102); neither can Leggatt see "the use [of] telling [the captain]" because "[he] knows" (124).

Nevertheless, the captain's apparent disregard for knowledge of the other does not necessarily, as pointed out in the previous chapter, mean he is "unintellectual";[13] nor does it mean that the whole text resists epistemological exploration. On the contrary, the text undoubtedly invites us to delve deeper into the heart of darkness to find some explanation for the young captain's strong attachment to the mysterious stranger, but it does so self-reflexively. The captain-narrator himself cannot thoroughly escape the epistemological tendency when he asks himself "how that absurdly whiskered mate would 'account' for [his] conduct" (97) of taking an anchor watch on himself dismissing his officers from duty. He soon becomes "vexed with [himself]" (97) to find himself duplicating his chief mate's manner of "accounting to himself for everything that came in his way." Moreover, the captain is curiously observant and perceptive about Leggatt's "concentrated, meditative" expression under the inspecting light of the lamp, "such as a man thinking hard in solitude might wear" (100); he even goes further to say that "[he] could imagine perfectly the manner of this thinking out" (106). One may hazard the guess that like Leggatt, the captain may also have "thought out" (106) "in solitude" about what happened to him, "only afterwards" (120), perhaps "almost to the point of his insanity" (114), to the point of a suicidal depression. The captain of the British ship *Cutty Sark*, the model of the captain of "The Secret Sharer," in fact committed suicide by jumping overboard into the sea when he found his first mate who had murdered the cook disappeared from the ship.[14] One would not be surprised if Leggatt's case "exercised [the young captain] infinitely," as if to copy the "tenacity" of his terribly whiskered chief mate as cited earlier, to such an extent that the narrator thought of killing himself. If the captain-narrator "sticks to the point" after the fashion in which what he calls "tenacious beasts" do, then his narrative would have been more like a "confession" of or even an "excuse" for his "guilt,"[15] which is, in fact, how most critics

13 See Ressler, *Joseph Conrad*, 81, 97.
14 "Arrest and Trial of Sidney Smith," *The Times*, Wednesday, July 5, 1882, in Leiter, "Echo Structures," 53.
15 For the reading of the captain's narrative as an excuse, see Schwarz, "'The Secret Sharer' as an Act of Memory," 98, and as a confession, see Miller, "Sharing Secrets," 235; Ressler, *Joseph Conrad*, 94; Phelan, "Sharing Secrets," 143.

have read his story. And yet, his aversion to Archbold's manner of "criminal making a reluctant and doleful confession" (116) reveals his disillusion with and departure from a confessional mode, or the grand narrative of crime and punishment, as it were. The narrator instead makes a different confession, a confession that he "should have been perfectly incapable of" "this thinking out—a stubborn if not a steadfast operation" (106). Hence his suppression of Archbold's accounts of Leggatt's case in his retelling as "[i]t is not worth while to record his version" (117).[16]

Well in accordance with the captain-narrator's skeptical attitude toward totalization, the "stubborn operation" of "sticking to the point" is repeatedly interrupted by chance throughout his narrative. On the *Sephora*, Leggatt had the time to "think all those matters out" while he was under arrest in his cabin for nearly seven weeks. His act of "thinking out" could have been continued longer if it were not for the unexpected combination of events as follows. When the ship is anchored among the islets around Carimata, "[Leggatt] [doesn't] know how it [is]," but the steward leaves the door unlocked after bringing him his supper. After he finishes it and strolls out on the quarter-deck, again, "[he doesn't] know that [he] [means] to do anything," but then "a sudden temptation" comes over him, and he jumps in the water "before he [makes] up [his] mind fairly" (108). Now that he is clear of the ship, as he tells the captain-narrator, he is not going back; he "can't see the necessity" to stand in court (like Jim) "before a judge and jury on that charge [of murder]" (101, 131). Taking off all his clothes, he then strikes out for the riding light of the captain-narrator's ship. Going on swimming "with no place for scrambling out" or going back (109), Leggatt, again unexpectedly, finds the ladder left hanging on the ship's side: he later tells the captain, "Who'd have thought of finding a ladder hanging over at night in a ship anchored out here!" (110) In other words, Leggatt is only fortuitously relieved from captivity and saved by the captain-narrator.

We may also add here the case of the mutinous sailor killed by Leggatt as another variation on "spiritless tenacity" in the story. The sailor was "just simmering all the time with a silly sort of wickedness" (101) about what happened, instead of doing his duty or letting anybody else do theirs during the awful

---

[16] For the suppression of all rival accounts of Leggatt, see Richardson, "Construing Conrad's 'The Secret Sharer,'" 307–308.

weather. On the diegetic level, to be sure, we cannot be indifferent to a sort of class prejudice of an ex-*Conway* boy, a member of British social and maritime elite.[17] For Leggatt, the sailor is just one of those "[m]iserable devils that have no business to live at all" (101), and for the captain as well, the case looks as if Leggatt's "strung-up force" "crushed an unworthy mutinous existence" (124–125). On the extra-diegetic level, the level of the narrative's telling, however, we find here another silencing of "a tenacious beast," by extension, another interruption of the act of "sticking to the point." The captain never interrupts Leggatt whose narrative has "something that [makes] comment impossible" (109), whereas the captain's narrative, despite its appearance as a confession of his past behavior, recurrently interrupts and represses the act of "thinking out." Unable to reconcile himself by "sticking to the point," the captain forgets, or slips, as it were, out of the context that must have "exercised him infinitely."

To give an account of what happened to us, or to put it in words, amounts to neutralizing and ultimately naturalizing it into what we generally call "an (empirical) experience." If our memory of an experience is something that an individual subject safely and securely looks back and returns to again and again, it means that those naturalized events as such are firmly located in our memory.[18] In the case of the captain-narrator, however, what happened between Leggatt and him can hardly be temporally localized in his memory. The narrator as an individual subject does not claim his past experience as wholly his own. Spatially and temporally unanchored, as we have seen in the previous chapter,[19] the event is not entirely accommodated in his memory; it is not a fixed, safe place that he can come back to, time and again, in his telling. Little wonder, as I have said at the outset, that there has been a critical disagreement as to the sense of the past in "The Secret Sharer."

* * *

Critical opinion has also been divided over the symbolism of the white floppy hat, the captain's last-minute gift to Leggatt when they part. When the captain and Leggatt slip to the sail locker where Leggatt gets ready to ship out and lowers himself overboard, the captain suddenly imagines himself "wandering

---

[17] Richardson, "Construing Conrad's 'The Secret Sharer,'" 313.
[18] Mari Oka, *Kioku/Monogatari* (*Memory/Narrative*) (Tokyo: Iwanami, 2000), 8.
[19] Regarding the spatial and temporal unspecificity in "The Secret Sharer," see Phelan, "Sharing Secrets," 128–144, and Miller, "Sharing Secrets," 235.

barefooted, bareheaded, the sun beating on [his] dark poll" (138) and snatches off his hat to ram it on his other self. Then, the captain sets out to come as close as possible to land to allow Leggatt to swim to the island of Koh-ring. In this passage from the closing scene, the captain's eye again roams over the water, as it does in the opening, and then all at once, his strained, yearning stare spots a white object floating within a yard of the ship's side:

> White on the black water. A phosphorescent flash passed under it. What was that thing? … I recognized my own floppy hat. It must have fallen off his head … and he didn't bother. Now I had what I wanted—the saving mark for my eyes. But I hardly thought of my other self, now gone from the ship, to be hidden forever from all friendly faces, to be a fugitive and a vagabond on the earth, with no brand of the curse on his sane forehead to stay a slaying hand … too proud to explain.
>
> And I watched the hat—the expression of my sudden pity for his mere flesh. It had been meant to save his homeless head from the dangers of the sun. And now—behold—it was saving the ship, by serving me for a mark to help out the ignorance of my strangeness. Ha! It was drifting forward, warning me just in time that the ship had gathered sternway. (142)

Now that the ship is successfully around and all hands wait for the captain's order on the deck, the floppy hat, fallen off Leggatt's head, drifting on the water, seemingly serves the captain as "a mark" to help his "eyes" distinguish black from white, strangeness from sameness, thereby "saving" himself, his ship, and his crew. This climax scene has been traditionally taken by many critics as an enactment of the captain's subjective recovery through exorcism of his hidden, morally darker, evil self, embodied in Leggatt,[20] and therefore the discarded white hat has been regarded as "an aid marking the position of the ship, enabling the narrator to recover his subject position as a member of the community."[21] Importantly, however, the ship is, as Eardinast-Vulcan rightly points out, not saved through the captain's navigational skills but by "a most unlikely miracle."[22] Accordingly, the fortuity of the hat's appearance is, for some critics,

---

[20] For Leggatt as a symbol, see, note 3 in Chapter 4.

[21] Erdinast-Vulcan, *The Strange Short Fiction of Joseph Conrad*, 45. Yelton regards the hat as a positive sign of the reciprocal relationship between the captain and his double. See Yelton, *Mimesis and Metaphor*, 284. For the view of the hat as a symbol of fidelity, see Stallman, "Conrad and 'The Secret Sharer,'" 103; on the other hand, for Phelan who thinks of the hat as an alternative for "a ring or any other token of remembrance and identification that one lover gives to another," the hat symbolizes an "unconsummated relationship" between the two men. See Phelan, "Sharing Secrets," 138.

[22] Erdinast-Vulcan, *The Strange Short Fiction of Joseph Conrad*, 45.

a weakness because it makes the captain's achievement of knowledge too much a matter of chance, turning the highest kind of seamanship into a tightrope of contingency.[23] Contingency, to be sure, creates a hole in the linear unfolding of the plot of captain's self-recovery through initiation. And yet, far from being a flaw in the work, what is taking place in this anticlimax, or gap, can better be reconsidered as what Derrida would call a gift, or an impossible event that at once supports and subverts the idea of an individual subject.[24]

In the passage cited above, as soon as the hat signifies itself as gift, that is, as soon as it is "meant [by the captain] to save [Leggatt's] homeless head from the dangers of the sun" (142) as "the expression of [the captain's] sudden pity for [Leggatt's] mere flesh," it is annulled without being repaid or even kept in memory by the recipient: "[The hat] must have fallen off his [Leggatt's] head … and he didn't bother." The captain, the donor, also barely retains the memory of his double, the donee and his gift: "I hardly thought of my other self"; "The great black mass brooding over our very mastheads began to pivot away from the ship's side silently. And now I forgot the secret stranger ready to depart" (141). This "radical forgetting," in Derrida's sense, exceeds a category of the individual psyche. For there to be gift, according to Derrida, not only must the donor or donee not perceive or receive the gift as such, have no consciousness of it, no memory, no recognition, but he or she must also forget it right away.[25] The gift as the symbol, that is, "the expression of [the captain's] sudden pity for [Leggatt's] mere flesh," immediately engages one in restitution, Derrida says; therefore the gift not only must not be repaid but also must not be kept in memory, retained as something symbolic:

> [The] simple intention to give, insofar as it carries the intentional meaning of the gift, suffices to make a return payment to oneself. The simple consciousness of the gift right away sends itself back the gratifying image of goodness or generosity, of the giving-being who, knowing itself to be such, recognizes itself in a circular, specular fashion, in a sort of auto-recognition, self-approval, and narcissistic gratitude.[26]

---

[23] Daleski, *Joseph Conrad*, 183; Ressler, *Joseph Conrad*, 93–94.

[24] In Erdinast-Vulcan's words, this "gift" of the hat is "an abortive gesture towards an empty topos of subjectivity." *The Strange Short Fiction of Joseph Conrad*, 46.

[25] Jacques Derrida, *Given Times: I. Counterfeit Money*. trans. Peggy Kamuf (Chicago and London: University of Chicago Press, 1992), 16, 24.

[26] Derrida, *Given Times*, 23, also see, 13.

This narcissistic "auto-recognition," I would suggest, entails the momentary illusion of "the perfect communion of a seaman with his first command" (143), thereby producing the effect of reality of the captain's self-recovery; and thus he apparently ceases to be a stranger to himself, "taking full possession of himself" in the end, as has been said.[27] A gift will take place only at the instant of "breaking and entering" in the circle of restitution; at the instant when all circulation will have been interrupted,[28] the captain's "I" is subjectivated, becoming a subject, entering into the realm of the calculable as subject.[29] The conditions of the possibility of the gift designate simultaneously the conditions of the impossibility of the gift: these conditions of possibility define the annulment, or discarding of the gift in the quotation above.[30] This condition of the impossibility of the gift concerns time but does not belong to it. Derrida writes: "*At the limit, gift as gift* ought *not appear as gift: either to the donee or to the donor.* It cannot be gift as gift except by not being present as gift. Neither to the 'one' nor to the 'other.'"[31] If the other perceives or receives it, if he or she keeps it as gift, the gift is annulled, as we have seen above. From the moment the gift would appear as gift, the moment it is "meant to save [Leggatt's] homeless head from the dangers of the sun," according to Derrida, it would be engaged in an economic structure that would annul the gift in the ritual circle of the debt.[32] If the donor sees it or knows it, as soon as he or she intends to give, he or she begins to gratify him- or herself, to congratulate him- or herself, to give back him- or herself symbolically the value of what he or she thinks he or she has given. This "temporalization of time (memory, present, anticipation … and so forth)," says Derrida, always sets in motion "the process of the destruction of the gift."[33] There would be a gift only at the instant, at "the paradoxical instant of decision that is madness, tears time apart"; the "present" of the gift is no longer thinkable as a now.[34] The white hat floats around the "shadow-line" between the possible (presence) and the impossible (absence), life and death, history and myth, opening up a hole, a gap of contingency, the impossible space beyond linear time sequence.

[27] Daleski, *Joseph Conrad*, 182.
[28] Derrida, *Given Times*, 9.
[29] Ibid., 12.
[30] Ibid., 16, 24.
[31] Ibid., 14.
[32] Ibid., 23.
[33] Ibid., 14.
[34] Ibid., 9.

The Koh-ring enterprise seems to encapsulate the captain's approach to the (im)possible. Before going on to dramatize the separation of the two, the narrator likens the "towering shadow" of Koh-ring (141) to "the very gateway of Erebus":

> The black southern hill of Koh-ring seemed to hang right over the ship like a towering fragment of everlasting night. On that enormous mass of blackness there was not a gleam to be seen, not a sound to be heard. It was gliding irresistibly towards us and yet seemed already within reach of the hand. (139)
>
> Then stillness again, with the great shadow gliding closer, towering higher, without a light, without a sound. Such a hush had fallen on the ship that she might have been a bark of the dead floating in slowly under the very gate of Erebus. (140)

With its mythical stature, the darkness here implies something more than "the hell of unredeemable moral failure."[35] Returning (as he came) to the primordial darkness with mythical fecundity,[36] Leggatt presents himself as a disappearing trace (witnessed only by the narrator and the reader) and keeps escaping verbal labeling. In its attempt to go as close as possible to what is unapproachable by word, or the thing-in-itself,[37] the Koh-ring enterprise stages the unnameable relationship between Leggatt and the captain. We may be tempted to ask here: "Who (or what) is '… too proud to explain' in the passage above? The captain or Leggatt? Or both?" If the gift cannot take place between two subjects exchanging objects, as Derrida thinks, then we may argue that the gap in "… too proud to explain" is the very space for "strange fraternity" to emerge, the space in which "[t]he question of the gift should … seek its place before any relation to the subject, before any conscious or unconscious relation to self of the subject."[38] The relationship (without relationship) between Leggatt and the captain might prompt a person with "'the Bless my soul—you don't say so' type of intellect" (101) (like that of the terrifically whiskered chief mate) to fill

---

[35] Ressler, *Joseph Conrad*, 90.
[36] For the fecund, primordial darkness, see Masao Yamaguchi, *Bunka to Ryogisei* (*Culture and Ambiguity*) (Tokyo: Iwanami, 2000), 1–2.
[37] For the idea of things and words, see Yuasa Hiroo, *Outousuru Yobikake* (*Responding Call*) (Tokyo: Miraisha, 2009), 178.
[38] Derrida, *Given Times*, 24.

in the blank space, but we readers might want to "proudly" leave it open for some mysterious arrival, some relationship to come.

Thus, in their inclination to go beyond the idea of an individual subject, the two overlooked episodes in "The Secret Sharer"—that of the miserable scorpion and that of the captain's white floppy hat—resonate with the captain-narrator's unconditionally hospitable gesture toward the other, an unexpected event that is not wholly available to subjective consciousness but underlies and makes possible every kind of plurality, as we have seen in the previous chapter. "The Secret Sharer," in its allusion to "the 'brand of Cain' business" (107), the alleged first fratricide in human history, engages not only with modernistic exploration into the secret of a closed, individual inner space of heart, but also with an exploration into an impossible space of "strange fraternity" in Conrad's words that surpasses conventional brotherhood.

6

Responding in a Duel

History as Responsibility in "The Duel"

Conrad began "The Duel" in late 1906 and completed it in 1907. The short story appeared in *Pall Mall Magazine* from January to May 1908, and it was included as the longest of the stories in *A Set of Six* (1908) with the added subtitle, "A Military Tale." "The Duel" is Conrad's first historical piece, one in which he attempted to "realize the spirit of the Napoleonic Era."[1] In a letter to J. B. Pinker, Conrad wrote that he had gone to the local library to read all he could discover there about Napoleon in Elba.[2] *Nostromo*, the history of a fictional state without an easily locatable referent, reveals some of Conrad's difficulty with the idea of chronological, referential history. "The Duel" shows that Conrad was already interested in the Napoleonic theme, not in the sense of straightforward history but in the sense of responsibility, as early as 1907, a year or two before he explored the possibility of the unconditional welcome of the other in "The Secret Sharer."

"The Duel" recounts a sixteen-year-long quarrel between two officers during the Napoleonic wars, a fight that originates in "a mysterious, unforgivable offence"[3]—unforgivable by Feraud, a hot-tempered, low-born lieutenant. The urbane, aristocratic lieutenant D'Hubert is sent to place Feraud under house arrest because of his involvement in a duel with a civilian. Feraud takes offence and challenges D'Hubert to a duel. Napoleon, meanwhile, notoriously remains "a shadowy off-stage presence"[4] in this novella as in Conrad's other

---

[1] Conrad, *The Collected Letters*, vol. 4, 29.
[2] Conrad, *The Collected Letters*, vol. 3, 409.
[3] Joseph Conrad, "The Duel: A Military Tale," *A Set of Six* (London: Dent, 1961), 211. Subsequent page references will be to this edition, preceded by *SS* where necessary.
[4] Avrom Fleishman, *The English Historical Novel: Walter Scott to Virginia Woolf* (Baltimore and London: Johns Hopkins Press, 1971), 219.

historical novels, and the author does not, as he did in so many of his major works, psychologically analyze the obsessive duelists. It is thus not surprising that, under the "achievement and decline" theory where the norm is psychological depth, the novella has been underrated as a "slight tale"[5] of "tiresome length and rhetoric" and also criticized for the author's "banal" treatment of the heroic theme.[6] However, some critics have highlighted the eccentricity of the duel between two officers in Napoleon's Grand Army. Edward H. Sparrow points out the "unorthodoxy" of the first duel, which starts "irregularly" in a "post-lapsarian" garden where everyone except D'Hubert is "looney";[7] Sean Gaston, more recently, remarks in a similar vein that the first two "unconventional" duels set the pattern for "the duel *without end*."[8] On closer observation, the feud between the two officers is far from being "banal." On the contrary, it strangely involves women from time to time, and it takes place in a "most unsuitable ground" (179) for a duel. One combatant answers to/ for the perpetual call of the other, but he does so not from "the sympathy of mankind" (195) but in a fight, laying himself open to a "cut" (208). In its challenge to "the justice of men" (195),[9] the duelists' "private contest" (165) without end is "at once a duel and not a duel,"[10] gesturing toward the realm of the impossible. Although Conrad's original plan for the novella was to make sweeping suggestions about the historical age, he in fact does something more than and different from simply relating history. Not surprisingly, therefore, one contemporary reviewer, W. L. Courtney, in the *Daily Telegraph*, missed the Napoleonic feeling, merely describing the story as "tedious through its unnecessary length."[11]

History, as Derrida writes in *Archive Fever*, is not simply the question of "a concept dealing with the past that might *already* be at our disposal," but rather "a question of the future ... the question of a response, of a promise and of a

---

[5]   Peters, *The Cambridge Introduction to Joseph Conrad*, 85.

[6]   Lawrence Graver, *Conrad's Short Fiction* (Berkeley and Los Angeles: University of California Press, 1969), 145–146.

[7]   Edward. H. Sparrow, "Conrad's Most Unsuitable Ground for A Duel," *L'Epoque Conradienne* 24 (1998): 49.

[8]   For the unconventionality of the duel, see Sean Gaston, "Conrad and the Asymmetrical Duel," in his *Derrida, Literature and War: Absence and the Chance of Meeting* (New York: Continuum, 2009), 128.

[9]   Lieutenant Feraud mistrusts the sympathy of mankind (191) and the justice of men, and he "by no means desire[s] a Court of Honour" (195).

[10] Tomás Juhász, *Conradian Contracts: Exchange and Identity in the Immigrant Imagination* (Plymouth: Lexington Books, 2011), 106.

[11] Norman Sherry, *Conrad: The Critical Heritage* (London: Routledge, 1973), 216.

responsibility for tomorrow."[12] "The Duel," a story of institutionalized mutual maiming and killing, makes—like most of Conrad's stories—impossible demands on its readers, calling for an answering singular response beyond any ethics and laws.[13] We readers are, in a way, summoned "to respond with [our] word in a duel," to open a "fight" or a "debate," to repeat Anne Dufourmantell's words in her invitation to Derrida in his seminar on the foreigner question:

> *The question that the foreigner will address to them [the laws of hospitality distinguished from* The *unconditional Law of hospitality] to open this great debate, which will also be a great fight, is nothing less than that of the political, of man as a political being," states Derrida from the beginning of the seminar. The question of the political is given there as being the question that comes to us from the other, the foreigner. If the political is one of the founding philosophical questions, operating since the first [Socratic] dialogues, in this seminar, as Derrida inscribes it, it is a new question, because it is signified to us from the place of the other, from the repeated, insistent breaking in of his question. From what, in that question, instructs us to respond. To respond to it, as you respond with your word in a duel, because what it is, is a fight.*[14] (emphasis in the original)

Thus, thinking Conrad's "history" less in terms of straightforward referentiality than in terms of responsibility, this chapter will discuss "The Duel" as a story of infinite response to the call of the other.

Let me start my response, my own duel with an excess that the story brings to our attention in its opening passage. As Myrtle Hooper persuasively argues in her discussion of the ethics of negativity in "The Duel," much of the action and the existential texture of the novella are defined less by what is than by what is not.[15] From the start, the text foreshadows that the story will not be about Napoleon but about the officers in his army:

[12] Jacques Derrida, *Archive Fever: A Freudian Impression*, trans. Eric Prenowitz (Chicago: University of Chicago Press, 1998), 36.

[13] Regarding an ethics that is not about prescriptions and moral codes, see Attridge, *Reading and Responsibility*, 146. Attridge also writes that responsibility is not a simple ethical concept and that it makes impossible demands (ibid., 4). Peters, on the other hand, points out that the irrationality of the duel calls Western values into question. See Peters, *The Cambridge Introduction to Joseph Conrad*, 85. One may surmise that Conrad might have been attracted by the polemically honorable nature, as it were, of the ritualized male intimacy, as is shown in Ferguson's quotation of the germ of the story from *Harper's Magazine* of September 1858: "[D]ueling was honorable; who should venture to punish the murderer, who was only [a] duelist?" See DeLancey Ferguson, "The Plot of Conrad's *The Duel*," *Modern Language Notes*, vol. 50, no. 6 (June 1935): 385.

[14] Derrida, *Of Hospitality*, 66, 68, 70.

[15] Myrtle Hooper, "The Ethics of Negativity: Conrad's 'The Duel,'" *L'Epoque Conradienne* 31 (2005): 111–112.

Napoleon I., whose career had the quality of a duel against the whole of Europe, disliked duelling between the officers of his army. The great military emperor was not a swashbuckler, and had little respect for tradition.

Nevertheless, a story of duelling, which became a legend in the army, runs through the epic of imperial wars. To the surprise and admiration of their fellows, two officers, like insane artists trying to gild refined gold or paint the lily, pursued a private contest through the years of universal carnage. (165)

Here we can hardly overlook the phrase "to gild refined gold or paint the lily," which is taken in slightly modified fashion from Shakespeare's tragedy *King John*, relatively unknown today but performed most frequently in the nineteenth century.[16] The phrase means "to do the superfluous,"[17] as in "To throw a perfume on the violet / To smooth the ice, or add another hue / Unto the rainbow, or with taper-light / To seek the beauteous eye of heaven to garnish" (4. 2. 11–15). It calls our attention to something that "[i]s wasteful and ridiculous excess" (4. 2. 16), something that overflows the expressed intention of the author: "[a] serious and even earnest attempt at a bit of historical fiction" (*SS* viii) of the Napoleonic era through rendering "the Spirit of the Epoch" (*SS* ix). The implication is that Conrad might have been aware of himself as an "insane artist" in his pursuit of the inconclusive, protracted "private contest" of Napoleon's two officers rather than of the emperor's own "duel against the whole of Europe." Despite Conrad's denial in the "Author's Note" of the novella's direct connection with his personal experiences (v), the line from *King John* already invokes his father, an adept translator of Shakespeare, and the drama's theme, the "foul revolt of French inconstancy" (3. 1. 249), is particularly interesting in our reading of the story of the Napoleonic era, or the decisive moment for the fate of Poland.[18] But I shall come back to the erasure of Polish experience later in my discussion. For now, invited by this Shakespearean verse to respond to an excess, I will look closely at the eccentricity of the duel between two officers.

The first duel, like the last one, happens "irregularly," to repeat Sparrow's word mentioned above, in an "unfit" ground without proper witnesses (*SS*

---

[16] For the history of this work's performance, see William Shakespeare, *King John*, ed. Yoshiko Ueno (Tokyo: Hakusuisha, 1983), 192.

[17] William Shakespeare, *King John. The Arden Shakespeare*, ed. E. A. J. Honingsmann (London: Bloomsbury, 2007), 97.

[18] It is also noteworthy that Napoleon is called a "usurper" in Conrad's "The Duel" (*SS* 244), as in *King John*, and that there is a character named Hubert in *King John*.

249). It takes place at dusk in "a private garden" (190) in what D'Hubert considers "most unsuitable ground" because his foothold is made "insecure by the round, dry gravel ... rolling under the ... soles of his boots" (179).[19] The last duel is also fought in a "poor" (250) ground in Provence without the presence of seconds because D'Hubert has only royalist friends from whom to choose, "[o]wing to the [reactionary] state of the people's minds" (249) in the southern part of the country. As D'Hubert regards it as "preposterous" (177) to get any of their comrades to serve as seconds for their first fight, Feraud seizes a deaf gardener by the throat, pushes him back against a tree and tells him to look on, and he sends word to an old maid to stick her head out of a window (177):

> The clash of arms filled that prim garden, which hitherto had known no more warlike sound than the click of clipping shears; and presently the upper part of an old lady's body was projected out of a window upstairs. She tossed her arms above her white cap, scolding in a cracked voice. The gardener remained glued to the tree, his toothless mouth open in idiotic astonishment, and a little farther up the path the pretty girl, as if spellbound to a small grass plot, ran a few steps this way and that wringing her hands and muttering crazily. She did not rush between the combatants: the onslaughts of Lieut. Feraud were so fierce that her heart failed her. (179)

The general exclusion of female presence amidst the ritualized male intimacy in this story has often been pointed out. Sparrow claims that the female characters in this story are "on stage mostly by way of contrast" and exist "to showcase, to condone and almost witness, a particular male problem."[20] Juhász, on the other hand, explains the exclusion of women in terms of homoeroticism.[21] Nevertheless, the "we" narrator inserts an old lady and a pretty young maid into the typically masculine setting, along with the deaf man, as witnesses.[22]

---

[19] Making a passing comment on Conrad's dueling story in terms of the procedure and etiquette of the duel, Kiernan writes that an accepted part of the duty of seconds is "to examine the facts of the case, and co-operate in seeking a peaceful solution, if this could comport with the self-respect of both disputants." "Most issues could be resolved," Kiernan continues, "by judicious management. Between them the seconds could constitute a small court of honour." Kiernan does not see unorthodoxy in Conrad's duel. See V. G. Kiernan, *The Duel in European History: Honour and the Reign of Aristocracy* (Oxford: Oxford University Press, 1989), 139.

[20] Sparrow, "Conrad's Most Unsuitable Ground," 58–59.

[21] Juhász, *Conradian Contracts*, 105.

[22] "By introducing numerous minor characters," Ferguson writes, "Conrad not only enriches the social and military panorama of the background but achieves such details of pattern as the Alsatian maid's attempted intervention for Feraud in the first duel and Adèle's for D'Hubert in the last." Ferguson, "The Plot of Conrad's The Duel," 388.

Furthermore, the intervention by the women is rendered rather comic. When D'Hubert hastily drops to his knees alongside Feraud's prostrate body to stop its bleeding, his gallant indulgence in a "memory of the right good-will he … put into the blow" is "ridiculously impeded" (181) by the pretty young maid:

> Rending the air with screams of horror, she attacked him [D'Hubert] from behind and, twining her fingers in his hair, tugged back at his head. Why she should choose to hinder him at this precise moment he could not in the least understand. He did not try. It was all like a very wicked and harassing dream. Twice to save himself from being pulled over he had to rise and fling her off. He did this stoically, without a word, kneeling down again at once to go on with his work. But the third time, his work being done, he seized her and held her arms pinned to her body. Her cap was half off, her face was red, her eyes blazed with crazy boldness. He looked mildly into them while she called him a wretch, a traitor, and a murderer many times in succession. This did not annoy him so much as the conviction that she had managed to scratch his face abundantly. (182)

Whereas the slash on Feraud's arm has been inflicted by his male adversary, the scratches on D'Hubert's face and hands come mainly from the pretty maid. The Alsatian young girl is, in her frenzy, the very embodiment of "a perfect singleness of intention," or "a homicidal austerity of mood," which is demanded in "[a] duel, whether regarded as a ceremony in the cult of honour, or even when reduced in its moral essence to a form of manly sport" (180). Even when D'Hubert tells her to fetch a surgeon for Feraud, "her sobbed out intention [is] to remain in the garden, and fight tooth and nail for the protection of the vanquished man" (183). She struggles all the time "not with maidenly coyness, but like a pretty, dumb fury" (183), kicking D'Hubert's shins now and then, until he releases her and she rushes to crouch by Feraud's side. It may be customary to see, along with Sparrow, that the battle ends when D'Hubert cuts Feraud on the arm and Feraud loses his balance on the gravel, falls, and hits his head.[23] But the first duel in fact ends not when Feraud falls but when "[t]he shades of the night [fall] on the little trim garden with this touching group" (*SS* 183) and D'Hubert goes away from "the group" to find a sergeant, "congratulat[ing] himself upon the dusk conceal- ing his gory hands and scratched face from the passers-by" (184).

---

[23] Sparrow, "Conrad's Most Unsuitable Ground," 49.

The burlesque tableau of "this touching group" suggests that the narrative concern lies less in a heroic, honorable one-to-one encounter between noble men than in a somewhat strange group of people, noble and common, including women. This sense of plurality is underscored by the unobtrusive "we" narrator. "The Duel" has generally been understood as a story told by an omniscient narrator,[24] but the seemingly omniscient narrator sometimes gives way to the first person plural "we" narrator when he is especially sympathetic to the two duelists:

> General Feraud, totally unable (as is the case with most of us) to compre-hend what was happening to him, received the Minister of War's order to proceed at once to a small town of Central France. ... (230)

> No man succeeds in everything he undertakes. In that sense we are all fail-ures. The great point is not to fail in ordering and sustaining the effort of our life. In this matter vanity is what leads us astray. It hurries us into situations from which we must come out damaged; whereas pride is our safeguard, by the reserve it imposes on the choice of our endeavour as much as by the vir-tue of its sustaining power.
> General D'Hubert was proud and reserved. He had not been damaged by his casual love affairs, successful or otherwise. In his war-scarred body his heart at forty remained unscratched. (233–234)

In this case, what happens between D'Hubert and Feraud is not simply a ser-ies of old-fashioned, gallant duels in the royalist memory of the old Chevalier, uncle of D'Hubert's fiancé Adèle, or the "fault" of a woman who "*would* [italics in the original] keep on playing" (243) with men. Women in this story are not the absent object of a male desire but something like what Derrida would call the *arrivant*, interrupting the male intimacy in the first duel (as we have seen above) and again in the last one. Learning of the duel, Adèle rushes to inter-fere, "over the field, two miles—running all the way" (260). Sparrow regret-fully states that the Intended comes upon the scene "too little too late to make her a full character,"[25] but her inability to become "a full character" does not necessarily point to her weakness; rather, it enhances her "to-comeness" by the

---

[24] As for the omniscient narration in "The Duel," see, for example, Middleton, *Joseph Conrad*, 77. We can add here another instance of "we" narration: "[I]f true courage consists in going out to meet an odious danger from which our body, soul, and heart recoil together, General D'Hubert had the opportunity to practise it for the first time in his life" (248).

[25] Sparrow, "Conrad's Most Unsuitable Ground," 58.

repeated allusions to her "running all the way" (260, 261, 263, 266) without finally reaching the fight scene.[26] "[T]he wonder of her existence" (235) always baffles D'Hubert, yet this "mysterious" creature's (234) "crazy boldness," like that of the pretty maid depicted above, at last prompts the inexperienced man of forty not so much to find "his true self," as Addison Bross asserts,[27] as to "find [her] out" (264, 266) after the last duel, and he welcomes her. Nevertheless, her "inaccessible nearness" (236), or her otherness, has not been eliminated but merely assuaged, as is implied in the "we" narrator's depiction of her transformation after the last duel: "her transcendental beauty [becomes] much less mysterious, much more accessible to a man's comprehension" (262).

Nor is Feraud totally detranscendentalized despite his otherized image as a hot-tempered, low-born little Southerner in contrast with the reflective, dandy, tall nobleman from the north. Their difference, in a way, reflects the democratization of armies that resulted from the implementation of mass conscription during the French Revolution, which was at first applied only to the poor but gradually drew many of higher station into its net.[28] For an aristocrat like Adèle's royalist uncle who tries to talk D'Hubert out of "mixing [himself] up with" (244) the son of a blacksmith (Feraud), and for a statesman like Joseph Fouché, the Minister of Police of the second Restoration who has his "choice of thousands [of names]" (226), people like Feraud and those mutilated Bonapartist veterans "do not exist" (244, 245); for them, the name of Feraud stands for "The People," the other(s) to historiography.[29] Despite their contribution to Napoleon's victory over European monarchies, the life or death of those "obscure" people "[doesn't] matter to France" (227), and thus they are abandoned by history. For Feraud himself, being "[n]o longer in the army" means, both literally and figuratively, that "[i]t [is] impossible to exist" (230). Imperial wars enable Feraud to surface on the stage of history, but he is again reduced to the status of "a man who, as far as [D'Hubert is] concerned,

---

[26]   In the chapter 9, I discuss another female intervention with men's heroic acts in *The Rover* in terms of Derrida's democracy to come.

[27]   Addison Bross, "A Set of Six: Variations on a Theme," in *Joseph Conrad: Critical Assessment*, ed. Keith Carabine (Robertsbridge, UK: Helm Information, 1992), 116.

[28]   "With wars nearly continuous from 1792 to 1815," Kiernan states, "Europe underwent a thorough militarization. Conscription spread everywhere; hitherto as a rule it had been practised only on the poor, like England's press-ganged Jack Tars or Holy Russia's serf-soldiers, but now many of higher station were drawn into the net." Kiernan, *The Duel in European History*, 194.

[29]   Michel de Certeau, *The Writing of History*, trans. Tom Conley (New York: Columbia University Press, 1975), 2–3.

does not exist" (258) when he loses in the last duel, outwitted by D'Hubert's mirror strategy. This may seem not very far from so-called incorporation of the other in the same, but the "serious difference" (189) between two officers is not settled in the end, as Feraud rejects D'Hubert's offer of reconciliation.

In thus doing justice to the other, the narrator presents the duel as an aporia, an impossible space that cannot easily be assimilated into the systematic representation of historiography, creating a rupture in the text of European history. The representational liminality of the duel may not be unrelated to the "forcible" closure of the third confrontation (204), for instance, as well as the premature ending of the fourth duel as follows:

> [A]t the very first set-to, Captain Feraud laid himself open to a cut over the forehead, which blinding him with blood, ended the combat almost before it had fairly begun. It was impossible to go on. Captain D'Hubert, leaving his enemy swearing horribly and reeling in the saddle between his two appalled friends, leaped the ditch again into the road and trotted home with his two seconds, who seemed rather awestruck at the speedy issue of that encounter. (208)

It is significant here that the fourth encounter is placed in an intermission of D'Hubert's epistolary writing. D'Hubert goes out to fight the fourth duel, throwing aside the long congratulatory letter that he is composing on his sister's marriage, but the "speedy issue of that encounter" brings him back home in the evening to finish the letter. In other words, the fourth duel literally "cuts" in and interrupts his epistle, thereby implicitly inviting us to connect Feraud's "cut" over the forehead with a gap in D'Hubert's letter—his writing—by extension, the text of "The Duel" written by Conrad.

Given "[t]he responsibility" of "the Man of St. Helena" regarding the Russian campaign, the importance of the analogy between a physical wound, that is, a "cut" in the body of a warrior, and a gap in the body of the text cannot be too strongly emphasized, but I shall return to this point later in the concluding part of my discussion. Before going further, let us look briefly at the ways in which the history of the Napoleonic campaigns is interrupted by the duelists' "private contests," or, to put it the other way around, the ways in which the actual wars cut in on their duels.

The battle of Austerlitz in 1805, one of Napoleon's greatest victories, happens in the interval between the second and the third duels, and Feraud arranges a meeting directly after the pressure of war eases. The third duel is then fought in Silesia, where both men suffer "many cuts" and bleed profusely:

> This duel [the third one] was fought in Silesia. If not fought to a finish, it was, at any rate, fought to a standstill. The weapon was the cavalry sabre, and the skill, the science, the vigour, and the determination displayed by the adversaries compelled the admiration of the beholders. It became the subject of talk on both shores of the Danube, and as far as the garrisons of Gratz and Laybach. They crossed blades seven times. Both had many cuts which bled profusely. Both refused to have the combat stopped, time after time, with what appeared the most deadly animosity. (204)

Covered with gore and hardly able to stand, the duelists are at last led away "forcibly" (204) by their seconds. The quarrel is not settled, but the necessities of service separate the two officers again until the following year, when they come together again during the war with Prussia: "Detached north after Jena, with the army commanded by Marshal Bernadotte … they entered Lübeck together" (205). This statement obviously refers to the twin battles of Jena and Auerstedt in 1806, in which Napoleon's army defeated Prussia decisively and Bernadotte occupied Lübeck, where the fourth duel, on horseback, ends almost as soon as it begins, with "a cut" over Feraud's forehead, as we have already seen. Then, between the fourth duel and the last one, a series of important battles against Russia transpire:

> He [Captain D'Hubert] saw the fields of Eylau and Friedland, marched and countermarched in the snow, in the mud, in the dust of Polish plains, picking up distinction and advancement on all the roads of North-eastern Europe. Meantime, Captain Feraud, despatched southwards with his regiment, made unsatisfactory war in Spain. It was only when the preparations for the Russian campaign began that he was ordered north again. He left the country of mantillas and oranges without regret. (209–210)

The bloody and inconclusive battle of Eylau in 1807 prolonged Napoleon's war with Russia until the Battle of Friedland in 1807 forced Tsar Alexander I to the peace table at Tilsit, where the Grand Duchy of Warsaw was instituted. The Treaties of Tilsit in 1807, traditionally regarded as the height of Napoleon's empire, were followed by the defeats of the Emperor's army in the Peninsular War in Spain and then by the Russian campaign, which ensured Napoleon's downfall.

As is again textually encapsulated in the last correspondence between the two, in which Napoleon's name comes up one last time, the Emperor and his duels always "stand in between" Feraud and D'Hubert.[30] Long after the last duel, D'Hubert, now happily married, writes a letter to Feraud, but Feraud rejects D'Hubert's attempt at reconciliation, declaring that the latter has *"never* loved the Emperor"*:

> If one of your boy's names had been Napoleon—or Joseph—or even Joachim, I could congratulate you on the event with a better heart. As you have thought proper to give him the names of Charles Henri Armand, I am confirmed in my conviction that you *never* loved the Emperor. The thought of that sublime hero chained to a rock in the middle of a savage ocean makes life of so little value that I would receive with positive joy your instructions to blow my brains out. From suicide I consider myself in honour debarred. But I keep a loaded pistol in my drawer. (265)

Curiously enough, Napoleon is called *"The Other"* (223) in this novella, as in Conrad's last unfinished novel of Napoleonic times, *Suspense*, in keeping with the Emperor's peculiar absence in the text, which I noted at the outset of this chapter. Thus literally "the other" to the text, Napoleon is incessantly called into an aporia, an impossible space of another justice, a gap in the text, which intermittently opens like many bleeding "cut[s]." Those gaps, overlapping with the wounds of the old veterans who lost an eye or left "the tip of his nose in Russia" (232), mutely point to "[t]he responsibility" of "the Man of St. Helena in view of his deplorable levity in the conduct of the Russian campaign," to borrow Conrad's own words in *A Personal Record*.[31]

Here we should perhaps recall what Gaston terms the "impossible proximity of a non-duelling duel" during the Russian campaign.[32] When the disastrous retreat from Moscow again brings D'Hubert and Feraud together in the winter

---

[30] Gaston, *Derrida, Literature and War*, 124.

[31] Joseph Conrad, *The Mirror of the Sea and A Personal Record* (Oxford: Oxford University Press, 1988), 32. Further page references will be to this edition, preceded by *PR* where necessary. Importantly, Ukai Satoshi observes that the wounds, gaping silently, point to those who invade and to the singular event that inflicted the wound. See Satoshi Ukai, *Otosuruchikara (Responsibility): Kitarubekikotoba tachi e (Towards Words that Are to Come)* (Tokyo: Seidosha, 2003), 353, 355. Juhász, on the other hand, argues "the imperfect nose" (259) of a veteran in "The Duel" in terms of the Lacanian phallic connotations of the nose in cultural history. Juhász writes that "the bearer of the nasal wound can be seen as standing for the ability to stay within the Symbolic order, to use signifiers in ways that are reflective of law and of desire, too." See Juhász, *Conradian Contracts*, 109.

[32] Regarding the "impossible proximity of a non-duelling duel" during the Russian campaign, see Gaston, *Derrida, Literature and War*, 123.

of 1812, they "make common cause" against the Cossacks instead of dueling.[33] Marching in the ranks of "the sacred battalion of skeletons" (213), the two officers never exchange a casual word, except when they find themselves cut off in the woods by a small party of Cossacks. Colonel Feraud's "taciturnity" is noticeable compared to D'Hubert's show of camaraderie in the narrator's "faithful record of speeches exchanged during the retreat from Moscow by Colonels Feraud and D'Hubert" (214). His reticence draws our attention to an opposition, a duel, buried and erased under the appearance of the two "indomitable companions" (214) making "common cause." Feraud's rage and feelings of "perfidy towards the sublime Man of Destiny" (214) are indeed "submerged … in a sea of disaster and misery" (211).

Here the Polish author, perhaps in the guise of the unobtrusive "we" narrator, is trying to open a "cut," a fight, interrupting the history to involve us readers in the history, opening the text to alterity, as if at once to review and renew the Russian campaign and the ensuing Congress of Vienna from 1814 to 1815. It can hardly be mere coincidence that "many cuts" bled profusely in Silesia, a historical region now located mostly in Poland, though its borders and national affiliations have changed over time. Conrad, "son of a land … bedewed with … blood," as he states in *A Personal Record* (35), incessantly recalls Napoleon, "*The Other*," into the great debate about "the Polish Question," which has a "practical bearing" on the future of Europe, as the author insists in his political essays.[34] However, in citing this inclination I do not to imply that Conrad simply looks back upon the period as "an era of hope that ended definitively" with Napoleon's retreat from Moscow.[35] Rather, I would suggest that he (more precisely, his text) simultaneously looks forward to an uncertain future to come, as I said when quoting Derrida at the outset. Conrad's "archive" of European history awaits the coming of the other, of what is coming, but not

---

[33] Owen Knowles and Gene Moore, eds., *Oxford Reader's Companion to Conrad* (Oxford: Oxford University Press, 2000), 97.

[34] I make a similar point in my discussion of *Suspense* in the final chapter. See Joseph Conrad, "A Note on the Polish Problem," in *Notes on Life and Letters*, 137; O. Halecki, *A History of Poland* (London and Henley: Routledge and Kegan Paul, 1978), 217–228. Derrida repeatedly reminds us of history as the responsibility of Europe. See Jacques Derrida, *The Gift of Death and Literature in Secret*, trans. David Willis (Chicago and London: University of Chicago Press, 1999), 5. For Europe's responsibility for itself, for the other, and before the other, see Jacques Derrida, *The Other Heading: Reflections of Today's Europe*, trans. Pascale-Anne Brault and Michael B. Naas (Bloomington and Indianapolis: Indiana University Press, 1992), 4–83.

[35] Niland, *Conrad and History*, 169.

in religious terms.[36] The specter of Napoleon is incessantly evoked to answer his "messianic" responsibility to Poland[37] not as what Niland calls "a failed Messiah"[38] but as what Derrida calls "the messianic without identifiable messiah." In this sense (without sense), the Polish author, like an "insane artist,"[39] recalling the "foul revolt of French inconstancy"—the theme of *King John* that we noted earlier in this chapter—"pursue[s]" (165) "[t]he responsibility" of the Man of St. Helena (*PR* 32). This "messianic opening to what is coming," this welcome of the other, into a great debate (or a great fight) is what Derrida would think the very condition of "history":

> Awaiting without horizon of the wait, awaiting what one does not expect yet or any longer, hospitality without reserve, welcoming salutation accorded in advance to the absolute surprise of the *arrivant* from whom or from which one will not ask anything in return and who or which will not be asked to commit to the domestic contracts of any welcoming power (family, State, nation, territory, native soil or blood, language, culture in general, even humanity), *just* opening which renounces any right to property, any right in general, messianic opening to what is coming, that is, to the event that cannot be awaited *as such*, or recognized in advance therefore, to the event as the foreigner itself, to her or to him for whom one must leave an empty place, always, in memory of the hope—and this is the very place of spectrality. It would be easy, too easy, to show that such a hospitality without reserve, which is nevertheless the condition of the event and thus of history ... , is the impossible itself, and that this condition of possibility of the event is also its condition of impossibility, like this strange concept of messianism without content, of the messianic without messianism, that guide us here like the blind.[40]

---

[36] Derrida distinguishes "the messianic" from religious "messianism." See Jacques Derrida, *Spectres of Marx: The State of the Debt, the Work of Mourning, and the New International*, trans. Peggy Kamuf (London: Routledge, 1994), 28.

[37] The original duel starts at the time of the French Revolution. By advancing the initial date from 1794 to 1800, Conrad, as the "we" narrator, focuses more intensely on his own duel with Napoleon. Thus Conrad, according to Ferguson, "gives unity of background with the glamor of Napoleon always a part of the picture." See Ferguson, "The Plot of Conrad's *The Duel*," 388.

[38] Niland, *Conrad and History*, 169.

[39] With regard to the "insanity" of artistry, Gaston interestingly contends that "[c]ontrary to Clausewitz's dictum that 'war is nothing but a duel on a larger scale' Conrad suggests that in times of war, literature is a kind of insane artistry, an asymmetrical duel with the asymmetric war, a war that is always more or less than the representation of war itself." See Gaston, *Derrida, Literature and War*, 138.

[40] Derrida, *Spectres of Marx*, 65.

We readers, as "the other" to the text, are also addressed here as "the unborn" (*NN*, xlii)[41] and made Conrad's "spectral interlocutors."[42] The sense of spectral interlocution, as it were, is all the more heightened by the "we" narrator, who invites us "to respond with [our] word in a duel" (to borrow Dufourmantell's words again) to this singular story, to open a fight or a debate with Napoleon's specter and with other ghostly Bonapartist veterans and royalists who haunt the text,[43] thereby opening "an empty place," "the very place of spectrality."[44] We readers are summoned both to bear witness to "the most agitated ten years of European history," to quote from Conrad's *Suspense*,[45] and to move beyond them, as Gaston did in his brilliant discussion of the asymmetrical encounter between the two officers, in which he compares Napoleon's global war to the contemporary endless war on terror. Gaston concludes his reading of "The Duel" by quoting the proposal made by an Iraqi vice president at the time that Saddam Hussein and George W. Bush should fight a duel to settle their differences. In doing so, Gaston engages his own reading in a dialogue, a duel, with the world's current highly asymmetrical encounters with the military superpower.[46] In responding to Conrad's text "The Duel," we answer for, or take responsibility for, the call of the "we" narrator—the call of his/Conrad's European memory—making it a new question in our own time, which seems more and more like another period of "universal carnage."

---

41 Hooper stresses the writing of the reader into the story as a narrative structuring agent, pointing out that the erasure of ethical as well as factual authority ... consequently places an obligation upon the reader to find a point of ethical reference. See Hooper, "The Ethics of Negativity," 108.

42 I borrow the expression "spectral interlocutors" from Derrida, *Archive Fever*, 43.

43 The text is indeed full of specters of veterans of Napoleon's army: "The sacred battalion of skeletons" (213), lean, shadowy "ghost[s] of *ancien régime*" (234, 243, 246) and "unsubstantial wraiths" (239). Ghostly veterans of Napoleon's army invite D'Hubert to the last duel, "as though they had been shot up with a snap through a trap door in the ground" (238–239). Feraud also feels that he is "like a disembodied spirit" (230).

44 For a "spectral messianicity" and the concept of the archive, see Derrida, *Archive Fever*, 36.

45 Joseph Conrad, *Suspense: A Novel of Napoleonic Times* (London: Dent, 1968), 91. Further page references to *Suspense* will be given parenthetically in the text, preceded by *S* where it might otherwise be unclear.

46 Gaston, *Derrida, Literature and War*, 139.

7

"The Warrior's Soul" and the Question of "Community"

Written in 1916 and published posthumously in 1925 as one of the stories in *Tales of Hearsay*, "The Warrior's Soul" is a tragic story told by an old Russian veteran to a group of young Russians about the young soldier Tomassov who has to honor his earlier pledge by obeying an order to kill a French officer during Napoleon's retreat from Moscow in the winter of 1812. Apart from "rather unexpected" sympathy toward the Russians and the Russian army,[1] "The Warrior's Soul" would seem at first glance to be characteristically Conradian in its dramatization of the moral ordeal of a young hero who has to choose between two nightmares. However, unlike Conrad's earlier personal narrators, the old Russian veteran who for the most part speaks for Tomassov, provides no satisfactory clues to his hero's conduct, thereby incurring Lawrence Graver's criticism of his "inadequate powers of explanation."[2] The absence of what Albert Guerard would call "the journey within," the introspective journey into the self,[3] a privileged theme of the "achievement and decline" paradigm, merely intensifies the theatrical, overdramatized aspect of Tomassov's commitment to a chivalric code of honor, and the story has inevitably been dismissed as a nostalgic reworking of Conrad's old theme of an isolated hero caught in a moral dilemma.[4]

However, the presentation of "a warrior's soul" in this story is too subtle to be taken simply as a failed attempt at the mimetic portrayal of an individual

---

[1] Najder, *Joseph Conrad*, 476.
[2] Graver, *Conrad's Short Fiction*, 196.
[3] See Guerard, *Conrad the Novelist*, 1–59.
[4] Regarding the nostalgic reworking of Conrad's old theme, see Peters, *The Cambridge Introduction to Joseph Conrad*, 116. Here Peters emphasizes the story's "psychological" power. See also Graver, *Conrad's Short Fiction*, 193; Geddes, *Conrad's Later Novels*, 116.

identity by an author who allegedly exhausted his creative energy in his later years. The transformation of this story's original title from an individually focused "The Humane Tomassov" to a more general "The Warrior's Soul" implies a shift in Conrad's emphasis from individuality to something beyond the self, or a sense of plurality that is also intensified by the old narrator's use of the "we" form of narration. With the cumulative effect of the repetitions of the phrase "the warrior's soul," the story links the word "soul" with something relational, undermining a concept of self—an autonomous, morally responsible individual human being whose inner life is fully known through introspection.

And yet, this is not to say that the story is a nostalgic glorification of a bygone mentality of a lost community of warriors, as most traditional critics have claimed,[5] linking such a nostalgic affirmation of the chivalric code of honor with Conrad's artistic deterioration. Instead, this chapter will reread "The Warrior's Soul" as a story of singular plurality, or Jean-Luc Nancy's idea of "community" that is not predicated on the organic model of community based on an individual subject.

* * *

"The Warrior's Soul" has been read as "an exemplary tale" of a legendary warrior, Tomassov,[6] but the narrator's presentation of the young Russian soldier alerts us from the start against the conventional "novelistic" portrayal of his protagonist. In the introduction of Tomassov after the veteran takes over the narrative from the seemingly omniscient, impersonal narrator of the opening few lines, he presents an image of Tomassov sitting erect in the saddle, emerging from "a crawling, stumbling, starved, half-demented mob" of French stragglers in the frozen battlefield. The narrator as a young warrior sees "[t]hat multitude of resurrected bodies with glassy eyes" seething round Tomassov's horse (*THL* 4–5). Then he goes on to emphasize Tomassov's youth, drawing us "near enough to have a good look into his eyes," which "were blue, something like the blue of autumn skies, dreamy and gay, too—innocent, believing eyes.

---

[5] See, for instance, Graver, *Conrad's Short Fiction*, 195; Daniel Schwarz, *Conrad: The Later Fiction* (London: Macmillan, 1982), 99–100.

[6] Graver, *Conrad's Short Fiction*, 195. Likewise, Schwarz contends that the old Russian officer defends the performance of the Russian army against Napoleon with "a parable about the complexities of honour in wartime." See Schwarz, *Conrad*, 99.

A topknot of fair hair decorated his brow like a gold diadem in what one would call normal times" (5).

Readers might expect this kind of external description of a character to be followed by the representation of his personality through exploration of psychological depth especially when Tomassov's inertia here, in sharp contrast with his troopers "pointing and slashing" the enemy, needs some explanation. However, instead of allowing us to look into Tomassov's inner feeling, the narrator's self-reflexive address to the audience of younger warriors—"You may think I am talking of him as if he were the hero of a novel"—prevents us modern readers from naively trusting the reality of this particular warrior.[7]

Suspending the image of a paralyzed Tomassov on the battlefield, the narrator introduces an episode of passionate love and friendship in France three months before the war, where Tomassov had an affair with a French woman and was saved from arrest by a gallant French officer, De Castel, who was also in love with her. At her request, De Castel ascertained the real truth about a rumor that Emperor Napoleon had made up his mind to have the Russian envoy arrested, and he warned Tomassov to escape from France immediately. In deep gratitude for the generosity of someone who was later to become, in fact, his enemy, Tomassov swore that if it ever became necessary he would give up his life for De Castel.

The narrative then again abruptly returns to the scene of battlefield from which the young narrator and Tomassov ride after the charge against the main column of Napoleon's Grand Army. Immediately after the temporal and spatial dislocation, the narrator states, "So I had not been very surprised to see our Tomassov sheathe deliberately his sword right in the middle of the charge" (17), as if to make us believe that the French episode caused Tomassov to show less fight in the battlefield than compassion for the enemy who had died without even trying to defend themselves. Tomassov was resting on a

---

[7] In his attempt to assess Tomassov's "humanity," the narrator contrasts a novelistic characterization of Tomassov with the image of "our Tomassov" in the gossip, the "banter" (5) shared among the Russian warriors, and later with the Tomassov buried in the historical records. The narrator thus makes us see "how people's mere gossip and idle talk pass into history": "In all the memoirs of the time if you read them you will find it stated that our envoy had a warning from some highly placed woman who was in love with him. Of course it's known that he had successes with women, and in the highest spheres, too, but the truth is that the person who warned him was no other than our simple Tomassov—an altogether different sort of lover from himself. This then is the secret of our Emperor's representative's escape from arrest. He and all his official household got out of France all right—as history records" (15–16).

horse, "sheathing his sword deliberately" (5), without even looking down at the multitude of dead bodies, while his comrades were engaged in "a mere butchery" (18). As Tomassov's comrades jeer at his tender sensibilities by dubbing him "the Humane Tomassov" (16), the emphasis on Tomassov's inaction could undermine the glorified image of the classical warriors of the past. But the narrator, contrarily, distances himself from his comrades' sneering attitude by defending Tomassov on the grounds that "[t]here is nothing incompatible between humanity and a warrior's soul" (16–17). If the veteran narrator neither simply aims to represent realistically an individual warrior nor a valorous mentality of warriors, what does he mean by the phrase "a warrior's soul"?

In the whole of traditional iconography, the soul tends to be represented as a little person, a little angel with wings, exiting the mouth of a dying person and taking off.[8] It is no wonder therefore if the title "The Warrior's Soul" is taken as referring either solely to the young soldier Tomassov or to three men: the narrator himself, Tomassov, and De Castel.[9] However, the "soul" in this story cannot always be contained within a single, individual subject as is implied in the picture of Tomassov emerging from "[t]hat multitude of resurrected bodies" (4–5) cited earlier. What Conrad seems to be doing in this story, in his images of those who died in the Napoleonic wars, is instead to deny the singularity of the "soul" as a subject. The singularity of those who are reduced to the nameless dead, "that human mass" (4) of stragglers attacked by the narrator's troop, cannot emerge as an individual. Rather, the text insistently evokes the impossibility of the isolation of a soul (as an individual subject) from the community. De Castel's honorable act of rescue of Tomassov from arrest in France can be viewed as a denial of the singularity of Tomassov's "soul," in that it prevents the young Russian from being "cut off from his country in danger, from his military family, from his duty, from honour, and—well—from glory, too" (16). Furthermore, the rumor among the soldiers that Tomassov has shot an unarmed prisoner denies him the chance to become an exile, obstinately pursuing him even after he resigns from the army.

The impossibility of the separation of the individual from the collective is repeatedly inscribed in Conrad's texts: Kurtz, Jim, Razumov, and Heyst all try

---

[8] Nancy, *Corpus*, trans. Richard A. Rand (New York: Fordham University Press, 2008), 126.
[9] Schwarz, *Conrad*, 99.

but fail to keep aloof from the "we" community. Michael Greaney observes that Conrad's fiction is "haunted by the dream of a community of speakers sharing a language of transparent referentiality and self-present meaning," such as "an intimate circle of storytellers or the close-knit crew of a merchant vessel," and counts "The Warrior's Soul" as one of those tales like *Heart of Darkness* in which Conrad's nostalgia for a lost era of authentic storytelling finds expression.[10] However, the old Russian narrator differentiates himself from the Russian soldiers' sense of "we" in his defense of the humane Tomassov and even goes beyond such an idealized speech community as the "we" in the following extract, where the narrator recalls the night when Tomassov brought in a French prisoner, none other than De Castel. While Tomassov went off on a round of the outposts, the young narrator and other Cossacks dozed off as they sat in front of the fire and he woke up into "a startled consciousness" (19):

> I was no longer sleepy. Indeed, I had become awake with an exaggerated mental consciousness of existence extending beyond my immediate surroundings. Those are but exceptional moments with mankind, I am glad to say. I had the intimate sensation of the earth in all its enormous expanse wrapped in snow, with nothing showing on it but trees with their straight stalk-like trunks and their funeral verdure; and in this aspect of general mourning I seemed to hear the sighs of mankind falling to die in the midst of a nature without life. They were Frenchmen. We didn't hate them; they did not hate us; we had existed far apart—and suddenly they had come rolling in with arms in their hands, without fear of God, carrying with them other nations, and all to perish together in a long, long trail of frozen corpses. I had an actual vision of that trail: a pathetic multitude of small dark mounds stretching away under the moonlight in a clear, still, and pitiless atmosphere—a sort of horrible peace. (20)

It is not easy to see this awakening of the narrator as his purely subjective experience. This is indeed an "exceptional" moment in which the young narrator's "exaggerated mental consciousness of existence" extends beyond the boundary of his "immediate surroundings," or the "sweep of the horizon" of his self (*TLS* 92), to repeat the captain-narrator in "The Secret Sharer." This does not exclusively happen to him but to the whole of "mankind." In his "intimate" communication with "the earth in all its enormous expanse

---

[10] Greaney, *Conrad, Language, and Narrative*, 2–3.

wrapped in snow," the boundary between the inside and the outside, man and nature, life and death, the visual and the auditory, dissolves, and he "suddenly" sees human existence as plural, with individuals "perishing together," *en masse*, at this moment, however much they have so far "existed apart." Overwhelmed by this sense of "general mourning," the narrator cannot isolate any single friend or even enemy from "a pathetic multitude of small dark mounds stretching away under the moonlight." Neither does the reader's "soul" remain detached from this sense of "general mourning," for the narrator prepares us for this "startled consciousness" (19) after a short doze by the repetition of the second person "you" (addressed to his young Russian audience) in the following lines:

> You know what an impermanent thing such a slumber is. One moment you drop into an abyss and the next you are back in the world that you would think too deep for any noise but the trumpet of the Last Judgment. And then off you go again. Your very soul seems to slip down into a bottomless black pit. (19)

The opposition between a body and a soul is brought up, only to be blurred in the narrator's description of the French warriors' "souls doubly riveted inside their bodies to carry them out of Russia through that frost fit to split rocks" (2) and also of De Castel's "suffering soul in that mere husk of a man" (23).[11] The "soul" in this story is drawn out and goes beyond itself, exposing itself to alterity. Tomassov feels in his warrior's soul a "boundless gratitude" (16) to the two people who helped him escape what would have been a cruel ordeal in France just before the war. It is, indeed, "boundless" in its transcendence of national borders, not to say of the boundaries of the self; his experience in France affected his attitude not only toward De Castel and the lady but also toward Frenchmen "in general." Tomassov is "naturally indignant at the invasion of his country, but this indignation [has] no personal animosity in it" (16). Though he is a "great patriot," his grief is not confined to the loss of his countrymen and extends well beyond to "the appalling amount of human suffering he saw around him" (16). Thus, his compassion can be seen as embracing all humanity beyond the binary opposition between friend and enemy,

---

[11] For another example, see the depiction of De Castel: "The prisoner sat between us like an awful gashed mummy as to the face … in a body of horrible affliction, a skeleton at the feast of glory" (23).

"we" and "they". Tomassov is "full of compassion for all forms of mankind's misery in a manly way" (16).

Now we begin to doubt Schwarz's claim that Tomassov's passionate love is merely an "anachronistic" form of the "romantic worship of an unattainable woman."[12] Rather than mere anachronism, love in this story also opens up the possibility of "community." In love, as Jean-Luc Nancy says, the subject finds itself *beyond itself.* Love's "singularity does not belong to a self—it is the singularity of the opening of one to another. It exposes the singularity of a being, its finitude, *in its community.*"[13]

The narrator attributes the inadequacy of his explanation to Tomassov's ostensibly platonic reservation about his lover's "mere physical impressions" (8). And yet, it is the narrator himself who is not concerned with describing her "in set terms" and "[keeps] such details out of his discourses wonderfully well" (8). The narrator's reticence concerning "how she looked," as he himself admits, is in fact "strange," considering his supposedly privileged position as Tomassov's "special confidant" (7). Rather than creating an illusion of the lady's reality by accumulating the "details," however, the narrator conjures up a magical atmosphere of her beauty, observing that Tomassov was "ready to swear that in her presence everybody's thoughts and feelings were bound to circle round her" (8). The narrator goes on to add that "the assertion, the power, the tyranny of sheer beauty" flowed "unheard like a mysterious strain of music" (8) running through wonderful conversations in her distinguished salon. I would suggest that the word "tyranny" is crucial here, because on the one hand it tellingly conveys how she irresistibly attracted men to her salon; but on the other hand, more importantly, for Conrad the word "tyranny" bears a heavy weight of personal anguish, associated with his feelings toward the Russian Empire. Given his Russian experience, things "tyrannical" could not be a mere object of "romantic worship" for the Polish author. Her "tyrannical" beauty flowing "unheard like a mysterious strain of music" (8) resists the visual, even aural, appropriation. Accordingly, it is no wonder that we can see, in Tomassov's love, something more and other than mere adoration for a beautiful woman as a separate, "unattainable" object of masculine desire or fear as the following extract will show. After the French officer went out at the request of the lady to confirm

---

[12] Schwarz, *Conrad*, 99.
[13] Nancy, *The Inoperative Community*, xviii.

the rumor, Tomassov is left alone with her in her salon and experienced an ecstatic moment:

> The lady turned to Tomassov and said: "You may stay with me."
>
> This express command made him supremely happy, though as a matter of fact he had had no idea of going.
>
> She regarded him with her kindly glances, which made something glow and expand within his chest. It was a delicious feeling, even though it did cut one's breath short now and then. Ecstatically he drank in the sound of her tranquil, seductive talk full of innocent gaiety and of spiritual quietude. His passion appeared to him to flame up and envelop her in blue fiery tongues from head to foot and over her head, while her soul reposed in the centre like a big white rose .... (11–12)

What is happening here appears to be the ecstatic merging of lovers, yet it is not merely an amorous union between already existing subjects, such as a man and a woman or the self and the other. As is implied in the narrator's oxymoron, their ecstatic love obviously goes beyond the horizon of signification: it would be almost impossible to hear the "sound" of "silence" or the "sound" of "talk," which is at once "seductive" and "innocent". Therefore it is "unheard," but Tomassov seems to be listening to what still remains "unheard," drinking in that "sound." He does not seem to be simply fascinated with something preexisting; but rather, he seems to be calling for something beyond this, something still "unheard." Driven out of himself by her glance, his boundless passion almost devours and envelops her, but this is neither an appropriation of the other by the self nor their merger into some higher substantial identity "we." Instead of being completely consumed by passion, in the midst of an ecstatic communion, her soul remains blank and at rest, with her tyrannical beauty "like a big white rose," in the way that recalls Nancy's account of "the sovereignty of lovers." According to Nancy,

> lovers are neither a society, nor *the* community effected through fusional communion .... The sovereignty of lovers is no doubt nothing other than the ecstasy of the instant; it does not produce a union, it is nothing—but this nothing itself is also, in its "consummation," a communion.[14]

The singular being is, in Nancy's terms, not properly the subject of ecstasy, for ecstasy has no "subject." Ecstasy is "community," which is not a description of

---

[14]   Nancy, *The Inoperative Community*, 37.

the classical, preexisting association of individual subjects but "happens *to*" the singular being that does not have the nature or the structure of individuality.[15]

Conrad's idea of this singular community is nowhere better epitomized than in "that appalling dark group" of Tomassov and De Castel at the end of the story. On the night of the charge, Tomassov captures a French prisoner, only to discover that it is the officer De Castel who saved his life before the war, and he finally shoots his captive. As the narrator reports, the French officer apparently calls on Tomassov's "warrior's soul" to "pay the debt" "with one liberating shot" (23). This tragic ending, however, does not simply present "the supreme expression of chivalry"[16] but rather shows that it is through death that the community, the shared nature of finite existence, reveals itself, as Nancy says. If community is revealed in the death of others, according to Nancy, it is because death itself is "the true community of *I*'s that are not *egos*."[17] It is not "a communion that fuses the *egos* into an *Ego* or a higher *We*" but rather "the community of *others*"; "death as community" in Nancy establishes their impossible communion, occupying a singular place, assuming "the impossibility of a communitarian being in the form of a subject."[18]

The old veteran ostensibly bases his narrative on the opposition between culture and savagery, between "us" and "them," more than once accentuating the cultural superiority of France over "*Des Russes sauvages*" (5): "You of the present generation, you cannot conceive how much prestige there was then in those names [Paris and France] for the whole world. Paris was the centre of wonder for all human beings gifted with imagination" (6). Thus he seems to define France in relation to Russian otherness. When Tomassov was saved from arrest by the forewarning from the Frenchman, "the primitive young Russian youth" (13) said "in an extremity of gratitude," "I swear it, you [De Castel] may command my life" (15). The hierarchy between "the exquisitely accomplished man of the world" (13) and "the unsophisticated young barbarian" (9) is inverted after the war, when the French officer is captured as a "fugitive" by the Russian "pursuers"; but this is more than an inversion of the antithetical order between the self and the other. Tomassov and De Castel "existed far apart," having nothing in common,

---

15   Ibid., 6–7.
16   W. F. Wright, *Romance and Tragedy in Joseph Conrad* (New York: Russell & Russell, 1966), 168.
17   Nancy, *The Inoperative Community*, 15.
18   Ibid.

and Tomassov's act of shooting De Castel obviously tears them farther apart than ever before. The act of giving death, however, highlights the inseparability of the two in the sense that the death of a French captive cannot be given without Tomassov. The French officer, held as prisoner of war, cannot kill himself. Tomassov sees "this miserable thing [De Castel] that cannot die" (24) with "all [his] being recoil[ing] from [his] own degradation" (23). In his desperate begging for a merciful killing, the French prisoner shows that death does not belong to an individual subject, necessarily demanding and dependent upon the existence of others. He cannot realize death as the action of an "I" in an instant of death.[19] The extreme situation enacts the impossibility of an individual's crossing over to "my death." As if to underscore that what happens between Tomassov and De Castel is impervious to personal interests, the narrator says that he saw "the event approaching [him], not that [he] knew it or had the slightest premonition" (21). In his inability to close his self, De Castel, together with Tomassov, constitutes "that appalling dark group" in the following citation, where the narrator depicts the hero's young face for one last time, but here we no longer expect the conventional novelistic description:

> Yes. He [Tomassov] had done it. And what was it? One warrior's soul paying its debt a hundredfold to another warrior's soul by releasing it from a fate worse than death—the loss of all faith and courage. You may look on it in that way. I don't know. And perhaps poor Tomassov did not know himself. But I was the first to approach that appalling dark group on the snow: the Frenchman extended rigidly on his back, Tomassov kneeling on one knee rather nearer to the feet than to the Frenchman's head. He had taken his cap off and his hair shone like gold in the light drift of flakes that had begun to fall. He was stooping over the dead in a tenderly contemplative attitude. And his young, ingenuous face, with lowered eyelids, expressed no grief, no sternness, no horror—but was set in the repose of a profound, as if endless and endlessly silent, meditation. (26)

---

[19] Drawing on Jacques Derrida and Maurice Blanchot, Wake persuasively discusses the impossibility of the formulation "my death" and mentions the self "outside the self." Wake's concern is more with the structural implications of suicide for narrative, in particular, in *Lord Jim* than with the idea of "community," which is the main concern of mine. Paul Wake, *Conrad's Marlow: Narrative and death in "Youth," Heart of Darkness, Lord Jim and Chance* (Manchester and New York: Manchester University Press, 2007), 66–75.

Tomassov "stooping over the dead in a tenderly contemplative attitude" shows him in a state of "repose" and thus duplicates his image when he rested on horseback on the battlefield as mentioned earlier. His fair hair shining "like gold in the drift of flakes" is also a repetition of "a topknot of fair hair decorated his brow like a gold diadem" (5) when he first appeared. The narrator finally leaves Tomassov's personality open, thus posing another challenge to the idea of character development. Neither Tomassov himself nor the narrator as his "special confidant" (7) is certain about whether Tomassov's final tragic act is performed from a brotherly feeling for another soldier or not. When the Frenchman urged Tomassov to kill him mercifully, saying, "Haven't you got the soul of a warrior?" Tomassov simply replied, "I don't know" (23). Tomassov does not (and possibly will not) know if he really achieved some higher, collective identity "we" through soldierly communion. The narrator only sarcastically says, "You know what the world's justice and mankind's judgement are like," and he stays aloof from the "hypocritical" moral judgement of "a vague story of some dark deed [which] clung to him [Tomassov] for years" (26). As Tomassov's young face expresses "no grief, no sternness, no horror," there seems to be no simple feeling of loss in this moment of separation. Rather, what prevails in this scene is an unnameable, serene atmosphere—"a sort of horrible peace"—as we have seen in the passage of that "pathetic multitude of small dark mounds stretching away under the moonlight" (20). During his "endlessly silent" meditation, Tomassov remains possessed by De Castel, but this "endless" possession does not, as in the case of other heroes of Conrad's earlier works, arise from a sense of guilt or remorse. Nor does this profound meditation lead Tomassov's soul to any divine revelation. He is together with the dead in the blank space ("on the snow") in an endless suspension in which his soul is always open to, exposed to, death.[20] Tomassov and De Castel are referred to in the passage above in the book version simply as the "dark group," apparently with more emphasis on

---

[20] As David Lodge succinctly remarks, the religious idea of the individual immortal soul is seen as intimately connected with the more secular idea of the self, which humanism developed from the Judeo-Christian religious tradition. See David Lodge, *Consciousness and the Novel* (Milan: Rizzoli, 2005), 4–5, 89. It is no wonder, then, the ecstatic images of "a big white rose" and Tomassov "stooping over the dead" in the scenes cited above evoke Christian symbols, such as the white rose and Pietà. Conrad's use of the Western traditional frame of reference all the more draws our attention to the subversive nature of his narrative attempts to go beyond the conventional idea of the "soul," which is, as we have seen so far, more than the individual self. I am very grateful to John H. Stape, Allan H. Simmons, and Don Rude for helpful suggestions about the iconography.

their togetherness than as "that appalling dark group of two" in the serialized version.[21] I would think that the deletion suggests the irreducibility of the "dark group" to its two separate individual subjects.

It is hard not to see some similarities between Conrad's "dark group" and Alphonso Lingis's "community in death," or "another community" that, as cited below, subverts and goes beyond a "community" usually conceived of as a number of individuals with something in common:

> To catch sight, beyond kinship, of this *community in death*, we should have to find ourselves, or put ourselves through imagination, in a situation at the farthest limits from kinship—in a situation in which one finds oneself in a country with which one's own is at war, among foreigners bound in a religion that one cannot believe or which exclude one, with whom one is engaged in no kind of productive or commercial dealings, who owe one nothing, who do not understand a word of one's language, who are far from one in age (for even being of the same age-groupe is a commitment)—and on whom one finds oneself completely dependent, for one's very life.[22]

From the very start, the old Russian narrator "put[s] himself in a situation at the farthest limits from kinship." Addressing the unsympathetic young listeners, he places himself in a situation where his audience are those "who do not understand a word of one's language, who are far from one in age."[23] The impersonal narrator of the first few lines before the introduction of the aged Russian narrator has been largely ignored, but he is more than a "nominal" narrator who contributes a few sentences to establish the scene before yielding to the officer's monologue.[24] The first sentence of "The Warrior's Soul" is

---

[21]   Joseph Conrad, "The Warrior's Soul," *The Lagoon and the Other Stories,* ed. William Atkinson (Oxford: Oxford University Press, 1997), 251. This is the first edition to reprint the stories including "The Warrior's Soul" as they first appeared in popular magazines of the time.

[22]   Alphonso Lingis, *The Community of Those Who Have Nothing in Common* (Bloomington and Indianapolis: Indiana University Press, 1994), 157–158. See also Blanchot's account of "community in death": "'The basis of communication' is not necessarily speech, or even the silence that is its foundation and punctuation, but the exposure to death, no longer my own exposure, but someone else's, whose living and closest presence is already the eternal and unbearable absence, an absence that the travail of deepest mourning does not diminish." Blanchot, *The Unavowable Community*, 25.

[23]   Niland historicizes "The Warrior's Soul" as registering Conrad's response to generational conflict in English society at the time of the Great War. "The Warrior's Soul," according to Niland, treats perceived public enthusiasm for the Great War. See Niland, *Conrad and History*, 154–155.

[24]   Schwarz, *Conrad*, 99. While Graver points out that the function of the omniscient narrator in "The Tale" is, like those of *Youth* and *Heart of Darkness*, to "introduce and later punctuate the remarks of the commanding officer," he gives just a passing comment on the omniscient narrator of "The Warrior's Soul": "Except for three short sentences at the start, 'The Warrior's Soul' is entirely in the

revealing in its directness in enacting the somewhat "abrupt" contact between the narrator and his hearers:

> The old officer with long white moustaches gave rein to his indignation.
>
> "Is it possible that you youngsters should have no more sense than that! Some of you had better wipe the milk off your upper lip before you start to pass judgment on the few poor stragglers of a generation which has done and suffered not a little in its time."
>
> His hearers having expressed much compunction the ancient warrior became appeased. But he was not silenced.
>
> "I am one of them—one of the stragglers, I mean," he went on patiently. (1)

The veteran is indignant with his young hearers for passing judgment on "the poor stragglers," that is, his comrades who suffered during Napoleon's retreat from Moscow. Much compunction expressed by his ignorant hearers appeases him, yet by no means silences him. Despite the lack of sympathy, he goes on telling the story of his war experience "patiently". Though they are all Russian, there is no bond of friendship or brotherhood between them, which would have been the case in an earlier generation, the narrator's generation that had "suffered nearly to the limit of their strength" (1). The narrator's summary of Tomassov's conduct, "He had done it. And what was it? ... I don't know. And perhaps poor Tomassov did not know himself," can hardly encourage us to suppose that his nostalgia for a lost community of a heroic past moves him to tell "an exemplary tale," as mentioned earlier, to a new generation.[25] For it seems that the disagreement between them is not overcome in understanding in the end. Offering just a possible interpretation of Tomassov's story that "one warrior's soul paying its debt a hundredfold to another warrior's soul by releasing it from a fate worse than death—the loss of all faith and courage," the aged Russian only remarks, "You may look on it in that way. I don't know. And perhaps poor Tomassov did not know himself" (26).

We may then wonder what makes the veteran tell the story to the young people and why they are together there at all. The ancient warrior and the

---

Russian voice." Significantly, he goes on to say concerning "The Tale," *Youth*, and *Heart of Darkness* that "the intimate byplay between the audience and the narrator is supposed to add suggestiveness to the events being described." I would argue that a similar point could be made about "The Warrior's Soul," but Graver thinks that the old Russian merely "answer[s] his listeners' deprecatory remarks about the Slavic capacity for heroism" with Tomassov's story. See Graver, *Conrad's Short Fiction*, 195.

[25] See note 6.

young hearers are simply "together" in the narrative "now" despite apparent communicative difficulty. Through indignation the aged Russian narrator does expose himself to the young hearers who share hardly anything with him. If it is an effort on the part of the narrator to reach "their [the hearers'] very soul" (19), this "violent relatedness" is exactly what Conrad needed when opening his story of "being-together."[26] The "togetherness" in this story is neither something preexisting nor a willed action, but rather, it always "suddenly" happens. The Russians and the French, as cited earlier, come "suddenly" to "perish together in a long, long trail of frozen corpses" (20). "The dark group" of Tomassov and De Castel as "the event," the old veteran puts it, "approached" him before "[he] knew it or had the slightest premonition" (21). We can argue therefore that the impersonal narration in the first few lines stages the author's strange idea of "community" that permeates the text.

In this context, this story's sympathetic treatment of the Russian military characters may not appear so "unexpected" as Najder observes.[27] "The Warrior's Soul" is Conrad's only story in which the Russian military characters are treated sympathetically; a young Russian officer is, to Najder's surprise, presented even as a "noble and idealistic hero."[28] Conrad's lifelong friend Cunninghame Graham also states in the Preface to *Tales of Hearsay* that in "The Warrior's Soul" the Polish author "rises above nationality" and even forgets "his hatred of the hereditary tyrants of his country" (*TLH* xiv). However, unlike the "humane" Tomassov, the historical Conrad might never have overcome his "personal animosity" (16). In his political essays, such as "Autocracy and War," Conrad himself shows an unmistakable dislike of Russia, which is for him "the [very] farthest limits from kinship." Even if through the mediation of a narrator, to feel for the oppressor, as Graham says, would be "no light thing for a Pole to do" (*TLH* xiv). Therefore, the story's sympathy toward the Russians is, I believe, all the more worthy to be considered. It was the fact of Conrad's being a Pole, an émigré, who "find[s] himself, or put[s]

---

[26]   Cf. Nancy's idea of "com-passion," which is not "a pity that feels sorry for itself and feeds on itself. Com-passion is the contagion, the contact of being with one another in this turmoil. Compassion is not altruism, nor is it identification. It is the disturbance of violent relatedness." See Nancy, *Being Singular Plural*, xiii. Considering that "The Warrior's Soul" is thus structured through Nancy's "com-passion," the narrator's defense of Tomassov's compassionate nature against his comrades' sneer seems quite natural, at least, to me.

[27]   Najder, *Joseph Conrad*, 476.

[28]   Ibid.

himself through imagination, in a situation at the farthest limits from kinship," which made it possible for him to appreciate what Nancy was to call the idea of "being-together." As the old Russian narrator lays himself open to his unsympathetic young hearers and, in turn, Tomassov to his thoughtless comrades' banter, Conrad, for the first and only one time in his writing career, finds himself prepared to use the Russian "we," in Lingis's words above, putting himself "in a situation where one finds oneself in a country with which one's own is at war." Najder suggests that it is "as if Conrad were trying to show his lack of prejudice as a writer,"[29] but Conrad the skeptic might have anticipated this kind of criticism, fully conscious of the fine line between his notion of strange "community" and mere pretension or sentimentalism. Deliberately assessing his notion of "community" against Tomassov's comrades' jeering of his compassion, Conrad continues his narrative search for a possible form of "we," not as a nostalgic return to lost human solidarity but rather as a sharing of "humanity" beyond the classical, preexisting association of individual subjects. This story thus parallels recent debates by Nancy and others on our "being-together" in today's society. Such parallelism means that we avoid the risk of reducing the story to merely an evocation of national military solidarity (the mentality of a people, for instance) in his great uncle Nicholas's day, or during the Great War when it was being written.[30] "The Warrior's Soul," with its narrator's repeated address to young listeners, "You of the present generation" (6), appeals greatly to us who still share a world full of seemingly irresolvable conflict and war.

---

[29] Ibid.

[30] For a reading of "The Warrior's Soul" in relation to Nicholas Bobrowski's experience during the Napoleonic conquests, see, in particular, Wright, *Romance and Tragedy*, 168. "The Warrior's Soul" has generally been read as slight "war-time products" along with "The Tale." See, for instance, Graver, *Conrad's Short Fiction*, 193; Jocelyn Baines, *Joseph Conrad: A Critical Biography* (London: Weidenfeld, 1960), 406; and Peters, *The Cambridge Introduction to Joseph Conrad*, 116. Schwarz points out that Tomassov's "macabre act of chivalry" has been responsible for "crystallising the grotesqueness of war." See Schwarz, *Conrad*, 100. Regarding the historicization of "The Warrior's Soul" in the context of the Great War, see note 23.

8

An Art of Palpation

Plastic Imagination in *The Arrow of Gold*

Traditional Conrad criticism has called *The Arrow of Gold: A Story between Two Notes* the "weakest"[1] or "worst"[2] pseudo-autobiographical novel among the underestimated Mediterranean historical fiction written during the final years of his literary career. Recent critics, however, have rediscovered the novel as a self-conscious, modernist text, paying more attention to gender politics. Accordingly, there has been an increasing focus on the question of the gaze and the central female character Doña Rita's position as the object of male possessive desire, as Andrew Michael Roberts, for example, rigorously discusses in *Conrad and Masculinity*.[3] While largely acceding to the charge of objectification of Rita in these gender-conscious readings, as the visual and pictorial are indeed present everywhere in the pages of *The Arrow of Gold*, I will argue in this chapter that, at points in the text, plastic imagination interrupts the visual to open up a space for another perception of reality.[4] Unlike the painter Henry Allègre, a detached observer of an art object, Monsieur George, often cast as a sculptor, attempts to approach, touch, and identify with Doña Rita. The identification between George and Rita, however, tends to be dismissed simply as melodramatic in the overall underestimation of

---

[1] Najder, *Joseph Conrad*, 60.
[2] Eloise Knapp Hay, *The Political Novels of Joseph Conrad* (Chicago and London: University of Chicago Press, 1963), 322.
[3] Roberts, *Conrad and Masculinity*, 163–185. For a similar discussion of the gaze, see Geddes, *Conrad's Later Novels*, 115–143; Hampson, *Joseph Conrad*, 251–281, to name but a few.
[4] I shall principally discuss "an intrusion" of plastic imagination into the visual one in this chapter, while Daphna Erdinast-Vulcan claims that "an intrusion of self-consciousness, doubt, scepticism into the heart of romance" undermines the generic conventions. See Daphna Erdinast-Vulcan, *Joseph Conrad and the Modern Temper* (Oxford: Oxford University Press, 1991), 198.

Conrad's later works, yet it could well be reconsidered in the light of the sensation of palpability that the sculptor feels toward his carving. The artist's identification with the object, as we shall see later, entails not so much appropriation of the other into the self as his or her surrender of the "I" to the object (the other).

In his philosophical history of the sense of touch for the past two centuries, *On Touching—Jean-Luc Nancy*, Derrida writes that the pleasure of touching besets us with questions regarding the individual subject "I": "What is this pleasure? What is that? Where does it come from? From the other or from me? Am I taking it? Am I giving it? Is it the other who gives it to me? Or takes it from me? The time of this pleasure—is it that I am giving *it myself*?"[5] Thus disturbing the subject of a sense, the sense of touch is, for Nancy as well as for Derrida, not a matter of a self, an identity, or a subject as the interior of an exterior;[6] rather, it is inseparable from his thinking of a "community": "We are in touch with ourselves insofar as we exist. Being in touch with ourselves is what makes us 'us,' and there is no other secret to discover or bury behind this very touching, behind the 'with' of coexistence."[7] Insisting on the plural singularity at the moment of touching, Nancy repeats that only touch (contact, caress, kiss) can interrupt the "the reflexive or specular autonomy of self-presence."[8]

The considerable factual discrepancies between Conrad's life in Marseilles and the events described in the novel have been pointed out, but Conrad, I would argue, obliquely reveals himself in his identification with Rita through the tactile perception of his younger self, Monsieur George.[9] This is not, however, to repeat what has already been said about authorial identification with George,[10] or the feminist argument of Conrad's sympathy with the female

---

5   Derrida, *On Touching—Jean-Luc Nancy*, 75.
6   Nancy, *Corpus*, 131.
7   Nancy, *Being Singular Plural*, 13.
8   Derrida, *On Touching—Jean-Luc Nancy*, 290.
9   According to John Batchelor, "M. George" was one of the names by which Conrad had been known in Marseille. Therefore, Batchelor writes, it is "an acknowledgement in fiction, incidentally, of Conrad's non-English identity." See John Batchelor, *The Life of Joseph Conrad* (1994; Oxford: Blackwell, 1996), 259. Najder, on the other hand, warns us against treating *A Personal Record*, *The Mirror of the Sea*, and *The Arrow of Gold* as autobiographically authentic. See Najder, *Joseph Conrad*, 48. Erdinast-Vulcan wonders "[w]hy ... Conrad felt the need to mislead his wife, his friends, his biographer, and his readers about the autobiographical authenticity of the novel," but she believes nonetheless that *The Arrow* is "an important autobiographical document." See Erdinast-Vulcan, *Joseph Conrad and the Modern Temper*, 196.
10 Hampson, *Joseph Conrad*, 253. Schwarz observes that Conrad is immersed in George's emotions to the point at which discrimination between them is usually impossible. See Schwarz, *Conrad*, 126, 133, 137.

characters in his later novels.[11] Rather, I wish to suggest that plastic imagination offers us a glimpse of how Conrad's personal remembrance of the past can be linked to his engagement with strange plurality in his later historical novels, plurality that could also include women.

* * *

In his seminal book *Conrad's Later Novels*, Gary Geddes rightly asserts that Conrad's awareness of other forms of art informs every aspect of *The Arrow of Gold*, and he discusses the allusions to sculptures in the novel in relation to the spells and curses in classical and romance literatures. He then proceeds to suggest that the metaphor of sculpture is more important in Conrad's last completed historical novel, *The Rover*, in terms of the paralysis and the immobility of traumatized characters.[12] However, Conrad's interest in plastic art is not limited to these later works. As early as his celebrated preface to *The Nigger of the "Narcissus,"* Conrad states: "[Fiction] must strenuously aspire to the plasticity of sculpture, to the colour of painting, and to the magic suggestiveness of music" (*NN* xli). Toward the end of Conrad's earlier, experimental "historical" novel, *Nostromo*, we see, though only briefly, an Italian sculptor and his "[r]emarkable piece of statuary" of an old bishop.[13] In addition, in a long letter to William Blackwood in 1902, Conrad expresses his hope to "find his place in the rear of [his] betters" such as the painter James Abbot McNeill Whistler and the sculptor Auguste Rodin, the artists who "had to suffer for being 'new.'"[14]

Conrad's appreciation of Rodin's modernity is remarkable because, since Rodin's time, sculpture has indeed emerged as virtually a new art, according to Herbert Read, an eminent poet and critic of literature and art. Read observes that sculpture has always had difficulty in establishing its independence as an art, partly due to the lack of any clear formulation of the requisite autonomous laws.[15] Sculptors themselves, as Read continues, have all too readily submitted to the rules of the architect or the painter. The full consciousness of the need

---

[11] For the author's identification with the central female characters in his later fiction including Rita, see Ruth Nadelhaft, *Joseph Conrad* (Atlantic Highlands, NJ: Humanities Press International, 1991), 124–125.

[12] Geddes, *Conrad's Later Novels*, 132, 134; on the metaphor of sculpture in *The Rover*, see ibid., 179.

[13] Joseph Conrad, *Nostromo* (Oxford: Oxford University Press, 2007), 341. I would suggest that this Italian sculptor and his "[r]emarkable piece of statuary" of an old bishop at the end of *Nostromo* may be counted as another indication of the link between Conrad's historical imagination and the tactile sensation.

[14] Conrad, *The Collected Letters*, vol. 2, 418.

[15] Herbert Read, *The Art of Sculpture* (1956; Princeton, NJ: Princeton University Press, 1977), ix.

for liberation came only with Rodin. Since then there has arisen the concept of a piece of sculpture as a three-dimensional mass occupying space and apprehended only by senses that are alive to its volume and ponderability, as well as to its visual appearance.[16]

Equally in most readings of *The Arrow of Gold*, the plastic perception has not been strongly differentiated from the visual sensation, which is represented in the wealthy French Henry Allègre's possessive, "Olympian gaze"[17] of the male artist and the "collector of fine things."[18] The novel's landscape has been likened to a "gallery" of fine arts and curios,[19] and paintings and sculptures have been lumped together under the general label of "art objects"—for instance, those "priceless items" that Henry accumulated in the exclusive house in Paris, among which Rita is his "most admirable find" (23). Ruth Nadelhaft, for example, does not distinguish between the two arts in her otherwise stimulating feminist critique of the novel's "regular tendency" to "depersonalise Rita, to turn her into an image or a statue."[20]

And yet, the key difference between the two arts lies in the tactile sensation, a sense of touch that is essential to sculpture, as Read emphasizes below:

> For the sculptor, tactile values are not an illusion to be created on a two-dimensional plane: they constitute a reality to be conveyed directly, as existent mass. Sculpture is an art of *palpation*—an art that gives satisfaction in the touching and handling of objects. That, indeed, is the only way in which we can have direct sensation of the three-dimensional shape of an object. It is only as our hands move over an object and trace lines of direction that we get any physical sensation of the difference between a sphere and a square; touch is essential to the perception of subtler contrasts of shape and texture. A genuine sculptor is continually passing his hands over the work in progress, not to test its surface quality, though that may be one purpose, but simply to realize and to assess the shape and volume of the object.[21]

[16]   Ibid.
[17]   On "the male artist's Olympian gaze," see Greaney, *Conrad, Language, and Narrative*, 52; Geddes, *Conrad's Later Novels*, 140; Jones, *Conrad and Women*, 185.
[18]   Joseph Conrad, *The Arrow of Gold: A Story between Two Notes* (London: Dent, 1947), 22. Further page references will be to this edition, preceded by *AG* where necessary. Roman numeral references are to Conrad's "Author's Note."
[19]   Paul L. Wiley, *Conrad's Measure of Man* (New York: Gordian Press, 1966), 163. Similarly, see Greaney, *Conrad, Language, and Narrative*, 44; Schwarz, *Conrad*, 136; Geddes, *Conrad's Later Novels*, 133; Nadelhaft, *Joseph Conrad*, 123.
[20]   Nadelhaft, *Joseph Conrad*, 123.
[21]   Read, *The Art of Sculpture*, 49–50.

Read's observations might encourage us to notice Conrad's preoccupation with the tactile sensation, which begins with his "Author's Note" to *The Arrow of Gold*.

> The subject of the book I had been carrying about with me for many years, not so much a possession of my memory as an inherent part of myself. It was ever present to my mind and ready to my hand, but I was loth to touch it, from a feeling of what I imagined to be mere shyness but which in reality was a very comprehensible mistrust of myself. . . .
>
> . . . The present work [*The Arrow of Gold*] is not in any sense an attempt to develop a subject lightly touched upon in former years. (vii–viii)

Then, in the very beginning of the First Note, we find the irruption of plastic imagination in the form of a sculptor in an operatic costume. In a Marseilles café on the night of the carnival, as Mr. Mills and Captain Blunt intend to draw an innocent young sailor, Monsieur George, into the Carlist plot, three men are interrupted by the theatrical appearance of Prax, a sculptor and a leader of the bohemian circle. George becomes annoyed when he sees his friend enter the café in a sort of Faustian costume and stride "theatrically" up to their table (13). Theatrical images of Prax are indeed notable, as Geddes argues,[22] but here I would rather highlight the fact that Prax is a sculptor, followed thirty pages later by yet another sculptor, Old Doyen, who is moved to tears in his first encounter with Henry Allègre's "adopted" daughter Rita. This self-proclaimed "great sculptor of women" thought his life as an artist was finished, and then Rita came along with his friend Allègre, who, the old sculptor puts it, "isn't a bad smearer of canvases—but it's marble and bronze that [Rita] want[s] ..." (43).

These preliminary insertions of sculptors, creating a space for the perception of palpation and thus marking a rift, as it were, in the midst of the visual perception, prepare us for the emergence of Monsieur George as a sculptor. Whereas Rita is regarded and presented predominantly in painterly terms, as most critics assert,[23] she is for George not simply a visually defined object of

---

[22] Geddes, *Conrad's Later Novels*, 127. Erdinast-Vulcan also points to theatrical figure regarding Rita and George as play-acting in a stage romance. See Erdinast-Vulcan, *Joseph Conrad and the Modern Temper*, 192.

[23] John Peters sees the differing views of Rita from the multiple perspectives by various characters as a redeeming aspect of *The Arrow of Gold*. But I would contend that by claiming that the narrative methodology of *The Arrow of Gold* "harks back to Conrad's earlier method of presenting material from differing perspectives," he nevertheless subscribes to the "achievement and decline" theory that marginalizes such works as *The Arrow of Gold*. See Peters, *The Cambridge Introduction to*

desire. More like a sculptor than a disengaged and detached observer of an art object such as Henry, George responds to her volume, weight, and gravity;[24] his relationship with Rita is an experience of "plasticity that develops not [only] through observation but [also] through identification."[25]

Before going any further, it might be worth noting here that our definition of sculpture against painting drawing on Herbert Read is part of the paragone debate that set different arts against each other.[26] The paragone is the theoretical discussion on the relative merits of sculpture versus painting in which the sense of touch is prioritized over that of vision.[27] Passing through Read, this discourse continues to be the source of keen debate.[28] More recent philosophers such as Mauris Merleau-Ponty and Michel Foucault have considered tactility, especially in contrast to vision,[29] the sense of sight to which traditional Western aesthetics has given priority over touch.[30] Nevertheless, the specificity of the connection between touch and sculpture grounded on such a clear-cut division of the senses, touch and vision, as Read's, is left unexamined. As Hagi Kenaan points to a constant intertwining and intersection of the senses, sculpture is uniquely rooted in the visual.[31] Far from espousing the belief in immediacy of contact, therefore, following Nancy, we attempt to think of touch as breaking with immediacy, with "the immediate given wrongly associated with touch and on which all bets are always placed, as on self-presence."[32] As Conrad mentions the untouchableness of his past in

---

Joseph Conrad, 111. My underscoring of the plastic imagination is, I hope, a way of challenging the hegemonic theory in Conrad criticism, which has not been unconnected with what Martin Jay calls "scopic regimes of modernity," as I will observe later in this chapter. See Jay, "Scopic Regimes of Modernity," 3–23.

24   Henry Moore writes that the sculptor "identifies himself with its [the sculpture's] centre of gravity, its mass, its weight; he realizes its volume, as the space that the shape displaces in the air." See Henry Moore, "Notes on Sculpture," *Henry Moore: Sculpture and Drawings* (London: Lund Humphries, [1944]1949), xl.

25   In explaining how far the Greek sculptor, for whom out of sight was generally out of mind, was from the integral conception of a work of art that we now regard as essential to any complete aesthetic achievement, Read states that the Greek sculptor remained the spectator *ab extra*, whereas plasticity (as Read quotes Austrian poet, dramatist, and essayist Hugo von Hofmannsthal's aphorism) "develops not through observation, but through identification." See Read, *The Art of Sculpture*, 78–79.

26   Peter Dent, "Introduction," *Sculpture and Touch*, ed. Peter Dent, (Surrey: Ashgate, 2014), 14.

27   Geraldine A. Johnson, "A taxonomy of touch: tactile encounters in Renaissance Italy," ed. Dent, *Sculpture and Touch*, 92.

28   Dent, "Introduction," 14.

29   Johnson, "A taxonomy of touch," 91.

30   Michael Paraskos, "Bringing into being: vivifying sculpture through touch," ed. Dent, *Sculpture and Touch*, 62.

31   Hagi Kenaan, "Touching sculpture," ed. Dent, *Sculpture and Touch*, 46.

32   Derrida, *On Touching—Jean-Luc Nancy*, 293.

his "Author's Note" cited earlier, to write an autobiography, that is, to "touch" "an inherent part of [himself]"(viii), is for him the experience of "touching on what is untouchable" in a certain way. Conrad's use of tactile metaphors is highly evocative of what Nancy would call "self-touching,"[33] that is not, as such, something that can be touched. The body is, Nancy writes, the experience of indefinitely touching on the untouchable, but in the sense that the untouchable is not anything that would be back behind, anything interior or inside, or a mass, or a God. The untouchable is, as Nancy goes on, the fact that it touches. It is "a structure of being set outside," according to Nancy, "such that we cannot speak of the body without speaking about it as an *other*, an other indefinitely other, indefinitely outside."[34] If the young captain is thrown out of himself and extends toward the other, Leggatt, Conrad's narrators after "The Secret Sharer" cannot, of course, speak of the body without speaking about it as an indefinitely other, indefinitely outside, the untouchable. Hence the loathness to touch lightly upon the past in the "Author's Note" to *The Arrow of Gold*.

The repetitive allusions to George's feeling of intimacy and identification with Rita, similar to the relationship of the young captain and Leggatt in "The Secret Sharer," seem so redundant that they unavoidably draw the reader's attention. For example, when George was first introduced to Rita, he felt a "sense of solidarity" with her in their youth and "therefore no misunderstanding between [them] was possible and there could be nothing more for [them] to know about each other" (*AG* 70). On one of the many occasions when George looks upon her, he sees her leaning on her elbow on the couch with her face "veiled in firm immobility and … so appealing that [he has] an insane impulse to walk round and kiss … that strong, well-shaped forearm" (74); "So familiar ha[s] [he] become already with her in [his] thoughts!" (74). At another time, again seeing Rita lying on the couch, he feels "the insensible phantom of the real [her] that is in [him]" (296). George's "consciousness of [Rita] always being present in [him]" is "complete to the last hair, to the faintest shade of expression, and that not only when [they] are apart but when [they] are together, alone" (296). He tells her, "You exist in me. I don't know where I end and you begin. You have got into my heart and into my veins and into my brain" (224). And finally, the distance between them seems to be completely

---

33 Nancy, *Corpus*, 134–135.
34 Nancy also calls this "self-sensing." See Nancy, *Corpus*, 135.

removed in the famous kiss at the end of the First Note, in a way suggestive of the sculptor's identification with "the thing" itself. As George opens his lips, pressing her arrow of gold to his breast, Rita, who knows "what [is] struggling for utterance in his breast," cries as follows:

> "Speak no words of love, George! Not yet. Not in this house of ill-luck and falsehood. Not within a hundred miles of this house, where they came clinging to me all profaned from the mouth of that man. Haven't you heard them—the horrible things? And what can words have to do between you and me?"
>
> Her hands were stretched out imploringly. I said, childishly disconcerted:
>
> "But, Rita, how can I help using words of love to you? They come of themselves on my lips!"
>
> "They come! Ah! But I shall seal your lips with the thing itself," she said. "Like this . . . . " (336)

The caress, inviting a question of whether it comes from the other or "me," as George does not know where he ends and Rita begins as cited earlier, cannot be reduced to simple contact. The caress, Derrida writes, "carries beyond phenomenality, indeed beyond any contact sensation, or any contact as sensation, and does not share with sight [the] being enclosed within a totality."[35] The text's emphasis on the closeness between George and Rita's bodies might then be productively rethought in the light of what art historian Jonathan Crary calls disembodiment of vision in the nineteenth century. Crary argues that in the nineteenth century, vision comes to be known as produced in the body and it becomes regarded as somehow autonomous, separated from any referent; he goes on to suggest that this is a precondition of the modernist move that culminates in abstraction.[36] Read also mentions the isolation of the *objet d'art* as "a peculiarly modern conception" and "a consequence of [the] growth of a

---

[35] Derrida, *On Touching—Jean-Luc Nancy*, 75, 77.

[36] Regarding the production of the observer in the nineteenth century, see Jonathan Crary, *Techniques of the Observer: On Vision and Modernity in the Nineteenth Century* (Cambridge, MA: MIT Press, 1992), 112. Crary explains that the subjective vision (and the separation of senses) that endowed the observer with a new perceptual autonomy coincides with the making of the observer into a subject of new knowledge and new techniques of power. Ibid., 79, 81. Crary and art historian Hal Foster repeatedly emphasize in the discussion portion following Crary's essay "Modernizing Vision" in *Vision and Visuality* that the modernist move is usually seen in terms of disembodiment of vision, and that many modernist articulations of autonomous vision or of pure visibility totally excluded the body. See Jonathan Crary, "Modernizing Vision," in *Vision and Visuality*, ed. Hal Foster, 48.

sense and of a philosophy of individualism,"[37] that is, what intellectual historian Martin Jay would call Cartesian perspectivalism, which is "*the* reigning visual model of modernity."[38] In this sense, the text's emphasis on bodily contact and intimacy could be taken less as a mere reactionary gesture toward something anachronistically romantic than as a radical attempt to go beyond modernity and the modern era, which have been allegedly dominated by the sense of sight.[39] Therefore, it may be proper to consider the lovers' apparently melodramatic reunion after the failed gun-running mission as the sculptor's grasp of the object, rather than as the disembodied and detached seer-master's assimilation of the object. Returning to Marseilles in tatters, George is surprised to discover that Rita is also back in the house, and he approaches her on the couch to touch her hand as before:

> When I have you before my eyes there is such a projection of my whole being towards you that I fail to see you distinctly. It was like that from the beginning. I may say that I never saw you distinctly till after we had parted and I thought you had gone from my sight for ever. It was then that you took body in my imagination and that my mind seized on a definite form of you for all its adorations—for its profanations, too. Don't imagine me grovelling in spiritual abasement before a mere image. I got a grip on you that nothing can shake now. (298–299)

In a clear opposition between the senses of touch and sight, George attempts here to present his grasp of her not as "an image" but rather as something tangible and three-dimensional. George seems to identify with Rita so fully that he cannot see her distinctly despite her presence "before his eyes"; her absence, on the contrary, makes her all the more palpable to him. This identification may indeed, as has often been pointed out, seem as though Rita as alterity is finally subsumed under George as the self-same.[40] Nevertheless, George's unshakable grasp of Rita, which occurs in his giving up his "whole being" to her, is something more than a visual impression of a woman formed in an individual consciousness. Rita, whom George described as "the insensible phantom of the real [her] that is in [him]" (296), "takes body" and has "a definite form" in his "imagination," becoming more real and substantiated than

---

[37]   Read, *The Art of Sculpture*, 57–58.
[38]   Jay, "Scopic Regimes of Modernity," 3–27.
[39]   Ibid., 3.
[40]   On the depersonalization of Rita, see Nadelhaft, *Joseph Conrad*, 121, 123; Hampson, *Joseph Conrad*, 256; Geddes, *Conrad's Later Novels*, 123.

the real her. This "surrender of the 'I'" is, again, not so very far from what is at the heart of Read's idea of "immediacy," which is achieved by the projection of the sculptor's whole being toward the object, as the art theorist elaborates:

> As long as objects are to you merely an antithesis to your 'I,' you will never grasp their real essence, and no amount of intensive observation, description or copying will help you to do so. You may succeed, however, if you are able to divest yourself of your 'I' by projecting it into the object so that the object can begin to speak in your stead. For you yourself, a single individual facing a single object, have only your subjective impressions, have thus like the animal-soul hardly a language, at best mere sounds of terror and delight, of warning and enticement, at most exclamations such as *Oh!* And *Ah!*; whereas real language perpetuates not only the momentary impression of objects but their essence, hence requiring a far more intimate, richer, more subtle relationship with them than animals have. And this ... immediacy ... is achieved exclusively by the surrender of the 'I' to the object. He, however, who is satisfied with subjective exclamations is no artist, no poet: confession is nothing, insight is everything.[41]

As George feels Rita's existence in him so intensely that he tells her, "I don't know where I end and you begin" (224), their relationship cannot be "a single individual facing a single object," and therefore his grasp of her cannot be understood simply as his "subjective impressions." Moreover, it is interesting that Read links the art of sculpture to confession, a linkage evocative of Conrad's criticism of the "artlessness" of Jean-Jacques Rousseau's self-sufficient and self-justifying confessions in *A Personal Record* (95). Conrad's biographers view that *The Arrow of Gold* could not possibly have had the authenticity that the author claimed for it.[42] But in our reading of *The Arrow of Gold* as an art of palpation, we may perhaps be allowed to think that "a writer of imaginative prose," as Conrad says in *A Personal Record*, "stands confessed in his work[s]" (95), not through romantic self-justification in a manner of Rousseau but rather through "surrendering" the "I" to the other, or in "solidarity" with the other.

George's "sense of solidarity" with Rita, as we have seen earlier, is inseparable from his youthful feeling: "I felt no longer alone in my youth. ... that

---

[41] Read, *The Art of Sculpture*, 79. Here Read cites Austrian modernist Hermann Broch's interpretation of Hugo von Hofmannsthal.

[42] Erdinast-Vulcan, *Joseph Conrad and the Modern Temper*, 196.

woman was revealed to me young, younger than anybody I had ever seen, as young as myself (and my sensation of my youth was then very acute); revealed with something peculiarly intimate in the conviction, as if she were young exactly in the same way in which I felt myself young" (*AG* 70). In those moments of identification like this one, in which "[he] [feels] no longer alone in [his] youth," the present might be connected to the past in Conrad. In other words, Conrad's own youth is, as is repeated here as a form of self-persuasion, "revealed" in Rita through George, to the author himself and the reader alike. George's tactile perception thus enables him to surrender the "I" to the object and grasp Rita's reality firmly, whereby the author in turn might have achieved immediacy, albeit only momentarily, with "an inherent part of himself," which has not been a "possession of [his] memory" and which he was so far "loth to touch," as he writes in the "Author's Note" (viii).

Given Conrad's notion of confession in *A Personal Record*, the oblique, clandestine nature of authority in *The Arrow of Gold* is not surprising. In the First Note, Captain Blunt tells a story (whose "author" is Rita) that she was discovered by Henry Allègre in his "private garden." Here is the scene of the discovery of the Basque peasant girl from her native Pyrenees:

> "As a matter of fact, Henry Allègre caught her very early one morning in his own old garden full of thrushes and other small birds. She was sitting on a stone, a fragment of some old balustrade, with her feet in the damp grass, and reading a tattered book of some kind. She had on a short, black, two-penny frock (*une petite robe de deux sous*) and there was a hole in one of her stockings. She raised her eyes and saw him looking down at her thoughtfully over that ambrosian beard of his, like Jove at a mortal. They exchanged a good long stare, for at first she was too startled to move; and then he murmured, '*Restez donc.*' She lowered her eyes again on her book and after a while heard him walk away on the path. Her heart thumped while she listened to the little birds filling the air with their noise. She was not frightened. I am telling you this positively because she has told me the tale herself. What better authority can you have …?" Blunt paused.
>
> "That's true. She's not the sort of person to lie about her own sensations," murmured Mills above his clasped hands. (34)

Henry Allègre finds Rita "sitting on a broken fragment of stone work buried in the grass of his wild garden," "adopt[s]" her and reveals "[her] existence to the world at large" (41); later she sits again as a model for Allègre's paintings.

The "collector of fine things" (22) discovers and acquires her "like some unique object of art" (37). As Mills sarcastically puts it, she is "the most admirable find of his [Henry's] amongst all the priceless items he had accumulated in that house [the Pavilion in Paris]" (23). It is no wonder that this extract is cited as presenting her as "the startled captive of the male artist's Olympian gaze,"[43] yet at the same time it interestingly raises the question of authority. As in the case of *Under Western Eyes*, the "immediacy" of the subject of the book to the author, I would suggest, makes the scene of her discovery a highly complex self-reflexive moment. By "authority," Captain Blunt here literally means Rita's, but to us readers it also evokes Conrad himself, the author behind the story.[44] It is interesting to note that Rita is here reading "a tattered book of some kind." By implication, the worn-out book is an emblem of Conrad's autographical writing, itself contained in a book, *The Arrow of Gold*, another autographical novel though somewhat excessive in its metafictionality.

As Conrad begins the "Author's Note" "at the risk of some confusion" (vii) with the ensuing two notes, the discovery of Rita in Henry's "private garden" cannot help but remind us Conrad's reference to his "private garden" in his justification of belated confession in the "Author's Note": "In plucking the fruit of memory one runs the risk of spoiling its bloom, especially if it has got to be carried into the market-place. This [the subject of the book] being the product of my private garden my reluctance can be easily understood" (viii). Thus, the boundaries between the inside and the outside, between words and things, are constantly blurred, and what slowly emerges "between two notes," or from "the shadow-line," if you like, is the memory of Conrad's youth embodied in Rita.

Unlike the art object in Read's argument, however, Rita does not speak much in place of the artist and she eventually departs. In the concluding note, George, having won Rita, fights a duel with Blunt and is severely wounded. She nurses him back to health and then disappears forever. Her exit might imply on the one hand, as Susan Jones states, the heroine's release from the fixed modes of representation imposed upon her throughout the novel,[45] thereby pointing to the authorial

---

[43] Greaney, *Conrad, Language, and Narrative*, 52.

[44] George, the author's younger self, also wishes "to deal with that embodied mystery [Rita], to influence it, to manage it … and long for the gift of authority" (*AG* 312).

[45] Jones, *Conrad and Women*,185–186. Jones contends that Conrad's frequent reference to the framed image in his late novels could be viewed as an endorsement of the prescribed codes of romantic fiction; however, she continues, the experimental nature of his later fiction—for instance, using the framing device to question the boundaries between reader and text—demonstrates that he moved toward an account of the construction of gender within the limitations and possibilities of romance.

awareness of Rita's aestheticization (and thus her depersonalization), as is repeatedly evoked in her mutilated and "mangled" dummy "like the model of some atrocious murder" (189).[46] On the other hand, it might indicate that the author sensed something "insane" about an art of palpation, about the unshakable "firm grip" on reality cited above; the old sculptor Doyen is described by Henry Allègre as "a little mad all his life" (44), and George is convinced that "[he] soon [will] be [mad]" when he becomes almost unable to distinguish between Rita's dummy and an "illusion of the original" (241). Doyen's "deferential roar of the sea very far away" (43) might have encouraged Conrad to relive his youthful moments on the sea, while the "remote power" (44) of that "booming" (43) voice of the old sculptor perhaps constantly reminds him of the "insanity" of attempting to touch the untouchable, or to get in touch with palpable reality, if there is any such thing. This locus of untouchable is, according to Derrida, "the place of confession, that place of a thinking of touch as thinking of the untouchable or intangible, the very place of what happens … when one touches on, tampers with the limit."[47] There in the limit, or "the shadow-line," "the untouchable becomes tangible."[48]

If Konrad Korzeniowski's youthful follies in Marseilles did actually contain something like a suicidal act, then, as Najder says, even the young Konrad himself may not have known the whole truth of his actions.[49] Perhaps unavoidably, therefore, Conrad's stay in Marseilles, which is the least documented period of his life, defies simple insertion into a continuity. Instead of gathering it up into a meaningful whole by filling in a gap between his Polish past and his seafaring life, the author finally releases it as he does with Rita's departure. Then, despite the accusation of Conrad's tendency of self-fictionalization,[50] despite "suspicion of facts concealed, of explanations held back, of inadequate motives," he seems to be speaking with some sincerity in the "Author's Note" when he writes: "I never tried to conceal the origins of the subject matter of this book which I have hesitated so long to write" (viii); "the only assurance I can give my readers is, that as it stands here with all its imperfections it is given to them complete" (ix).

* * *

---

[46] Cf. also *AG* 45, 48, 66, 70, 85, 91, 93.

[47] Derrida, *On Touching—Jean-Luc Nancy*, 295–296.

[48] Ibid.

[49] Najder, *Joseph Conrad*, 67.

[50] Regarding Conrad's tendency of self-fictionalization and self-definition, see Erdinast-Vulcan, *Joseph Conrad and the Modern Temper*, 197.

Conrad's protagonists, however hard they struggle, cannot be complete own-
ers of a memory; constantly delayed and, in the end, denied the romantic individual possession of the past, they are nevertheless traumatically possessed by
the past. Therefore, we are not surprised when Conrad states in the "Author's
Note" that the subject of *The Arrow of Gold* is "not so much a possession of
[his] memory as an inherent part of [himself]" (vii–viii). This does not necessarily mean, however, that the memory is vague and ambiguous; on the contrary, it means that the past experience cannot easily be reduced to a memory
but still lingers palpably in the present. The subject of the book was, as the
author puts it, "ever present to [his] mind and ready to [his] hand," but he was
"loth to touch it" (viii). Thus his sense of the past is connected with that of
palpation. This traumatic sense of the past, which I shall discuss at length in
subsequent chapters, constitutes an important part of Conrad's sense of existence and, by extension, what is later to be developed as his sense of "history."
Trauma, according to Cathy Caruth, already describes the individual experience as something that extends beyond the confines of the individual psyche.
Something more than a clinical case of an individual, a traumatic experience
has a collective, intercultural, or intergenerational structure in the sense that
the witnessing of the trauma can take place in cultures and in future generations. One's own trauma is never, as she insists, simply one's own; it is tied up
with the trauma of another. Thus, she sees the possibility of "history" arising in
the very way we are implicated in each other's traumas; for her, events are only
historical to the extent that they implicate others.[51]

In this sense, I would suggest that *The Arrow of Gold* is not simply a
personal reminiscence. The individual in this story is inseparable from the
plural in plastic imagination, thereby opening up a space that is singularly
plural. George's sense of "solidarity" with Rita arises simultaneously with his
confidence in himself: the sense of identification "seemed to have kindled
magically somewhere within [him] a glow of assurance, of unaccountable
confidence in [himself]: a warm, steady, and eager sensation of [his] individual life beginning for good there ... in that sense of solidarity ..." (70). To take
another example, when George first sees Rita coming down the stairs after he
has heard so much about her, he feels something more than the pictorial in

51   Cathy Caruth, *Unclaimed Experience* (Baltimore: Johns Hopkins University Press, 1996), 18, 24,
     42, 124.

"that face, which … made you think of remote races, of strange generations, of the faces of women sculptured on immemorial monuments and of those lying unsung in their tombs" (66). What Rita stands for accords well with her "plebeian abruptness" (210) as opposed to the Blunts' aristocratic refinement. We may add here her intolerance, or, more precisely, abhorrence of the Italian banker Azzollati who "trample[s] on the poor" (99) and of George's mockery of her maid Rose; Rita orders the Italian financier to "take himself off from her presence for ever," and she remonstrates with George about his "infantile" inability to comprehend the minds of people other than "a certain class of people" (202).

In my reading of *The Arrow of Gold* as an art of palpation rather than that of vision, I have tried to show that the novel is at once deeply personal and singularly plural in its sense of the past, a feature that is to be developed further as "strange fraternity." Conrad in his later years, perhaps like Prince Roman, responding to the call of "something louder than [his] grief and yet something with a voice very like it" (*THL* 42), is gravitating toward the "history" of the Napoleonic era. Plastic imagination in *The Arrow of Gold* gives us a glimpse of how far Conrad, in this phase of his writing career, has moved away from the subjective impressionism of his major works. If the roots of the priority that traditional aesthetics has given to non-tactile sense, particularly to sight, can be found in the long history in Western society of elevating thinkers above doers,[52] then it further encourages our comparison between Conrad and Hannah Arendt in the next chapter. Conrad is preoccupied with tactility in contrast to vision in *The Arrow of Gold*—a sense of touch that goes beyond an individual consciousness. Likewise, Hannah Arendt rethinks the traditional prioritization of solitary contemplation over action, which demands a plurality of men, that is, "the human condition."

---

[52] Paraskos locates the fear of tactility and the prioritization of sight in the long history in Western society of elevating thinkers and non-physical cerebral work above doers and physical manual labor. Paraskos, "Bringing into being: vivifying sculpture through touch," 61–62.

9

Arendtian Action and "Strange Fraternity" in *The Rover*

In his last years, Conrad wrote two historical novels of the Napoleonic era, *The Rover* (1923) and *Suspense: A Napoleonic Novel* (1925). Conrad began *Suspense* in 1920, his last unfinished novel set primarily in Genoa in 1815, just before Napoleon's return from Elba for the Hundred Days that ended at Waterloo. *Suspense* was eventually set aside for the sake of *The Rover*, a novel spanning the years from 1796, a turning point for the French Revolution, to 1804, shortly before the Battle of Trafalgar. In *The Rover*, Master-Gunner of the Republic, Jean Peyrol, returns home from his long and adventurous life at sea, yet "suddenly" turns into a committed patriot toward the end of the story.[1] A retired, nonpolitical sailor's climactic metamorphosis into a national hero has been the greatest riddle in the narrative of Conrad's last completed novel, which is, as Robert Hampson rightly states, constructed as a series of "overlapping mysteries."[2] In rereading what Albert Guerard called "the slightest" of Conrad's full-length novels,[3] critics have tended to fill in those textual gaps, first of all, by trying to find out Peyrol's motive for his abrupt, final commitment. Whether they construe the protagonist's final action as motivated by patriotism,[4] or by love and friendship for the younger generation,[5] in their efforts to grasp an individual character as a totality through psychological speculation

---

[1] Moser's argument of Peyrol's sudden change is later echoed by many others. See, Moser, *Joseph Conrad*, 200 and also Schwarz, *Conrad*, 143–5.

[2] Hampson, *Joseph Conrad*, 274.

[3] Guerard, *Conrad the Novelist*, 284.

[4] Critics have agreed that Peyrol sacrifices himself for the national cause. See, for instance, Schwarz, *Conrad*, 144; Fleishman, *The English Historical Novel*, 151; Hampson, *Joseph Conrad*, 280.

[5] On Peyrol's death for the younger generation, see Hampson, *Joseph Conrad*, 280; Fleishman, *The English Historical Novel*, 215. And also see Schwarz, *Conrad*, 152–153.

(which has been the norm in the "achievement and decline" theory), they only reiterate and even reinforce rather than subvert the still dominant paradigm that favors Conrad's major works marked by "epistemological dilemmas" of the male protagonists.[6] The protagonist in *The Rover* is, however, characterized as "a stranger" to "melancholy" and "introspection"; unlike Conrad's heroes in his earlier stories, Peyrol lacks "intimate inward sense of the vanity of all things, that doubt of the power within himself" (173).

Ellipses in Peyrol's characterization, along with other holes in this story, far from corroborating the traditional idea of exhaustion of creative energy in later Conrad,[7] defy instead our totalizing desire to appropriate Peyrol in a static, intellectual way. Indeed, Conrad's major works are marked primarily by their epistemological exploration into their heroes' "heart of darkness," but at the same time the exploration is always challenged and thwarted. As we have seen in the previous chapters, "The Secret Sharer," among others, with its overt indifference to epistemological questions as to who the secret sharer is or why the captain-narrator hides him at the risk of his ship and crew, seems to compel us to think otherwise, to think beyond the knowledge of self/other.

Arguing against the epistemological and psychological trend, therefore, this chapter reassesses Peyrol's final commitment in the light of Hannah Arendt's political insight into an "action," which demands a plurality of men, "the human condition" in her terms. Arendt famously cites Conrad's *Heart of Darkness* to elucidate the critique of imperialism in her monumental *The Origins of Totalitarianism* (1951). In Conrad studies, correspondingly (and indeed appropriately), the relationship between Arendt and Conrad has mainly been discussed in the context of European imperialism. Yet more fundamentally, as this chapter hopes to demonstrate, Arendt's distrust of the cult of individuality that seeks to attribute all meaning to the single consciousness in favor of "action" can be interestingly compared with the later Conrad's preference for political actions rather than solitary contemplation.[8] Action, for Arendt,

---

[6] Jones, *Conrad and Women*, 1.

[7] Regarding Peyrol's characterization as a sign of Conrad's later deterioration, see Moser, *Joseph Conrad*, 198; Hay, *The Political Novels of Joseph Conrad*, 315–317; Zdzisław Najder, *Conrad's Polish Background* (London: Oxford University Press, 1964), 28; Andrew Busza, introduction to *The Rover*, by Conrad, xxvii; Palmer, *Joseph Conrad's Fiction*, 253; Geddes, *Conrad's Later Novels*, 179.

[8] On the relationship between Arendt and Conrad from the colonial perspective, see, Patrick Blantlinger, *Rules of Darkness: British Literature and Imperialism, 1830–1914* (Ithaca, NY and London: Cornell University Press, 1988), 268; Eloise Knapp Hay, "Nostromo," in *The Cambridge Companion to Joseph Conrad*, ed. J. H. Stape (Cambridge: Cambridge University Press, 1996),

is "never possible in isolation; to be isolated is to be deprived of the capacity to act."[9] Instead, she emphasizes "the boundlessness of action," that is, the tendency of an action to "establish relationships cut[ting] across all boundaries."[10] In this respect, Peyrol's final voyage through Nelson's blockade can be regarded more as the very Arendtian action of "cutting across" a boundary than as a deliberate, willed action resulting in a belated, patriotic self-realization.[11] Far from a willed action of a responsible individual self, Peyrol's final action, as we shall see in this chapter, takes place inexplicably as a response to the call of the other, evoking "strange fraternity" (8), in contrast with the French Revolution idea of Fraternity.

* * *

The Rover opens with the hero's homecoming in Toulon Harbour from a long sea-roving life, followed by a series of acts of withdrawal until "his instinct of rest [finds] its home" in a remote farmhouse attic on the island of Porquerolles. Here, in what he believes is the scene of his childhood, "[h]e thought he would never want to get away from it, as though he had obscurely felt that his old rover's soul had been always rooted there" (31). As has frequently been quoted, Conrad in his letter to John Galsworthy in 1924 expresses his long-term wish to "do a seaman's 'return' (before [his] own departure)."[12] It is no wonder therefore that *The Rover* has been read as "a fictional version of *A Personal Record*," a story about the recovery of lost identity, which mirrors the author's own nostalgia.[13]

On closer inspection, however, the illusory nature of his "home," his former self, is implied from the outset. The very name "Peyrol" is not, in fact, his own but is borrowed from a farmer who hired him and his mother, and as a boy he did not even know that he had his own name. The name of the farmer,

---

84–85·Christopher GoGwilt, "Joseph Conrad as Guide to Colonial History," in *A Historical Guide to Joseph Conrad*, 148–152; Simon Swift, *Hannah Arendt* (London and New York: Routledge, 2009), 104–107, 110, 115. Arendt makes a mention of Conrad's *Victory* (1915) with respect to imperialist bureaucracy in *The Origins of Totalitarianism*, but she makes no mention of *The Rover*. See Hannah Arendt, *The Origins of Totalitarianism* (New York: Harcourt, [1951]1976), 180–190.

[9]   Hannah Arendt, *The Human Condition* (Chicago and London: University of Chicago Press, [1958]1998), 188.

[10] Ibid., 190–191.

[11] Hampson and Schwarz regard Peyrol's sacrificial death as reassertion of his former identity. See Hampson, *Joseph Conrad*, 280 and Schwarz, *Conrad*, 142.

[12] Conrad, *The Collected Letters*, vol. 8, 318.

[13] Schwarz, *Conrad* 141; Hampson, *Joseph Conrad*, 280; Fleishman, *Conrad's Politics*, 151.

Peyrol, was "attached to his person on account of his inability to give a clear account of himself" (8) when he was found by the crew in Marseilles after he had run away from the farm terror-struck by his mother's death; "[H]e didn't know very well how to talk to people, and they [the crew] must have misunderstood him. Thus the name of Peyrol stuck to him for life" (7–8). One is tempted to assume that nostalgia may propel him from Toulon toward his childhood home, but Peyrol is not, in fact, sure about his birthplace, as we are told: "He had an idea that he had been born on Porquerolles, but he really did not know" (6).

In keeping with his actual attempts to return to his roots, Peyrol's mental tendency to withdraw into himself is also underscored: his "self-command amounting to placidity" (33) was caused by the early traumatic experience of his mother's death. All he wanted was "a quiet nook, an obscure corner out of men's sight where he could dig a hole unobserved" (12). Peyrol withdraws, however, only to discover the impossibility of a quiet retreat both for his soul and body. Suspected of being an antirevolutionary traitor on his untimely homecoming, Peyrol immediately sneaks away from the port of Toulon into the Escampobar Farm, but the life among people traumatized by revolutionary violence barely provides the retired sailor with a safe refuge from the memory of the nation's revolutionary past. Against his intention to stay aloof from political involvement, he again faces "a treason-hunter" (180), Citizen Scevola, a farmer and a fanatic Jacobin, who (and whose mere presence) never stops demanding a reason for Peyrol's absence during the revolution. Scevola's so-called wife, Arlette, a psychologically damaged orphan of the revolution, renders Peyrol speechless at their first meeting by asking abruptly if he ever "carried a woman's head on a pike" (22). Peyrol's "self-command" (33) fails both in the presence of Scevola, "the only patriot left," who is still hunting for "the enemies of the Republic" (80), and in the presence of the deranged young woman's "provokingly pagan" beauty and vitality (149). The young Arlette's seductiveness has often been noted by critics,[14] yet Peyrol's feeling for her is

---

[14]   For Arlette's seductiveness, see, Palmer, *Joseph Conrad's Fiction*, 254–255. Schwarz, *Conrad*, 149. Palmer regards her as "the final type of Conrad's long line of love goddesses and metaphysical seductresses." See ibid., 254. Geddes sees the "humorous contrast" between Arlette's vitality and Peyrol's complete lack of control in the face of her seductiveness. See Geddes, *Conrad's Later Novels*, 180, 190. Using an anthropological model of father/daughter/lover triangle, Hampson suggests that Peyrol's feeling for Arlette is paternal rather than sexual. See Hampson, *Joseph Conrad*, 280.

something more troubling than sexual attraction; he finds in her "the first problematic human being he [Peyrol] had ever been in contact with" (88).

Here on the farm, "the soul of the returned Peyrol" (25) is not only thrown out of itself by the presence of the residents, but it also exerts a miraculous power over them. Peyrol, "unforeseen, unexpected, inexplicable," gives "a moral and even a physical jolt to all her [Arlette's] being" (219), a being that has been imprisoned in her own home, not only by Scevola who waits for a chance to "have her for his own" (167) but also by her horrific memories of participation in the Toulon massacre in which her royalist parents were slaughtered. Drawn out of her terrified silence by Peyrol, Arlette's "true self" "return[s] matured in its mysterious exile, hopeful and eager for love" (159), not to herself; rather, it turns to the other, to another orphan of the revolution, Lieutenant Réal, who comes to stay at the farm to monitor the English vessel lying in the Hyères roadstead. Peyrol is "the first human being to break through" Réal's "schooled reserve" (71), opening up his heart to his love for Arlette. The love between the orphans of the revolution may seem too melodramatic to draw much critical attention,[15] but Réal's affection for Arlette nonetheless serves to put into relief Scevola's hidden, egoistic impulse for her. Whereas Arlette is, for the old Jacobin who watches for an opportunity to kill the young aristocrat and "have her [Arlette] for his own," an object of obscure desire, she seems to remain an alterity for Réal (even after his marriage to Arlette) that is not reappropriable into a static knowledge, as he later says to her: "[Y]ou [Arlette] … are not so simple as some people would take you to be" (284). Scevola's lust for her, however, is held in check by the mere presence of Peyrol and Arlette's aunt Catherine; they recognize fanatic Jacobin's selfish desire behind his declared "republicanism" (171), which, he insists, motivated him to bring home the youthful Arlette as a "patriot" (33) from the Toulon massacre. Likewise, Catherine's "watchfulness" (90) stands in the way of Peyrol's "intimate emotion" aroused by Arlette. He sometimes feels himself "an object of observation to Catherine, whom he used to detect peeping at him round corners or through half-opened doors" (88). The visual emphasis in *The Rover* has been discussed in the context of the sexual power situation,[16] but I would suggest

---

[15] Jones analyzes the romantic moment of Réal and Arlett in the light of Conrad's aim "to attract lucrative film contracts for his fiction." See Jones, *Conrad and Women*, 165–169.

[16] For a discussion of the nature of the gaze in terms of the sexual power situation, see, in particular, Robert Hampson, "The late novels," in *The Cambridge Companion to Joseph Conrad*, ed. J. H. Stape

that it can better be rethought in terms of one's exposure to others in Hannah Arendt's political sphere where no one should be shielded against the public eye. We shall return to this later as regards Peyrol's final political action. For now though, it suffices to say that the farm residents are all dislocated from themselves; they cannot possess themselves any more than they can possess the other(s). In their efforts to return to themselves, they cannot but open themselves to the other(s). Thus the Escampobar Farm can neither be a home to Peyrol nor to any of its inhabitants who are uneasily exposed to each other.

* * *

Given the dislocation from selfhood of all those people at the farm, one would not be surprised if some mainstream critics have complained about their "unself-consciousness."[17] Under the realist assumption of unified and purposeful selfhood, those "unself-conscious" characters whose selves are, as we have seen above, not firmly situated at the center of consciousness, may indeed appear "feeble-minded"[18] or "unconvincing."[19] The mimetic presupposition such as this, I would think, has most critics look to Peyrol's eight years on land to find the reason behind his abrupt final political decision. They claim that family ties might have been slowly reestablished among the farm residents, and matured and developed his character.[20] However, the farm residents are neither communicative nor cooperative enough to build such a close bond; nor have they anything in common with each other. Strangely, no real work is done or produced in the farm. The "working-day" aspect of Scevola, the master of the Escampobar Farm, has in Peyrol's eyes somehow "an air of being a manifestation," but the patriot crosses the field "in a way no real worker on the land would ever do at the end of a day of toil. Yet there [are] no signs of debility about his person" (39–40).[21] Their weird relationship in what Jean-Luc

---

(Cambridge: Cambridge University Press, 1996), 152–153. With particular emphasis on Peyrol's "extraordinary power of seeing," Fleishman argues that *The Rover* develops "the advanced position [from *Victory*'s purely spectatorial attitude] that the best spectator is he who can both see clearly from a distant perspective *and* engage in historical activity." See Fleishman, *The English Historical Novel*, 216–218.

17 As regards the "unself-conscious" characters, see Schwarz, *Conrad*, 139.
18 Guerard regards *The Rover* as "at its worst a coarse-grained study of feeble-minded and inarticulate people," with its tone of "the dull consciousness" of Peyrol. See Guerard, *Conrad the Novelist*, 284.
19 For the "weariness" of "unconvincing" characters, see Moser, *Joseph Conrad*, 198–201.
20 Schwarz, *Conrad*, 152; Palmer, *Joseph Conrad's Fiction*, 254; Geddes, *Conrad's Later Novels*, 179.
21 Geddes discusses the sense of inertia and paralysis on the land as part of the romance pattern of the novel and within a mythical frame of the Gorgon's head, which, for him, stands for the French Revolution. See Geddes, *Conrad's Later Novels*, 177–179.

Nancy would call "the inoperative community"[22] is perhaps best illustrated in the passage of the supper scene cited below, which gives a sense of distance between them, instead of simply portraying a happy circle around the dinner table. After she slipped into Lieutenant Réal's room to find out if he was gone for good while he was off to Toulon to make arrangements for a secret mission from Napoleon, Arlette went down to kitchen to join others who seemed "shy of meeting each other's eyes,"

> and the evening meal of the Escampobar seemed haunted by the absent lieutenant. Peyrol, besides, had his prisoner to think of. His existence presented a most interesting problem, and the proceedings of the English ship were another, closely connected with it and full of dangerous possibilities. Catherine's black and ungleaming eyes seemed to have sunk deeper in their sockets, but her face wore its habitual severe aloofness of expression. Suddenly Scevola spoke as if in answer to some thought of his own.
>
> "What has lost us was moderation."
>
> Peyrol swallowed the piece of bread and butter which he had been masticating slowly, and asked:
>
> "What are you alluding to, citoyen?"
>
> "I am alluding to the republic," answered Scevola, in a more assured tone than usual. "Moderation I say. We patriots held our hand too soon. All the children of the ci-devants and all the children of traitors should have been killed together with their fathers and mothers. Contempt for civic virtues and love of tyranny were inborn in them all. They grow up and trample on all the sacred principles .... The work of the Terror is undone!" (165–166)

Against our expectation of the hearth, the relationship depicted here does not seem to rely on "the values of proximity, presence, gathering together, and communal familiarity which dominate the traditional culture of friendship"; on the contrary, it is "a friendship without hearth, resemblance, affinity and presence."[23] With little interaction with each other at the table, they are "haunted" by those who are not present and what is not there. The absent lieutenant has occupied

---

[22] Nancy's community commands action, but this action cannot take the form of production. Nancy writes: "Community necessarily takes place in ... 'unworking'. ... Community is made of the interruption of singularities, or of the suspension that singular beings *are*. Community is not the work of singular beings, nor can it claim them as its works, just as communication is not a work or even an operation of singular beings, for community is simply their being—their being suspended upon its limit. Communication is the unworking of work that is social, economic, technical, and institutional." See Nancy, *The Inoperative Community*, 31.

[23] Jacques Derrida, *The Politics of Friendship* (1994: London and New York: Verso, 1997), 155, 255.

the mind of Arlette since he kissed her hand when they were alone in the kitchen. Peyrol's mind is full of "dangerous possibilities," torn between the French lieutenant and the English "prisoner" who is one of the party the English Fleet put ashore at night for scouting; Peyrol knocked him out and locked him in the cabin of his ship hidden in the basin. Scevola's anachronistic eloquence, directed more toward himself than toward Peyrol, barely hides his jealousy to the son of a ci-devant couple murdered by "patriots." Thus invoked, the absent French lieutenant seems as ghostly as Catherine and Scevola. Catherine is no less locked up in the nation's revolutionary past than Scevola. Her eyes are "sunk deeper in their sockets," in accordance with her "aloofness" from (or more accurately, blindness to) what is presently happening around her. She is obsessed with the idea that her niece is "fit for no man's arms" (159) as "there is death in the folds of her [Arlette's] skirt and blood about her feet" (225). Feeling pity for her aunt, on the other hand, Arlette now knows better than Catherine does, with "a terrestrial revelation" (160) that came to her when the lieutenant kissed her. To these people we can add the homeless Michel who comes up to the farm only for dinner. Among them, Peyrol remains "unaffected by familiarity" and "invincible," and he eventually goes as he came in an "unforeseen, unexpected, inexplicable" manner (219).

The Escampobar community is, in effect, a "strangely assorted company served by the anxious and silent Catherine" (79), a group of socially invisible people for whom "there was no place" (82) in the life of the village. Michel, the homeless fisherman, walks up to the farm "to let himself be seen by Peyrol" (82) one day after his beloved dog's death. The Toulon sans-culotte Scevola, a horror and an abomination to the village people for years, keeps away from the village, frightened of their vengeance. The rumor of the village community has it that Arlette, the psychologically traumatized daughter of the Toulon royalists, has given herself and her property up to the Toulon sans-culotte who had either delivered her parents to execution or had murdered them himself during the first three days of massacres. Catherine as a handsome young girl was also hated by the village peasants' "poisonous tongues"; no one "would have looked at [her] if [she] had wanted to be looked at" (89). The ci-devant orphan Réal, having "no place in the world to go to" (71), keeps clear of social connections, with scorn and angry loathing for the revolution.

The Escampobar Farm was "the very accursed spot" for "hatching treacheries" (180) where the Toulon royalists met secretly with the officers of Lord

Nelson's fleet ten years before. The peace of the farm is "strained, questionable, and ominous in its origins" (127), and thus the relationships, as we have seen above, cannot be totally captured in terms of the values such as proximity or presence; it does not develop in a calculable, countable, and chronological way to some telos. The account of the group, correspondingly, does not conform to the preexisting order of systematic, linear representation and is necessarily repressed between chapters 3 and 4. Chapter 4 suddenly jumps forward eight years; thus, the years of political change that ended with the proclamation of Napoleon as consul for life are not covered. And yet, this does not, as Avrom Fleishman argues, necessarily mean a limitation in *The Rover*'s historicity,[24] but rather, it implies that the strange, "ghostly" relationship at the farm during the intervening years calls for another thinking of historicity.[25]

A similar point might also be made about the repression of another strange community, the Brothers of the Coast, to which Peyrol belonged before the story of *The Rover* begins. We can only have a brief glimpse of it when Symons, the captive English sailor, suddenly reminds the old rover of his time with the Brothers. Peyrol, though surprised, sees "nothing impossible" (133) in the fact that the youngster who once admired him had now turned into an English man-of-war's man, because

> You found Brothers of the Coast in all sorts of ships and in all sorts of places. Peyrol had found one once in a very ancient and hopeless cripple practising the profession of a beggar on the steps of Manila cathedral; and had left him the richer by two broad gold pieces to add to his secret hoard. There was a tale of a Brother of the Coast having become a mandarin in China, and Peyrol believed it. One never knew where and in what position one would find a Brother of the Coast. (133–134)

Regardless of nationality, race, class, profession, and physical ability,[26] this amorphous, "cosmopolitan" (132) piratical group appears unpredictably "in

---

[24] For the difficulty in assessing *The Rover*'s historicity mainly because of Napoleon's shadowy offstage presence, see Fleishman, *The English Historical Novel*, 219–220.

[25] For an extended argument of "another thinking of historicity beyond the opposition of the real presence of the real present or the living present to its ghostly simulacrum," see Derrida, *Spectres of Marx*, 70. Likewise, for "the uncanny" as what unsettles any "ordinary" sense or understanding of the "historical," see Royle, *The Uncanny*, 161. My discussion of the ghostliness both of Peyrol's "identity" and of the strange groups in *The Rover* is greatly indebted to this book.

[26] "The cripple of the Madrague," it should also be added here, "in his quality of Peyrol's friend (for the rover had often talked of him both to the women and to Lieutenant Réal with great appreciation—'C'est un homme, ça')" is welcomed as "a member of the Escampobar community" (285) at the closing of the story.

all sorts of ships and in all sorts of places." Peyrol underscores the strangeness of the Brothers' fraternity when his loyalty to the republic is doubted by the post-captain in the Toulon Port Office. The returned rover defends himself, saying, "we [Brothers] practised republican principles long before a republic was thought of; for the Brothers of the Coast were all equal and elected their own chiefs" (5). Interestingly, the Brother's "unthought-of," "strange fraternity," identifiable neither as entirely western nor as eastern, is not so dissimilar to the traditional Polish "szlachta" democracy known for its "social ideals of brotherly love and equality" and royal elections.[27] From the very beginning of the story, the Brother's "unthought-of," "strange fraternity" is contrasted with the slogan of the revolution that came floating from home, with the emphasis on its uniqueness:

> The name of the farmer Peyrol ... acquired a sort of reputation, both openly, in the ports of the East and, secretly, amongst the Brothers of the Coast, that strange fraternity with something masonic and not a little piratical in its constitution. Round the Cape of Storms ... the words Republic, Nation, Tyranny, Liberty, Equality, and Fraternity, and the cult of the Supreme Being came floating on board ships from home, new cries and new ideas which did not upset the slowly developed intelligence of the gunner Peyrol. They seemed the invention of landsmen, of whom the seaman Peyrol knew very little—nothing, so to speak. (8)

This opposition between the values of the French Revolution and those of the Brothers of the Coast has been taken by some critics as an example of how Conrad's political thinking has gone beyond "the abstract model" of his earlier works such as *The Nigger of the "Narcissus."*[28] Thus they discern later Conrad's mature appreciation of "particular human relationship" between the ex-freebooters,[29] but the notion of Conrad's later affirmation of human solidarity

[27] For Polish "szlachta" democracy, see Norman Davies, *Heart of Europe: The Past in Poland's Present* (Oxford: Oxford University, 2001), 291. The Polish nobles, indeed, "saw no contradiction between a political system based on the liberties of the ruling estate and a social system based on the complete subjugation of the lower orders," according to Davies, but in the era of partition, as he goes on, the ex-nobles shared the "democracy" of the oppressed and the deprived, and "the legal fiction of equality" became "the watchword of an embattled population, irrespective of social origin, but equally oppressed by the alien tyrannies." See ibid., 261, 292, 295, in particular. What Conrad's father Apollo calls "traditional *szlachta* democracy," Najder explains, meant that the heritage of citizens' personal liberties and responsibility for the community. See Najder, *Joseph Conrad*, 18.

[28] Hampson, *Joseph Conrad*, 281; Schwarz, *Conrad*, 145, 152.

[29] Ibid.

can hardly be tenable if it presupposes his artistic deterioration. Fleishman, for instance, obviously appreciates the resolution of the tension in *The Rover*, such as the one between egoism and community, while on the other hand he links what he calls the "increase in the simplicity" to Conrad's advancing age.[30] In *The Rover*, Conrad dates back to the very moment when the idea of "fraternity" predicated on the concept of nation-state sovereignty was being reshaped, but he does so neither with a view to rediscover the values of "particular," private attachments, nor indeed to resurrect classical concepts of community. Rather, Conrad might perhaps try to explore another possibility of community that overflows the contemporary idea of fraternity,[31] the possibility that could be rethought in terms of Arendtian action and the public sphere, as we shall see next.

* * *

Conrad's "strange fraternity" is not always a specifically locatable space, but it is, in nature, "potential." According to Arendt, however, what makes this onto-logically impossible space possible is "action."[32] Drawing on the Greek model of public sphere, Arendt claims as follows:

> The *polis*, properly speaking, is not the city-state in its physical location; it is the organization of the people as it arises out of acting and speaking together, and its true space lies between people living together for this pur-pose, no matter where they happen to be. "Wherever you go, you will be a *polis*": these famous words became not merely the watchword of Greek colonization, they expressed the conviction that action and speech create a space between the participants which can find its proper location almost any time and anywhere . . . .
>
> This space does not always exist . . . . No man, moreover, can live in it all the time.[33]

---

[30] Fleishman also associates *The Rover*'s simplicity with the social engagement in the contempo-rary scene of modern politics. See Fleishman, *Conrad's Politics*, 151; Palmer, *Joseph Conrad's Fiction*, 253.

[31] Conrad's attempt to explore another possibility of community is somewhat reminiscent of Derrida's juxtaposition between the fraternal figure of friendship during and after the French Revolution and his own notion of "friendship prior to friendship" that "does not allow itself to be . . . *presented* as a present-being (substance, subject, essence or existence) in the space of an ontology." See Derrida, *Politics of Friendship*, 249.

[32] Arendt, *The Human Condition*, 200.

[33] Ibid., 198–199.

A public realm, for Arendt, is not something preexisting, but rather, what is to be fabricated by human endeavor. Instead of simply describing a given space, she suggests the potentiality of a "space between the participants," which action can "create" "almost any time and anywhere." Conrad's strange communities, as we have seen, are also everywhere and nowhere: the Escampobar farm can be opened "almost any time and anywhere" on the arrival of "unforeseen, unexpected, inexplicable" Peyrol (219), and the "strange fraternity" of the Brothers of the Coast can be found "in all sorts of ships and in all sorts of places" (133).

In addition to these ubiquitous, strange groups, textual attempts to call for a possibility of the public space continue toward the end of the story, as we shall see below. Then, Peyrol's apparently impulsive final action, like Arendt's, could better be understood as another effort to open up a possible "fraternity" rather than as what has long been thought of by critics as "the culmination of movement that builds from the earlier descriptions of character."[34] In so far as Peyrol's "self" is dislocated at the farm, denied a quiet withdrawal from the world into itself, as we have seen earlier, we can no longer simply subscribe to the developmental view of a fictional character on the basis of the supposed unity and identity of a subject. Rather than being the "I" that is assumed to be responsible for "myself" and "my" action, Peyrol, in effect, involuntarily responds to the call of the other, Arlette, when she comes like a sudden storm. Peyrol does not answer for his self, his intention, nor indeed his action, but for Arlette, the other.[35] Lieutenant Réal, who had kept watch over the English fleet's movement with a plan to trick her out of position with a false dispatch signed by Napoleon, left the farmhouse while Arlette slept, to join Peyrol at the little basin. With "a feeble flicker of lightning and a faint crash, far away" (245), however, Arlette awoke from a bad dream in which Réal was set upon by a mob, all dripping with blood; then with "the first

---

[34] For Peyrol's final commitment as a logical, inevitable consequence of his former deeds, see Geddes, *Conrad's Later Novels*, 179, 186; Schwarz, *Conrad*, 146, 151–152; Hampson, *Joseph Conrad*, 277–279.

[35] On the question of response and responsibility in relation to the unity of the subject, see Derrida, *The Politics of Friendship*, 250–251. Derrida writes: on the one hand, "one does not answer for oneself in one's own name, one is responsible only before the question, the request, the interpellation, the 'insistence' of the other." On the other hand, "the proper name structuring the 'answering for oneself' is in itself *for the other*—either because the other has chosen it … or because … it implies the other in the very act of naming, in its origin, finality and use. The *answering* always supposes the other in a relation to self …" (ibid., 251; Derrida's italics).

heavy drop of rain striking the ground," Arlette flew down the slope, when "the rover alone heard and understood" her faint thin scream, "the first sign of her coming" (247). No sooner had Arlette in a desperate faint begged Peyrol to leave her beloved behind than a heavy squall enveloped the group of people on board the ship, "as if this had been the beginning of a destroying and universal deluge—the end of all things" (248). Sending Réal back to the house with Arlette in his arms, Peyrol replaced him on the dangerous mission to break through Nelson's blockade.[36]

Arendt also claims against the idea of the "I" as the origin of the actions. Defined by detachment from personal interest, Arendt's political "action" is different from that of a Western independent, responsible agent. Arendt, on the contrary, thinks of identity, "I," as the product of an act. "In acting and speaking," she observes, "men show who they are, reveal actively their unique personal identities and thus make their appearance in the human world."[37] This public appearance, or what Arendt calls "a second birth,"[38] cannot be a self-generated act: "[This disclosure of 'who'] can almost never be achieved as a wilful purpose, as though one possessed and could dispose of this 'who' in the same manner he has and can dispose of his qualities."[39] Conrad's choice of Marseille as the setting for Peyrol's postdiluvian "second birth," or revelation of "who he is," is particularly interesting if we recall the fact that it is also a place of "second birth" for the young Pole who left Russia to make a fresh start as a sailor.[40] Peyrol, who is supposedly "dead" (106), or "buried under a stack of blackened paper" (107, 241) in the Port Office after he vanished from Toulon, sails out aboard a tartane for a last voyage, "a second birth" after "a destroying and universal deluge—the end of all things" (248).

Before going further on Peyrol's public appearance, let us pause on the old rover's tartane, a narrow space in which nevertheless is also elaborately

---

[36] Significantly, replaceability, in itself, by implication, questions irreplaceable singularity of the individual subject, thus endorsing our discussion here of another responsibility as the possibility of the relationship to others. We may also recall another "replacement of the irreplaceable" in *Nostromo*, in which the titular hero is shot by his patron, Giorgio Viola, mistaken for Ramirez, a younger version of Nostromo, at the end of the story. On the replacement of the irreplaceable, see Jacques Derrida, *Rogues: Two Essays on Reason*, trans. Pascale-Anne Brault and Michael Naas (Stanford, CA: Stanford University Press, 2005), 7.

[37] Arendt, *The Human Condition*, 179.

[38] Ibid., 176.

[39] Ibid., 179.

[40] Fleishman alludes to Conrad's personal association with the Mediterranean coast as a scene of youthful adventures and a place of spectacular beauty. Fleishman, *The English Historical Novel*, 220.

inscribed the possibility of community. The "tragic craft" (85) took Arlette's parents to their death in the vengeful massacre of Toulon and brought the youthful Arlette and Citizen Scevola back to Escampobar where old Catherine waited for days for somebody's return, and later it was filled with mangled bodies of ci-devants who had tried unsuccessfully to flee the massacre. The associations of the Mediterranean small craft with the bloody memory of the revolution have been pointed out, and yet the vessel serves as something more than "a memory symbol,"[41] opening an unknown, possible space among people.

Desiring to get "something of his own that would float" (83, 97) ever since he arrived the farm, one day Peyrol finds the "neglected" tartane (84) lying perishing on the beach and soon starts to refurbish the "tragic craft" (85). Earlier on in the story, the old rover compares the farm to "a ship at sea": "I am old Peyrol and this place [the Escampobar farm], as lonely as a ship at sea, is like a ship to me and all in it are like shipmates" (44). The comparison then allows us to draw a parallel between the old rover's effort to renovate the craft into "something of his own" and his wish to retire to his "home," as we have noted at the outset. The narrative foregrounds the privateness of the tartane: "[H]is ship, the first really that he ever owned" was concealed at the bottom of a tiny basin surrounded by rocks within the cove; he "rejoiced at the idea that it [the tartane] was concealed from all eyes except perhaps the eyes of the goats" (99). Such words as "neglected" (84), "tragic" (85) and "desolate" (86) applied to the boat stained with blood of "fugitive traitors" (86), now turned into Peyrol's "home," cannot but evoke the image of Conrad's own "tragic" home country "neglected" by Napoleon who withdrew from Russia. Conrad addresses himself as "the son of a land ... bedewed with their blood (i.e., that of patriotic men like his grand-uncle Nicholas)" in an episode in *A Personal Record* where his uncle Nicholas, as Conrad puts it, ate a Lithuanian dog "to appease his hunger ... for the sake of unappeasable and patriotic desire" (*PR* 35) during his participation in Napoleon's retreat from Moscow in 1812. Then it makes some sense when Peyrol feels, upon clambering on board the renovated tartane, that "his true home [is] in the tartane" (99), gripped by the sense of "his origins from the crown of his head to the soles of his feet" (98).

---

[41]   Hampson, *Joseph Conrad*, 276. See also Geddes, *Conrad's Later Novels*, 184.

However, once he sets out to sea with his "old friends" (238), Scevola and Michel on board, the tartane, at first likened to "a jewel in a casket" reflecting his fantasy of retreat, is no longer his private space "meant only for the secret rejoicing of his eye" (121). Peyrol deftly plays decoy to the British corvette *Amelia*, nearly passing the blockade in the Petite Passe between Porquerolles Island and Cape Esterel; but, after a long chase, the British fleet finally fires on the tartane, shooting down "this infernal company" on board (238). The narrative suggests the liminality of the "infernal company." Scevola is awakened from the illusion of his "ownership" (251) not only of the farm but also of its heiress Arlette; and Michel, "man without friends" (100), has no tie on earth but Peyrol (268). "[A]t the end of [his] endurance … half dead already" (241), Peyrol sails out to sea with Scevola, "the very image of dejection" (252), and Michel "with the sense of his own insignificant position at the tail of all mankind" (253). Through the passage, it seems, they are crossing over to a nonhuman space, so to speak, as is shown in Peyrol's last vision: "He [Peyrol] felt himself removed far away from that world of human sounds, in which Arlette had screamed at him: 'Peyrol, don't you dare!' He would never hear anybody's voice again" (268)! In his gesture to break the English blockade through the passage, a passage beyond the binary opposition of friend and foe, Peyrol is again opening up the potentiality of plurality at once in the "infernal company" and among the French and the English. Daniel Schwarz points out the ambiguity of Peyrol's decisive action on the grounds that the consequences his "self-sacrifice" brings about to Michel and Scevola undermine the quality of his heroism.[42] But Peyrol's final voyage through the English blockade, with its "capacity for establishing relationships," is the very Arendtian act of "forc[ing] open all limitations and cut[ting] across all boundaries"[43] between friend and foe, human and nonhuman. Those relationships are, in their potential nature, again buried in the text just as the tartane is sunk into the Mediterranean by the *Amelia*'s crew, who give a respectful farewell to the worthy seaman and skillful adversary.

In the brief coda, which, as far as I am aware, has never attracted more attention than as a mere sequel to the climactic event, textual attempts to open the public space still go on, as if the author in turn tries to pass through the textual "blockade," or the limit of orderly, systematic representation. Lieutenant

---

[42] Schwarz, *Conrad*, 143, 151.
[43] Arendt, *The Human Condition*, 190–191.

Réal, wounded at Trafalgar, but escaping capture, retires from the eyes of the naval world in Toulon and also from the world altogether to a quiet and retired life. In the course of years, he becomes "the Mayor of the Commune" in that very same little village that looked on Escampobar as "the abode of iniquity, the sojourn of blood-drinkers and of wicked women." In addition, Peyrol's legacy, that is, a waistcoat lined with "a surprising quantity of gold pieces of various ages, coinages and nationalities" (283), is discovered at the bottom of the well, and Captain Réal decides with his wife's approval to give up Peyrol's hidden treasure to "the Government as the hoard of a man who [died] intestate with no discoverable relations, and whose very name [has] been a matter of uncertainty, even to himself" (284). Many years afterward, Réal and Arlette begin to talk of Peyrol and the episode of his gold. Her retrospective question, "What sort of man was he [Peyrol] really?" (286), poses (and suspends) the unanswered question of the individual subject one last time. The idea of redemptive self-sacrifice, as has been traditionalized by constant repetition in the discussion of *The Rover*, is still strongly attractive in its idealization of the old sailor as the author's heroic self-image. And yet, what Peyrol reveals in his final act, his public appearance, is instead, as is shown in the excerpt below, an apparition rather than some unique, singular identity as a self-presence. After the discovery of Peyrol's hidden treasure,

> the uncertain name of Peyrol found itself oftener and oftener on Monsieur and Madame Réal's lips, on which before it was but seldom heard; though the recollection of his white-headed, quiet, irresistible personality haunted every corner of the Escampobar fields. From that time they talked of him openly, as though he had come back to live again amongst them. (284)

Recovered from oblivion and silence, Peyrol's name becomes a frequent topic of conversation, but it is still "uncertain." Not entirely present but only latent, his "personality" is thus left open. The old rover does not only narcissistically "come back" as the same to himself but also to the others, to "live again amongst them," spectrally filling "every corner of the Escampobar fields" with his "irresistible personality." At issue here is neither what is called a typically Conradian moral choice between self-interest and self-abnegation[44] nor the

---

[44]   Situating Peyrol's sacrifice in the long line of "another, humane kind of fraternity," Schwarz argues that by his heroic act, Peyrol shows the meaning of "fraternity as self-sacrifice." See Schwarz, *Conrad*, 151.

self-relation predicated on the unity of an individual identity, but rather the relation to the other that exceeds a binary logic such as self/other. To put this into Arendtian formulation of "action" again, this is the very "revelatory quality of speech and action," that "comes to the fore where people are *with* others and neither for nor against them—that is, in sheer human togetherness." The person who unwittingly discloses himself in deed or word, in Arendt's terms, can neither be completely unselfish nor selfish: he can neither be "the doer of good works, who must be without self and preserve complete anonymity, nor the criminal, who must hide himself from others." "Both are lonely figures," she goes on to say, "the one being for, the other against, all men."[45]

Conrad's "strange fraternity," however, goes even further than Arendt's apparently androcentric public realm in its inclusion of women like Arlette and her aunt Catherine, and even of nature which is presented as a large mulberry tree mourning Peyrol at the end.[46] It appears more like Derrida's "democracy to come," which is beyond the living, open to the dead, animals, trees, and rocks:[47]

> [T]he mulberry tree, the only big tree on the head of the peninsula, standing like a sentinel at the gate of the yard, sighed faintly in a shudder of all its leaves, as if regretting the Brother of the Coast, the man of dark deeds, but of large heart, who often at noonday would lie down to sleep under its shade. (286)

Peyrol's deeds are "dark" not only in the sense that they are unlawful but also in the sense that no one can guess at what is in his "large heart." His heart is immeasurably "large," too "large" indeed to be totally captured by the logic of cause and effect, or the logic of the sameness. The only certain thing Réal and Arlette can say of Peyrol is that he was "not a bad Frenchman" (286). The cripple of Madrague, Peyrol's friend who became "a member of the Escampobar community" (285), sees everything in that summing-up "with fervent conviction," and "the silence [falls] upon Réal's words and Arlette's faint sigh of memory" (286). In words, Peyrol's "identity" may perhaps be ineluctably caught

---

[45]   Arendt, *The Human Condition*, 180.

[46]   In his discussion of "a fraternity ranging infinitely beyond all literal figures of the brother," Derrida points out the exclusion of the feminine in the philosophical, paradigm, in particular, in the Christian, fraternal friendship of the French Revolution. See Derrida, *The Politics of Friendship*, 237, 261.

[47]   On the question of "how far democracy is to be extended," see Derrida, *Rogues*, 54.

up within the dialectic of "a bad Frenchman"/"not a bad Frenchman," and yet Arlette's "faint sigh" *recalls* Peyrol, "an immense figure, like a messenger from the unknown entering the solitude of Escampobar; something immensely strong, with inexhaustible power" (219).

The *Rover* has generally been read as Conrad's "valedictory novel."[48] Though critics suggest that *The Rover*, Conrad's so-called fictional testament, gives us his final heroic self-image,[49] Peyrol's life can neither "reach completion,"[50] nor can he "fulfill himself" in his last home.[51] During his lifelong pursuit of "identity" in his allegedly autobiographical writings, Conrad repeatedly tries but fails to complete his image of self, and thus his "ghost" inevitably returns every time he sets his pen to paper, just as the revolutionary specter Haldin in *Under Western Eyes* interrupts Razumov's effort to establish his public self by writing a prize essay. At the end of the long line of Conrad's uncanny heroes, Peyrol has still an "inexhaustible power." From the very outset, *The Rover* is concerned with the ghostly; the story ends as it begins by Peyrol's coming back. He keeps coming back as a revenant, "with inexhaustible power," to haunt after his death, not returning safe to some fixed "identity." Conrad's "fictional testament" could better be understood in his affirmation of Peyrol's roving, spectral existence, over a being with a fixed identity like a national hero. Thus, the aptly titled *The Rover* refers less to Conrad's last will to break away completely from his wandering, rootless past than to his decision (without decision) to live on as a truly "free rover" (103), an indefinitely suspended being.

[48] George A. Panichas, *Joseph Conrad: His Moral Vision* (Macon, GA: Mercer University Press, 2005), 130.

[49] Schwarz, *Conrad*, 139, 141, 146, 153.

[50] Ibid., 146.

[51] Fleishman, *Conrad's Politics*, 151; Schwarz, *Conrad*, 145.

10

Toward a Possible Partage of Memory

"History" and "Solidarity" in *Suspense*

Cathy Caruth suggests in her discussion of the traumatic nature of history that events are only historical to the extent that they implicate others. Highlighting the intercultural and intergenerational structure of the witnessing of the trauma, she asserts the possibility of a "history" arising in the very way we are implicated in each other's traumas. What Caruth refers to as "history" is not directly referential, that is, no longer based on simple models of experience and reference but rather collective and exceeding individual bounds, allowing for an encounter that retains or does not fully erase difference.[1] Drawing on Caruth's notion of "traumatic history," this chapter aims to rethink Conrad's "history" not as a matter of referentiality but as that of responsibility, that is, partage of memory. Partage, as always with Nancy, signifying participation as much as "partition or separation, or a new departure,"[2] is "a sharing out without fusion, a community without community,"[3] which is already evoked as "strange fraternity" in the "separation, or a new departure" of the captain and Leggatt in the closing scene of "The Secret Sharer," as we have seen in Chapter 4. It is in fact Nancean "partage," sharing out as separation and sharing a secret. I shall begin by looking at the traumatic aspect of Conrad's nostalgic recollection and then

---

[1] By the implication of others, or the linking of traumas, to borrow Caruth's phrase, I do not mean some given, compassionate community of victims or witnesses. See Caruth, *Unclaimed Experience*, 18, 24, 42. Instead, the linking of traumas, as Caruth suggests, demands a different way of thinking that may not guarantee communication or acceptance. See ibid., 124. Thus "strange fraternity" and "history" in later Conrad can be combined in terms of Caruth's notion of trauma. As Kai Erikson also discusses, those who survived a catastrophic disaster are injured by the loss of a sustaining community. See Kai Erikson, "Notes on Trauma and Community," *Trauma: Explorations in Memory*, ed. Cathy Caruth (Baltimore: Johns Hopkins University Press, 1995), 183–199.

[2] Derrida, *On Touching—Jean-Luc Nancy*, 219.

[3] Ibid., 195.

link the notion of trauma to that of "history" as intercultural, or intergenerational implication in traumas. Then I shall finally show that his last unfinished historical novel, *Suspense: A Novel of Napoleonic Times* permits the possibility of "history" to emerge from the "solidarity" which, Conrad supposes, "binds ... the dead to the living and the living to the unborn" (*NN* xl).

* * *

Conrad is not usually thought of as a historical novelist, but in fact he wrote more historical fiction than any other major British novelist after Walter Scott. Throughout his career, Conrad had written many short stories on historical themes; and indeed his masterwork *Nostromo*, known primarily as one of the most experimental novels of the early modernist period, is a novel of the turbulent history of an imaginary republic in South America. In his last novels, *The Rover* and *Suspense*, Conrad deals with the period between the French Revolution and the Napoleonic wars. And yet, scholars say that they have found it difficult to "generalize about his historical sense or even to estimate the success of his historical novels."[4] Conrad's turn to the historical romance in his late career has often been associated with the exhaustion of his creative energy under the dominant paradigm that favors his earlier stories of individual psychological tensions.[5]

Recent historicist approaches, however, in their reassessment of Conrad's underrated, later historical works, situate them in new contexts, such as the contemporary market for the female novel of sensation in England, or the nineteenth-century European cult of Napoleon.[6] While I would agree, in large part, that Conrad's works "capture something powerfully real about the various histories to which they refer,"[7] I would nevertheless respond with a degree of caution to the assumption of a referential history, because Conradian experiences are, in most cases, "inconclusive," not necessarily guiding us toward a stable referent, or a certain point of the past on a linear time line. One example is the well-known episode of the attack on Marlow's steamboat by the native

---

[4] Fleishman, *The English Historical Novel*, 212.
[5] Regarding scholars' view of Conrad's creative exhaustion and his decision to write historical fiction as contributing factors to the weakness of his later work, see Niland, *Conrad and History*, 159.
[6] Regarding the female novel of sensation, see Jones, *Conrad and Women*, 192–220; for the cult of Napoleon, see Niland, *Conrad and History*, 183.
[7] GoGwilt, "Joseph Conrad as Guide to Colonial History," 137.

people hiding in the jungle in *Heart of Darkness* as cited below. Here, Marlow, terrified of running aground, is anxiously watching his poleman sounding in the bows just below him:

> I was looking down at the sounding-pole, and feeling much annoyed to see at each try a little more of it stick out of that river, when I saw my poleman give up the business suddenly, and stretch himself flat on the deck, without even taking the trouble to haul his pole in. He kept hold on it though, and it trailed in the water. At the same time the fireman, whom I could also see below me, sat down abruptly before his furnace and ducked his head. I was amazed. Then I had to look at the river mighty quick, because there was a snag in the fairway. Sticks, little sticks, were flying about—thick: they were whizzing before my nose, dropping below me, striking behind me against my pilot-house. All this time the river, the shore, the woods, were very quiet—perfectly quiet. I could only hear the heavy splashing thump of the stern-wheel and the patter of these things. We cleared the snag clumsily. Arrows, by Jove! We were being shot at! (109–110)

It is almost traditional to take this episode as a prime example of subjective rendering of surface phenomena, famously termed by Ian Watt as "delayed decoding," the narrative device that "combines the forward temporal progression of the mind … with the much slower reflexive process of making out their meaning."[8] The text, according to Watt, gives a chronological sequence of momentary sensations in the protagonist's mind; and the reader finds it quite natural that there should be delay before Marlow's brain finally decodes his impressions into their cause. We may therefore think that Marlow's initially inexplicable visual impression of a series of abrupt, odd changes in the posture of his men and then of the flying sticks is finally decoded in his mind into its cause—"Arrows, by Jove! We were being shot at!" But it is by no means, as has been understood, a mere perceptual mistake or confusion later to be corrected or decoded with conventional or traditional categories and explanations.[9] On the contrary, as Bruce Johnson importantly discusses, an initial unguarded perception—"Sticks, little sticks, were flying about"—is valuable to the author himself and may be revealing to the reader as well. Conrad is, Johnson states,

[8] Watt, *Conrad in the Nineteenth Century*, 175.
[9] Concerning the idea of the surface phenomena as mere perceptual "mistake," see Peters, *Conrad and Impressionism*, 37–40.

anxious to recreate those rare moments when we perceive something that is genuinely outside the usual frames of reference. In an atmosphere in which traditional meanings and names no longer function, there can be no secure decoding.[10] Hence "the terrific suggestiveness of words heard in dreams, of phrases spoken in nightmares" in Marlow's exchanges with Kurtz, whose soul, going "beyond the bounds of permitted aspirations," "knew no restraint, no faith, and no fear" (*HD* 144–145).

Watt contends that Conrad's use of "delayed decoding" reaches its climax in the Marlow stories, since this technique is based on the pretense that the reader's understanding is limited to the consciousness of the fictional observer, but at the same time he admits the technique, "delayed decoding," applies less well in *Lord Jim*.[11] As Marlow's deferred reaction to the incomprehensible phenomenon we have read above is already suggestive of Freudian traumatic belatedness, it is not simply a matter of seeing or knowing an empirical event occurring in time.[12] Rather, it can better be viewed as the temporal disjunction of trauma, in which the event is missed at the time that it happens, as is perhaps best illustrated by the ellipsis in Jim's private testimony to Marlow.[13] As Jim's case in *Lord Jim* makes clear, what happens to Conrad's heroes is not simply an experience in time but indeed a break in the mind's experience of time. With a cargo of 800 pilgrims bound from Singapore to Mecca, the *Patna*, a ship "eaten up with rust worse than a condemned water-tank," apparently strikes a submerged object and threatens to sink.[14] Terrified crew abandon her, leaving the pilgrims to their fate. Jim finally jumps overboard and finds himself joining the captain and the crew members in the lifeboat. The captain and

---

[10]   Bruce Johnson, "Conrad's Impressionism and Watt's 'Delayed Decoding,'" in *Conrad Revisited: Essays for the Eighties* (Tuscaloosa, AL: University of Alabama Press, 1985), 51–70, 53, 57, in particular.

[11]   Watt, *Conrad in the Nineteenth Century*, 270–271.

[12]   On the gaps and missing moments, see Peters, *Conrad and Impressionism*, 92 and also 37–40. Throughout his book, Peters discusses those missing moments not in terms of trauma that surpasses the confines of individual psyche but in terms of the subjective impressionism.

[13]   For the suggestion in some of Derrida's works that events are in some sense *traumatic*, see Geoffrey Bennington, *Not Half No End: Militantly Melancholic Essays in Memory of Jacques Derrida* (Edinburgh: Edinburgh University Press, 2010, 2011), 41. "[U]n événement," Derrida writes in *Papier Machine*, "est toujours traumatique, sa singularité interrompt un ordre et déchire, comme tout decision degne de ce nom, un tissue normal de la temporalité ou de l'histoire." See Jacques Derrida, *Papier Machine: Le ruban de machine à écrire et autres responses* (Paris: Galilée, 2001), 114.

[14]   Joseph Conrad, *Lord Jim* (Oxford: Oxford University Press, 2000), 10. Further page references to *Lord Jim* will be given parenthetically in the text, preceded by *LJ* where it might otherwise be unclear.

the crew disappear, leaving Jim to face an official inquiry alone, between sessions of which he tells his personal story to Marlow. Jim seeks to explain "the fundamental why" (*LJ* 41) behind the events, but his jump took place too suddenly, too unexpectedly to be fully grasped by his consciousness, as is shown in the ellipsis in his private testimony to Marlow as follows:

> He [Jim] raised his hand deliberately to his face, and made picking motions with his fingers as though he had been bothered with cobwebs, and afterwards he looked into the open palm for quite half a second before he blurted out—
>
> "I had jumped …" He checked himself, averted his gaze … . "It seems," he added.
>
> ….
>
> "Looks like it," I [Marlow] muttered.
>
> "I knew nothing about it till I looked up," he explained hastily. And that's possible, too. You had to listen to him as you would to a small boy in trouble. He didn't know. It had happened somehow. It would never happen again….
>
> "She [the ship] seemed higher than a wall; she loomed like a cliff over the boat … . I wished I could die," he cried. "There was no going back. It was as if I had jumped into a well—into an everlasting deep hole … ." (80–81)

It is, for Jim, a jump into "an everlasting deep hole," the endless "lack of direct experience" that becomes, according to Caruth, the basis of the repetition of the nightmare.[15] Jim's case echoes Caruth's description of the traumatic experience in terms of its temporal unlocatability:

> The breach in the mind … is not simply … the literal threatening of bodily life, but … the threat is recognized as such by the mind *one moment too late*. The shock of the mind's relation to the threat of death is thus not the direct experience of the threat, but precisely the *missing* of this experience, the fact that, not being experienced *in time*, it has not yet been fully known. And it is this lack of direct experience that, paradoxically, becomes the basis of the repetition of the nightmare … .[16] (italics in the original).

Jim is one of those traumatized Conradian heroes haunted by his unclaimed past and caught in a repetition-compulsion. My concern here is not, however, with what is individually remembered of the past within stories, regarding

---

[15] For the lack of direct experience, that is, "a missed experience," see Caruth, *Unclaimed Experience*, 62. Ann Whitehead would call it "a non-experience." See Anne Whitehead, *Trauma Fiction* (Edinburgh: Edinburgh University Press, 2004), 5–6.

[16] Caruth, *Unclaimed Experience*, 62.

which some psychoanalytical readings have already been attempted,[17] but rather with how the past is remembered across the whole of Conradian corpus. The subjective nature of Conrad's narrator's remembrance of the past has long been highlighted in Conrad studies, but the experiences of Marlow and Jim, as we have seen, remain unassimilable to their individual consciousness and thus they are not fully mediated through representation but rather through repetition from one story to another. Even in *Youth*, seemingly innocent in its nostalgic evocation of the past, Marlow's experience is nevertheless "inconclusive": following the spontaneous combustion of the cargo, the smoke of the "invisible" fire (*Y* 26) again and again comes up from "somewhere" (*Y* 21) at the bottom of the ship. Even after Marlow's exit, the haunting power of inconclusive experiences persists in Conrad's narrative. *Nostromo* portrays the history of a fictional South America as an unending cycle of repeated revolutions of the colonized indigenous people and almost futile counterrevolutionary projects of European colonizers. In *The Secret Agent*, "[a]n *impenetrable mystery*" of the attempted explosion of the Greenwich Observatory, as the newspaper says, "*seems destined to hang for ever over this act of madness or despair.*"[18] The Russian protagonist in *Under Western Eyes* is again inconclusively tossed between "the lawlessness of autocracy ... and the lawlessness of revolution" (77). Conrad's writing is thus preoccupied more with traumatic possession by the past than with romantic individual possession of the past.

Having said this, I do not mean to minimize the "glamour of youth" that Marlow recurrently evokes in *Youth* (*Y* 12, 26, 30, 42); nor do I play down the importance of the subjective nature of Conrad's narrator's remembrance of the past, particularly in the light of romantic tradition of personal identity, which is, as Anne Whitehead succinctly explains, identical with the remembering of one's own actions.[19] Still, Conrad's obsessive return to "inconclusive experiences" from time to time invites us to note some of their traumatic aspects, or what is in excess of reference to a past in his texts. Trauma, according to

---

[17] Cf. Jeffrey Mayers, *Joseph Conrad: A Psychoanalytical Biography* (Princeton, NJ: Princeton University Press, 1967). For a recent example of psychoanalytical reading, see Carola M. Kaplan, "Navigating Trauma in Joseph Conrad's *Victory*: A Voyage from Sigmund Freud to Phillip M. Bromberg," *Psychoanalytic Dialogues*, vol. 20, no. 4 (2010): 441–448. What I am trying to do in this chapter is to read Conrad's text not as a faithful reproduction of traumatic events that had actually happened in his life but as "traumatic history" that arises in the way we are implicated in each other's trauma.

[18] Conrad, *The Secret Agent*, 307.

[19] Anne Whitehead, *Memory* (London and New York: Routledge, 2009), 56–59.

Caruth, already describes the individual experience as something that extends beyond the confines of the individual psyche. Something more than the clinical case of an individual, a traumatic experience has the collective, intercultural, or intergenerational structure in the sense that the witnessing of the trauma can take place in cultures and in future generations. One's own trauma is never, as Caruth constantly stresses, simply one's own; rather, it is tied up with the trauma of another. Thus, she sees the possibility of "history" arising in the very way we are implicated in each other's traumas; events are only historical, for her, to the extent that they implicate others.[20] What Caruth refers to as "history" is, accordingly, no longer a straightforwardly referential history of a nation, a culture, or a generation; rather, it is a question of responsibility, a question of the possibility of passing on to another that would engage some notion of address.[21]

In this sense, *Lord Jim* can better be understood as a "survivor narrative," a series of survivors' testimonies to a traumatic event, the *Patna* case; it is a multilayered address to another, demanding a listening and a response, rather than a statement of an already given, empirical truth,[22] or the facts that the audience in the courtroom are "so eager to know" and that are "visible, tangible, open to the senses, occupying their place in space and time, requiring for their existence a fourteen-hundred-ton steamer and twenty-seven minutes by the watch" (*LJ* 22–23). Whereas the audience in the courtroom is "so eager to know" the mere facts (22), Jim tries to narrate to Marlow something more and other than the facts, that is, his trauma of survival. Marlow, the listener, in turn, survives Kurtz and Jim to pass on his own story of survival to his audience. Marlow is indeed an untypical nautical raconteur, according to the frame narrator in *Heart of Darkness* (*HD* 48); he sometimes sounds less like a seaman leisurely spinning a yarn after dinner than a witness to historical disasters that have national and international dimensions. The *Judea*, the ship

---

[20] Caruth, *Unclaimed Experience*, 18, 24, 42, and 124.

[21] Regarding the question of address, see also Shoshana Felman's articulation of the testimony as "an appointment to transgress the confines of that isolated stance, to speak *for* others and *to* others; it is '*addressed* to others, from within the solitude of his own stance … or a dimension *beyond himself*'" in her "Education and Crisis," in *Trauma: Explorations in Memory*, ed. Cathy Caruth (Baltimore: Johns Hopkins University Press, 1995), 15.

[22] On the "survivor narrative," see Cathy Caruth, introduction to *Critical Encounters: Reference and Responsibility in Deconstructive Writing*, eds. Cathy Caruth and Deborah Esch (New Brunswick, NJ: Rutgers University Press, 1995), 2.

"doomed to arrive nowhere" (*Y* 28) in *Youth*, symbolizes a nation for Marlow as he says, "it seems as though we had been born in her, reared in her, had lived in her for ages, had never known any other ship" (*Y* 18). The degradation of Kurtz, whose making (as Marlow puts it) "[a]ll Europe contributed to," implies the so-called decline of the West, as we are made to feel. Furthermore, "the real significance" of the maritime scandal in *Lord Jim* for Marlow is a "breach of faith with the community of mankind" (*LJ* 113). In this context, therefore, the panoramic vision of a fictional country in *Nostromo* can be regarded as a continuation and intensification of historical dimension of disasters already implicit in those earlier stories.

The success of Marlow's yarns becomes less and less unable to depend on "the bond of the sea" (*Y* 3), or "the solidarity of the craft" with his listeners (*LJ* 95), until finally in *Lord Jim* the listeners drift off as soon as Marlow ends his narrative, just carrying away with them "the last image of that incomplete story" (*LJ* 245). After staging the (im)possibility of address through the Marlovian narrative situation, Conrad then embarks on a new exploration into the possibility of sharing "history," making ever heavier demands on the reader, demanding our witness, as I shall be arguing next, with particular focus on the ending of his last, historical novel, *Suspense: A Novel of Napoleonic Times*.

* * *

Suspense: A Novel of Napoleonic Times is set in Genoa in 1815, just before Napoleon's escape from Elba for the Hundred Days. The story follows the actions of Cosmo, a young English veteran of the Peninsular War, who is on a grand tour to Genoa. "[T]he most agitated ten years of European history" (*S* 91) are compressed into Cosmo's three days' adventure, which begins with his encounter with an Italian conspirator Attilio, a member of a revolutionary group plotting to release Napoleon, and ends by helping the Italian to smuggle secret documents to a ship bound for Elba. Cosmo sees the social life of Genoa overshadowed by the suspense following the results of the Congress of Vienna and troubled especially by the "unseen presence" (93) of Napoleon on nearby Elba. However, the novel as we know it stops, in fact, before Cosmo reaches Elba and Napoleon heroically returns to France from exile.

We may tend to believe that Napoleon's return is absent because of the unfinished state of the novel caused by the untimely death of the author in 1924.[23] The author himself, Gene Moore remarks, prophetically had "an idea that [he would] never finish it [*Suspense*],"[24] a concern reflected in a surprising number of references to "unfinishedness" in the novel.[25] But if we note that the very suspension of *Suspense* has so far severely limited critical attention and led to almost unanimous critical agreement that Conrad's canon ends with his last competed novel, *The Rover*,[26] then we should perhaps pay due attention to "the sense of non-ending" of *Suspense*,[27] to borrow Moore's terminology, instead of further reinforcing the almost complete neglect of the novel by endorsing the assumption of a complete structure. I would argue contrarily that suspension is a constitutive feature of the novel that necessarily ends in suspension, or an open ending that permits the possibility of "history" to emerge.

The night scenes in the port of Genoa at the close of the novel are surrounded by "unbroken," "gravelike" stillness (233, 245): "A profound quietness reigned on the darkly polished surface of the harbour and the long, incurved range of the quays. This quietness that surrounded him [Cosmo] on all sides through which, beyond the spars of clustered coasters, he could look at the night-horizon of the open sea" (225). The silent darkness may seem yet another overused Conradian atmosphere, but in this story it is particularly heightened by the author's omission of a lofty lighthouse, the famed Lanterna. It is "most surprising," says Ugo Mursia, that Conrad never, in his description of the port, mentions this "outstanding feature of the town."[28] Cosmo, Attilio's secret documents concealed in his hat, is being transported across the harbor to be incarcerated. Suddenly he lets out a shout of "Boat ahoy" with all the

---

[23] For the absence of Napoleon's return and Conrad's untimely death, see Niland, *Conrad and History*, 183–184.

[24] Conrad to André Gide, August 20, 1919, vol. 6 of *Collected Letters*, 469–470.

[25] Gene Moore, "The Sense of Non-Ending: The Suspension of *Suspense*," in vol. III of *Joseph Conrad: Critical Assessments*, ed. Keith Carabine (Robertsbridge, UK: Helm Information, 1992), 681, 685. Moore, however, sees the authorial intention in the complete rounded structure of the novel, despite its unfinishedness (ibid., 682). Also, Richard Curle explained that Conrad "was himself quite undetermined as to how the novel should reach its climax: he left no notes, he left no hints; all he left, indeed, was this declaration of uncertainty." For Richard Curle's comment on Conrad's own uncertainty as to the ending, see Gene Moore, introduction to *Suspense*, by Joseph Conrad (Cambridge: Cambridge University Press, 2011), xlv.

[26] Gene Moore, "In Defense of *Suspense*," *Conradiana*, vol. 25, no. 2 (1993): 99.

[27] Moore, "The Sense of Non-Ending: The Suspension of *Suspense*," 678–688.

[28] Ugo Mursia, "Notes on Conrad's Italian Novel: *Suspense*," *Conrad's Cities: Essays for Hans van Marle*, ed. Gene Moore (Amsterdam-Atlanta, GA: Rodopi, 1992), 275.

force of his lungs (246), so that it seems to fill the whole of the harbor. Cosmo apparently is hailing the English man-of-war's boat outside the harbor, and yet it is Attilio who responds to his "extraordinary shout" (247) and comes to his rescue and then enlists him in the voyage to Elba.

Cosmo's psychological explanation for his shout is that he felt the necessity to assert himself as he had behaved like a frightened mouse before the Italian police officers and he could not resist the temptation to hail the English boat. Yet it is nonetheless "extraordinary" and startling enough not only for Attilio and the harbor authorities but also for us readers who are left in suspension in this perfect silence and profound darkness of the ending. Although Mursia asserts that the total darkness that surrounds the night scenes in the port is hardly believable,[29] I would suggest that it nevertheless strengthens the atmosphere that makes us, along with Cosmo and the other characters, attentive and anxious listeners. Cosmo's call awakens us, or even commands us, to depart from ourselves, from what we can know and understand,[30] when Cosmo and Attilio depart from Genoa for Elba. In this departure from our sense and understanding, we are first fully addressed by the text in ways we perhaps cannot yet fully understand. It is in this incomprehension and in our departure from sense and understanding that our own witnessing may indeed begin to take place.[31] The possibility of history arises, indeed, not as our mutual understanding but rather as the interruption of understanding in this total silence and darkness[32] that puts us in a position of exile, as it were. Thus dislocated, we readers become refugees or exiles like Napoleon who is interestingly called "the Other" (165) in this story as well as in *The Rover*. Refugees and exiles do not possess the memory of events as a story of a nation, that is, a national history, but rather they share—*partager*—the memory of events. Sharing of memory may happen when we become refugees in our departure from sense and understanding, starting to live as refugees.[33] Significantly, references to "the universe" (256)

---

[29]   Ibid.
[30]   Regarding the notion of address and departure, my reading here owes much to Caruth's stimulating interpretation of Marguerite Duras's film *Hiroshima mon amour* (1959) in her *Unclaimed Experience*. See, in particular, 24, 25–56.
[31]   Ibid., 56. My argument is greatly indebted to Caruth's idea of witness of a traumatic historical event.
[32]   Ibid., 42.
[33]   Oka argues that the possibility of sharing the memory of an event lies in our becoming and living dispossessed. See Oka, *Kioku/Monogatari* (*Memory/Narrative*), 112.

and "the constellation" of the sky (273, 274) toward the end of the story implicitly invite us to conflate Cosmo's vision with the cosmic vision of the fictional
world. Therefore, when Cosmo is destined for "the Other" (165) on Elba, we
are made aware that we readers, the other to the text, are addressed not only
by the protagonist but also by the fictional world, or more accurately, the text
itself.[34] This suspense or interruption of understanding, instead of empathy
or mutual understanding, paradoxically opens up the possibility of partage of
memory. In our departure from understanding, our own witnessing of "the
most agitated ten years of European history" (91) may indeed begin to take
place. The possibility of sharing the memory of events (far from possessing a
given, unified national history) arises from this "solidarity" in displacement,
or the "solidarity" in exile from ourselves, so to speak.[35]

I would like to think that this address is, through Cosmo and the microcosm of the suspended world of *Suspense*, spoken by Conrad in terms of "we,"
or the "solidarity" the author supposes in the famous "Preface" to *The Nigger
of the "Narcissus"* as follows:

> He [the artist] speaks ... to our sense of pity, and beauty, and pain; to the
> latent feeling of fellowship with all creation—and to the subtle but invincible
> conviction of solidarity that knits together the loneliness of innumerable
> hearts: to the solidarity in dreams, in joy, in sorrow, in aspirations, in illu-
> sions, in hope, in fear, which binds men to each other, which binds together
> all humanity—the dead to the living and the living to the unborn . . . . In a
> single-minded attempt of that kind, if one be deserving and fortunate, one
> may perchance attain to such clearness of sincerity that at last the presented
> vision of regret or pity, of terror or mirth, shall awaken in the hearts of the
> beholders that feeling of unavoidable solidarity; of the solidarity in mysteri-
> ous origin, in toil, in joy, in hope, in uncertain fate—which binds men to
> each other and all mankind to the visible world. (*NN* xl–xlii)

The celebrated passage of this preface—"My task which I am trying to achieve
is, by the power of the written word to make you hear, to make you feel—
it is, before all, to make you *see*. That—and no more, and it is everything!"
(*NN* xlii)—has on the one hand established Conrad as a master of subjective

---

[34]   On the notion of the Other as the third party, or the whole humanity, see Attridge, *Reading and
Responsibility*, 103. Also, see Levinas's concept of "solidarity" in his *Totality and Infinity*, 214.
[35]   My argument here draws on Oka's notion of the partage of memory by the others, or the survivors.
See Oka, *Kioku/Monogatari* (*Memory/Narrative*), 75, 112, in particular.

impressionism. This preface is on the other hand marked by an open, nonexclusive solidarity that extends beyond the living humanity even to "the dead" and "the unborn." We have earlier noted Ian Watt's skepticism about the "existential status" of this strange solidarity in our time,[36] and yet its latency, subtlety, and boundlessness indicate that we are dealing not with a straightforward declaration of communal concern of art based on some preexisting, traditionally understood fellowship, but rather with an impossible, ghostly relationship. This "we," addressed to "the unborn" by the author, makes us, as his future generations, his "spectral interlocutors." As such, we readers, being unborn and incapable of replying, cannot refuse the community thus proposed; we can only say "yes" to his "extraordinary" performative "we"[37] that summons us to bear witness to "the most agitated ten years of European history" (91). It is difficult not to recognize here the effacement of Polish history that is not directly told but only elliptically suggested as an address to the listening of another. In responding to Conrad's text, we answer for, and take responsibility for the call of European memory of the period when the fate of Poland was being decided at the Congress of Vienna. Cosmo's (or the text's) call is addressed not as a fact but rather as a question, asking for memory as a question.[38] For Conrad ("the living"), it is undoubtedly "the Polish Question" that has a "practical bearing" on the future of Europe,[39] as he insists in his political essays.[40]

The already dead Emperor is likewise summoned here by the author, but it does not simply mean that the Polish author recalls Napoleon as "a failed Messiah."[41] Conrad does not, as has been said, simply look back upon the period as "an era of hope that ended definitively" with Napoleon's retreat from Moscow;[42] but rather, he (or more precisely, the historical novel *Suspense*, his "archive" in Derrida's sense) simultaneously looks forward to the future, the

---

[36] See note 39 in Chapter 1.
[37] For the violence of this *communal* dissymmetry already inscribing the other person into the situation, see Derrida's argument of the spectral interaction between the historian Yerushalmi and Freud in his *Archive Fever*, 41–43. Also for the difficult question of the violence at the heart of any ethical relation, see Attridge, *Reading and Responsibility*, 29, 97–116.
[38] Regarding memory as a question, see Caruth, *Unclaimed Experience*, 35.
[39] Conrad, "Note on the Polish Problem," *Notes on Life and Letters*, 137. Cf. O. Halecki, *A History of Poland*, 217–228.
[40] For Europe's responsibility for itself, for the other, and before the other, see Derrida, *The Other Heading*, 4–83. Regarding the question of archive not simply as a question of the past but also as a question of the future, "the question of the future itself, the question of a response, of a promise and of a responsibility for tomorrow," see Derrida, *Archive Fever*, 36.
[41] Concerning the idea of Napoleon as "a failed Messiah," see Niland, *Conrad and History*, 169.
[42] Ibid., 169.

future to come. In Napoleon's "unseen presence," in his infinite "nearness" on Elba (*S* 93), Conrad's archive "summon[s] the very thing that will never present itself in the form of full presence";[43] the text awaits the coming of the other, what is coming, but it does so not in religious terms but "without identifiable messiah."[44] Despite our historical hindsight of what actually follows the ending, therefore, we can nevertheless discern here "messianic" promise and hope rather than "an ironic twist" to its suspense.[45] Indeed, the historical Napoleon failed in fulfilling his promises and betrayed the hopes of the Polish people; but, in our reading (or witnessing) of Conrad's archive of European history, which is epitomized in the "secret correspondence from Italy to the Island of Elba" (72), the specter of Napoleon, summoned by Conrad the historian, cannot refuse this "messianic" promise. The dead Emperor can only say "yes" to the "messianic" responsibility for tomorrow; since Conrad's solidarity, his "extraordinary" performative "we," is "unavoidable." Thus disrupting the linear historical time in implicating "the dead," "the living," and "the unborn," this "we" begins (unlike traditional communities) "in mysterious origin," opening to "uncertain fate" (*NN* xlii), to every possible promise and hope for anyone who comes (as I do) from another heading, another shore, European or non-European. In this implication, or "strange fraternity," arises the possibility of "history," "history" as responsibility.

---

[43] "[M]essianic opening to what is coming," Derrida writes, "to the event as the foreigner itself, to her or to him for whom one must leave an empty place, always, in memory of the hope—and this is the very place of spectrality." "[S]uch a hospitality without reserve" is, he goes on say, "the condition of the event and thus of history." See Derrida, *Spectres of Marx*, 65.

[44] Regarding the distinction between "the messianic" and religious "messianism," see Derrida, *Spectres of Marx*, 28.

[45] For "an ironic twist" to the "suspense," see Moore, "The Sense of Non-Ending," 686.

Conclusion

We have seen Conrad's gradual departure from the art of subjectivity to that of "strange fraternity," a process whereby his texts negotiate the question of distance between the subject and the object. In his or her unceasing struggle to close upon him- or herself as a single point of view, the observing subject distanced from the world simply takes the other(s) into account and is together with them despite disagreement and difference, expanding and flowing over him- or herself to reach toward the other(s). This is not to say that the self and the other(s) merge into some higher substantial identity "we," for instance, through soldierly communion; but rather, it is to suggest that a singular plurality takes place, a plurality that is something more than a collection of individuals having something in common and can only be described as "that appalling dark group" of Tomassov and De Castel in "The Warrior's Soul" or "strange fraternity" in *The Rover* that Peyrol's Arendtian action opens up as an involuntary response to the call of the other. We would not be too surprised then to find the expansive gesture of the self more connected toward his later years with touching that makes us "us," or "being singular plural" in Nancy, and with history as responsibility, or traumatic history that already describes the individual experience as something that extends beyond the confines of the individual psyche. To grasp history as responsibility, the self can no longer be separated and distanced from the world; rather, surrendering the "I" to the other, it touches and identifies with the other without appropriating the other into itself, which is what happened in *The Arrow of Gold*.

If the self in Conrad's later novels, exposed to and extended toward the other, is no longer "a pure interiority" but "a being in exteriority" in relation to itself,[1] in *Suspense* it is not simply the observing subject severed from the world, but rather it becomes the world, the universe itself. In his last, unfinished novel, the division between interiorized subject and exterior world as the object of knowledge is no longer a given condition; the model of an observer in an optically perceived world does not necessarily apply to the protagonist Cosmo as his name implies.[2] Cosmo is less an active, autonomous producer of his own visual experience than a being who finds himself enveloped in the world as a vast expanse,[3] "the wide world filled with the strife of ideas and the struggle of nations in perhaps the most troubled time of its history" (*S* 22). At the outset of *Suspense*, against the background of the terror in France, "the world of seas and continents … began at the edge of the long terrace [of Letham Hall, Cosmo's family home in Yorkshire] graced by gorgeous sunsets" (22). After the victory of Toulouse in 1814, one of the final battles of the Napoleonic Wars, Cosmo appears in Yorkshire to make up for past coolness by warmly shaking hands with his father. Then the son expresses his wish to leave the army "to see something of the world which [has] been closed to [them] so long" (39), referring to the Continental Blockade, effective between 1806 and 1814. In the closing scene, having narrowly won the race with the authorities' galley, on Attilio's boat, Cosmo does not simply give us an account or an impression of the world as a distanced perceiving subject; rather, he abandons himself to the "air and sea and stars enveloping" him:

> He [Cosmo] surrendered to the soft and invincible stillness of air and sea
> and stars enveloping the active desires and the secret fears of men who have
> the sombre earth for their stage. At every momentary pause in his long and
> fantastic adventure it returned with its splendid charm and glorious serenity,
> resembling the power of a great and unfathomable love whose tenderness

---

[1]   Nancy writes: "the subjectivity of [the] subject is clearly understood … as a 'self-sensing' that is exactly not … an appropriating of oneself to oneself in a pure interiority, but a being in exteriority in relation to itself. We sense ourselves as an outside." "Self being" is, according to Nancy, "necessarily being outside, on the outside, being exposed or extended." Nancy, *Corpus*, 132.

[2]   Regarding the division between interiorized subject and exterior world as a pre-given condition of knowledge about the world, see Crary, *Techniques of the Observer*, 46.

[3]   Ken-ichi Sasaki, *Nihontekikannsei—Shokkaku to zurashi no kōzō (Japanese Sensibility: Sense of Touch and Shifting Structure)* (Tokyo: Chuokoron, 2010), 92. I am greatly indebted to Sasaki's comparison between Eastern and Western senses of space.

like a secret spell lays to rest all the vividities and all the violences of passionate desire. (255)

Here how can we gauge the distance between men and the universe from a certain point of view when men can neither be simply opposed to nor distanced from the universe? The "stillness of air and sea and stars" is "soft" but "invincible" and it intermittently "returns" to envelope men; its tenderness is cast over men "like a spell," like a vast veil of love, covering them and their actions, even the "violences of passionate desire"; therefore, its love is "great and unfathomable." The wide "world of seas and continents" bordering on the terrace of Letham Hall cited previously now merges into "[t]he waste of waters [that] seem[s] to extend from the shores of Italy to the very confines of the universe, with nothing on it but the black spot of the galley which move[s] no more than the head of a rock" (256).

In Nancy's thinking of the body not as an interior but as an exterior, an other, the body is in fact "cosmic" and "touches on everything," going "through the atmosphere ... reach galaxies and finally the boundless limits of the universe."[4] As a being in exteriority is inseparable from a question of touch in Nancy, so in Conrad, given this atmospheric envelope, it is little wonder that the question of tactility becomes important in another historical novel, *The Arrow of Gold*. For, history in Conrad is more like something felt bodily than something seen from a detached viewpoint to be investigated and understood. It is something that can be apprehended by senses alive to its volume rather than something like a subjective visual impression. As Conrad puts it in the "Author's Note" to *The Arrow of Gold*, the subject of the story—his youthful life embodied in George and Rita—is not "a possession of [his] memory" but rather "an inherent part" of himself, a part that remains and disappears as a trace, "as though it were [his] absolute fate to be everlastingly dying and reviving to the tormenting fact of her [Rita's] existence" (*AG* 234). The "wild hope of finding a trace of Rita's passage, a sign or something" (233) that George felt when he heard she left for Paris with her maid Rose can be taken simply as his desire for something like a memento of the woman he loves; and yet, this may also give us a clue about how George grasps Rita. For George, she is "one of those beings that leave a trace" because he supposes she is "so unforgettable" (119);

[4] Nancy, *Corpus*, 154.

he knows he is destined to be "everlastingly dying and reviving to the torment-ing fact of her existence." She seems more "real" in her absence than in her presence; she "takes body" in his imagination and her absence makes her all the more palpable to him. Rita's reality is, for him, something more and other than "an image" or a subjective impression to be presented; rather, it is tan-gible and voluminous. But again their contact does not carry out any fusion. Plastic imagination instead creates a space for singular "solidarity" between George and Rita, as contrasted with pictorial perception predicated on indi-vidual perspective, thus making *The Arrow of Gold* not only a personal record but rather a unique historical account, enhancing the idea of Conrad's history as responsibility.

Interestingly, just as we are implicitly invited to take D'Hubert's letter to his sister as symbolizing the text of Conrad's "The Duel" itself, as we have seen in Chapter 6, so we might be tempted to see Cosmo's epistle to his innocent young sister Henrietta as standing for Conrad's unfinished novel *Suspense*. At a loss as to what to write to his sister about a lot of people he met in Italy, Cosmo ponders the difficulty of "describ[ing] the world outwardly" (70) by "piling up words which deal[s] exclusively with towns, roads, rivers, mountains, the col-ours of the sky." He thinks that it is a "vain thing" when he travels on, as it feels like "labouring the description of the scenery of a stage after a great play [came] to an end" (188). With his head full of Lady Jane, who attended him all the way from Paris to the morning of his arrival at Cantelucci's inn in Genoa, he won-ders how he can confide his "impressions" (71) of her to his sister Henrietta and asks himself if Lady Jane deserted him or if "[it was] his mind that . . . dropped her out of a haunting actuality into that region where the jumble of one's experi-ences is allowed to rest" (71). The protagonist's mock phenomenological ques-tion to himself, recalling Conrad's narrative treatment of past experiences, can also be interpreted as the text's self-reflexive meditation on how to convey the reality of "the most agitated ten years of European history" to his readership, which is comprised of the then-increasing number of female readers. Thus we might want to read *Suspense* less as a straightforward historical record of Napoleonic times than as a letter addressed to Messiah, the other still yet to come; that is, the dead emperor and a new readership in the future.

In thus submitting things to chance (since "The Secret Sharer") rather than to causal process in subjective perception and in permitting the history to arise from "strange fraternity" rather than faithfully reproducing the history, Conrad seems to share with surrealists a sense of a mismatch between words and the things to which they refer—along with a distrust (though not necessarily despair as in the case of Dadaists, for instance) of language's signifying capabilities.[5] And yet, unlike in the case of surrealists, Conrad's notion of "strange fraternity," in its potentiality, can hardly serve as an alternative or alternate reality for author and reader alike. Conrad's "strange fraternity," like Derrida's unconditional hospitality, neither simply condemns nor is opposed to the traditional community. Rather, the "strange fraternity" is indissociable from the traditional community, maintaining it "in a perpetual progressive movement."[6] We may therefore not be too sanguine about a possible alliance between Conrad and surrealists. Reminding us of the much discussed difficulty of locating Conrad in modernist tradition, Michael Levenson appropriately asserts, "It would be too strong to say that Conrad's standing in Modernism was ever in serious doubt, but right to hold that it had to await—and has always still to await—a fuller reckoning."[7] Conrad made the modernist "leap" into an individual consciousness from the Victorian sailing ship, to repeat Levenson's phrase cited in Introduction,[8] though perhaps only reluctantly,[9] but instead of making another "jump" from modernism to other artistic strands, he roves somewhere in between, ever-renewing his bonds of "community," his "strange fraternity."

[5] David Hopkins, *Dada and Surrealism. A Very Short Introduction* (Oxford: Oxford University Press, 2004), 64. Regarding Dadaist's conformity with chance, see ibid., 69–73.

[6] Derrida, *Of Hospitality*, 25, 27.

[7] Levenson, "Modernism," in *Joseph Conrad in Context*, ed. Simmons, 186.

[8] Levenson, *A Genealogy of Modernism*, 1–22, especially, 6.

[9] Greaney remarks that Conrad is "the most reluctant of modernists." See Greaney, *Conrad, Language, and Narrative*, 169.

Bibliography

Arendt, Hannah. *The Origins of Totalitarianism*. 1951. New York: Harcourt, 1976.

Arendt, Hannah. *The Human Condition*. 1958. Chicago and London: University of Chicago Press, 1998.

Attridge, Derek. *Singularity of Literature*. London and New York: Routledge, 2004.

Attridge, Derek. *Reading and Responsibility: Deconstruction's Traces*. Edinburgh: Edinburgh University Press, 2010, 2011.

Baines, Jocelyn. *Joseph Conrad: A Critical Biography*. London: Weidenfeld and Nicolson, 1960.

Batchelor, John. *The Life of Joseph Conrad*. 1994. Oxford: Blackwell, 1996.

Beer, Gillian *The Romance*. London: Methuen, 1970.

Bennett, Andrew. *The Author*. London and New York: Routledge, 2005.

Bennington, Geoffrey. *Not Half No End: Militantly Melancholic Essays in Memory of Jacques Derrida*. Edinburgh: Edinburgh University Press, 2010, 2011.

Blanchot, Maurice. *The Unavowable Community*, translated by Pierre Joris. 1983. New York: Station Hill, 1988.

Blantlinger, Patrick. *Rule of Darkness: British Literature and Imperialism, 1830–1914*. Ithaca, NY and London: Cornell University Press, 1988.

Bross, Addison. "A Set of Six: Variations on a Theme." In *Joseph Conrad: Critical Assessment*, edited by Keith Carabine. Robertsbridge, UK: Helm Information, 1992. 105–121.

Busza, Andrew. Introduction to *The Rover*, by Joseph Conrad. Oxford: Oxford University Press, 1992.

Cadava, Eduardo, Peter Connor, and Jean-Luc Nancy, eds. *Who Comes After the Subject?* New York and London: Routledge, 1991.

Caruth, Cathy, ed. *Trauma: Explorations in Memory*. Baltimore: Johns Hopkins University Press, 1995.

Caruth, Cathy. Introduction to *Critical Encounters: Reference and Responsibility in Deconstructive Writing*, edited by Cathy Caruth and Deborah Esch. New Brunswick, NJ: Rutgers University Press, 1995. 1–8.

Caruth, Cathy. *Unclaimed Experience*. Baltimore: Johns Hopkins University Press, 1996.

Caruth, Cathy. *Literature in the Ashes of History*. Baltimore: Johns Hopkins University Press, 2013.

Certeau, Michel de. *The Writing of History*, translated by Tom Conley. New York: Columbia University Press, 1975.

Conrad, Joseph. *The Arrow of Gold: A Story between Two Notes*. London: Dent, 1947.

Conrad, Joseph. "Autocracy and War." In *Notes on Life and Letters*. London: Dent, 1949. 83–114.

Conrad, Joseph. "The Crime of Partition." In *Notes on Life and Letters*. London: Dent, 1949. 115–133.

Conrad, Joseph. "Henry James." In *Notes on Life and Letters*. London: Dent, 1949. 11–19.

Conrad, Joseph. "A Note on the Polish Problem." In *Notes on Life and Letters*. London: Dent, 1949. 134–140.

Conrad, Joseph. *The Rescue: A Romance of the Shallows*. 1920. London: Dent, 1949.

Conrad, Joseph. "The Duel: A Military Tale." In *A Set of Six*. London: Dent, 1961. 165–266.

Conrad, Joseph. "Prince Roman." In *Tales of Hearsay and Last Essays*. London: Dent, 1963. 29–55.

Conrad, Joseph. "Stephen Crane." In *Tales of Hearsay and Last Essays*. London: Dent, 1963. 93–118.

Conrad, Joseph. *Under Western Eyes*. London: Dent, 1963.

Conrad, Joseph. "The Secret Sharer." In *'Twixt Land and Sea*. London: Dent, 1966.

Conrad, Joseph. *Almayer's Folly*. 1895. London: Dent, 1967.

Conrad, Joseph. *Youth / Heart of Darkness / The End of Tether*. London: Dent, 1967.

Conrad, Joseph. *The Sisters: An Unfinished Story*. Milan: U. Mursia, 1968.

Conrad, Joseph. *Suspense: A Novel of Napoleonic Times*. London: Dent, 1968.

Conrad, Joseph. *Chance*. London: Dent, 1969.

Conrad, Joseph. *Congo Diary and Other Uncollected Pieces*, edited by Zdzisław Najder. New York: Doubleday, 1978.

Conrad, Joseph. *The Secret Agent*. Oxford: Oxford University Press, 1983.

Conrad, Joseph. *The Nigger of the "Narcissus."* Oxford: Oxford University Press, 1984.

Conrad, Joseph. Preface to *The Nigger of the "Narcissus."* Oxford: Oxford University Press, 1984. xxxix–xliv.

Conrad, Joseph. *The Mirror of the Sea and A Personal Record*. Oxford: Oxford University Press, 1988.

Conrad, Joseph. *An Outcast of the Islands*. Oxford: Oxford University Press, 1992.

Conrad, Joseph. *The Rover*. Oxford: Oxford University Press, 1992.

Conrad, Joseph. "The Warrior's Soul." In *The Lagoon and the Other Stories*, edited by William Atkinson. Oxford: Oxford University Press, 1997. 231–251.

Conrad, Joseph. *Lord Jim*. Oxford: Oxford University Press, 2000.

Conrad, Joseph. *The Collected Letters of Joseph Conrad*, vols. 1–4, 6, 8, edited by
Frederick Karl and Laurence Davies. Cambridge: Cambridge University Press,
1987–2007.

Conrad, Joseph. *Nostromo*. Oxford: Oxford University Press, 2007.

Crary, Jonathan. "Modernizing Vision." In *Vision and Visuality*, edited by Hal Foster.
Seattle: Bay Press, 1988. 29–50.

Crary, Jonathan. *Techniques of the Observer: On Vision and Modernity in the
Nineteenth Century*. Cambridge: MIT press, 1992.

Critchley, Simon. *Continental Philosophy: A Very Short Introduction*. Oxford: Oxford
University Press, 2001.

Curley, Daniel. "Legate of the Ideal." In *Conrad's Secret Sharer and the Critics*, edited
by Bruce Harkness. Belmont, CA: Wadsworth, 1962. 75–82.

Daleski, H. M. *Joseph Conrad: The Way of Dispossession*. London: Faber and Faber, 1977.

Davies, Norman. *Heart of Europe: The Past in Poland's Present*. Oxford: Oxford
University, 2001.

Dean, Seamus. "Imperialism/Nationalism." In *Critical Terms for Literary Study*,
edited by Frank Lentricchia and Thomas McLaughlin. 2nd edn. 1990. Chicago and
London: University of Chicago Press, 1995. 354–368.

Dent, Peter, ed. *Sculpture and Touch*. Surrey: Ashgate, 2014.

Deresiewicz, William. "Conrad's Impasse: *The Nigger of the 'Narcissus'* and the
Invention of Marlow." In *Conradiana*, vol. 38, no. 3 (Fall 2006): 205–227.

Derrida, Jacques. *Of Grammatology*, translated by Gayatri Chakravorty Spivak.
Baltimore and London: Johns Hopkins University Press, 1997.

Derrida, Jacques. "Le facteur de la vérité." In *The Post Card: From Socrates to Freud
and Beyond*, translated by Alan Bass. Chicago: University of Chicago Press, 1987.
413–496.

Derrida, Jacques. *Acts of Literature*, edited by Derek Attridge. London and
New York: Routledge, 1992.

Derrida, Jacques. "Force of the Law: The 'Mystical Foundation of Authority.'" In
Deconstruction and the Possibility of Justice, translated by Mary Quaintance,
edited by Drucilla Cornell, Michel Rosenfeld, and David Gray Carlson. New York
and London: Routledge, 1992.

Derrida, Jacques. *Given Times: I. Counterfeit Money*, translated by Peggy Kamuf.
Chicago and London: University of Chicago Press, 1992.

Derrida, Jacques. *The Other Heading: Reflections of Today's Europe*, translated by
Pascale-Anne Brault and Michael B. Naas. Bloomington and Indianapolis: Indiana
University Press, 1992.

Derrida, Jacques. *Spectres of Marx: The State of the Debt, the Work of Mourning, and
the New International*, translated by Peggy Kamuf. London: Routledge, 1994.

Derrida, Jacques. *The Politics of Friendship*, translated by George Collins. 1994: London and New York: Verso, 1997.

Derrida, Jacques. *Archive Fever: A Freudian Impression*, translated by Eric Prenowitz. Chicago: University of Chicago Press, 1998.

Derrida, Jacques. *Adieu to Emmanuel Levinas*, translated by Pascale-Anne Brault and Michael Naas. Stanford, CA: Stanford University Press, 1999.

Derrida, Jacques. *The Gift of Death and Literature in Secret*, translated by David Willis. Chicago and London: University of Chicago Press, 1999.

Derrida, Jacques. *Of Hospitality*, translated by Rachel Bowlby. 1997. Stanford, CA: Stanford University Press, 2000.

Derrida, Jacques. *Papier Machine: Le ruban de machine à écrire et autres responses*. Paris: Galilée, 2001.

Derrida, Jacques. *On Touching—Jean-Luc Nancy*, translated by Christine Irizarry. Stanford, CA: Stanford University Press, 2005.

Derrida, Jacques. *Rogues: Two Essays on Reason*, translated by Pascale-Anne Brault and Michael Naas. Stanford, CA: Stanford University Press, 2005.

Di Piazza, Elio. "Conrad's Narrative Polyphony in *The Nigger of the 'Narcissus.'*" In *Beyond the Roots: The Evolution of Conrad's Ideology and Art*, edited with an introduction by Wiesław Krajka. Boulder, CO: East European Monographs; Lublin, Poland: Maria Curie-Skłodowska University Press; New York: Colombia University Press, 2005. 23–38. Vol. 14 of *Conrad: Eastern and Western Perspectives*, edited by Wiesław Krajka, 23 vols. to date, 1992–.

Dilworth, Thomas. "Listeners and Lies in 'Heart of Darkness.'" In *The Review of English Studies*. New Series, vol. 38, no. 152 (Nov., 1987): 510–522.

Erdinast-Vulcan, Daphna. *Joseph Conrad and the Modern Temper*. Oxford: Oxford University Press, 1991.

Erdinast-Vulcan, Daphna. *The Strange Short Fiction of Joseph Conrad: Writing, Culture, and Subjectivity*. Oxford: Oxford University Press, 1999.

Erikson, Kai. "Notes on Trauma and Community." In *Trauma: Explorations in Memory*, edited by Cathy Caruth. Baltimore: Johns Hopkins University Press, 1995. 183–199.

Felman, Shoshana. "Education and Crisis." In *Trauma: Explorations in Memory*, edited by Cathy Caruth. Baltimore: Johns Hopkins University Press, 1995. 13–60.

Fenves, Peter. Foreword to *The Experience of Freedom*, by Jean-Luc Nancy, translated by Bridget McDonald. Stanford, CA: Stanford University Press, 1988. xiii–xxxi.

Ferguson, DeLancey. "The Plot of Conrad's *The Duel*." In *Modern Language Notes*, vol. 50, no. 6 (June 1935): 385–390.

Fleishman, Avrom. *Conrad's Politics: Community and Anarchy in the Fiction of Joseph Conrad*. Baltimore: The John's Hopkins Press, 1967.

Fleishman, Avrom. *The English Historical Novel: Walter Scott to Virginia Woolf.* Baltimore: Johns Hopkins University Press, 1971.

Fogel, Aaron. *Coersion to Speak: Conrad's Poetics of Dialogue.* Cambridge, MA: Harvard University Press, 1985.

Gaston, Sean. *Derrida, Literature and War: Absence and the Chance of Meeting.* New York: Continuum, 2009.

Geddes, Gary. *Conrad's Later Novels.* Montreal: McGill-Queen's University Press, 1980.

GoGwilt, Christopher. *The Invention of the West: Joseph Conrad and the Double-Mapping of Europe and Empire.* Stanford, CA: Stanford University Press, 1995.

GoGwilt, Christopher. "Joseph Conrad as Guide to Colonial History." In *A Historical Guide to Joseph Conrad*, edited by John G. Peters. Oxford: Oxford University Press, 2010. 137–161.

Graver, Lawrence. *Conrad's Short Fiction.* Berkeley and Los Angeles: University of California Press, 1969.

Greaney, Michael. *Conrad, Language, and Narrative.* New York: Palgrave, 2002.

Guerard, Albert. *Conrad the Novelist.* Cambridge, MA: Harvard University Press, 1958.

Halecki, O. *A History of Poland.* London and Henley: Routledge and Kegan Paul, 1978.

Hampson, Robert. *Joseph Conrad: Betrayal and Identity.* London: Macmillan, 1992.

Hampson, Robert. "The late novels." In *The Cambridge Companion to Joseph Conrad*, edited by J. H. Stape. Cambridge: Cambridge University Press, 1996. 140–159.

Hampson, Robert. *Cross-Cultural Encounters in Joseph Conrad's Malay Fiction.* London: Palgrave, 2000.

Hawthorn, Jeremy. *Joseph Conrad: Narrative Technique and Ideological Commitment.* London: Edward Arnold, 1990.

Hawthorn, Jeremy. *Sexuality and the Erotic in the Fiction of Joseph Conrad.* New York and London: Continuum, 2007.

Hay, Eloise Knapp. *The Political Novels of Joseph Conrad.* Chicago and London: University of Chicago Press, 1963.

Hay, Eloise Knapp. "Proust, James, Conrad, and Impressionism." In *Style*, vol. 22, no.3 (Fall 1988): 368–381

Hay, Eloise Knapp. "Nostromo." In *The Cambridge Companion to Joseph Conrad*, edited by J. H. Stape. Cambridge: Cambridge University Press, 1996. 81–99.

Henricksen, Bruce. *Nomadic Voices: Conrad and the Subject of Narrative.* Urbana and Chicago: University of Illinois Press, 1992.

Hooper, Myrtle. "The Ethics of Negativity: Conrad's 'The Duel.'" In *L'Epoque Conradienne* 31 (2005): 107–117.

Hopkins, David. *Dada and Surrealism. A Very Short Introduction.* Oxford: Oxford University Press, 2004.

Hunter, Jefferson. *Edwardian Fiction*. Cambridge, MA: Harvard University Press, 1982.

Ihde, Don. *Listening and Voice: Phenomenologies of Sound*. Albany: State University of New York Press, 2007.

Jay, Martin. "Scopic Regimes of Modernity." In *Vision and Visuality*, edited by Hal Foster. Seattle: Bay Press, 1988.

Johnson, Bruce. "Conrad's Impressionism and Watt's 'Delayed Decoding.'" In *Conrad Revisited: Essays for the Eighties*, edited by Ross C. Murfin. Tuscaloosa, AL: University of Alabama Press, 1985. 51–70.

Johnson, Geraldine A. "A taxonomy of touch: tactile encounters in Renaissance Italy." In *Sculpture and Touch*, edited by Peter Dent. Surrey: Ashgate, 2014. 91–106.

Jones, Susan. *Conrad and Women*. Oxford: Oxford University Press, 1999.

Juhász, Tomás. *Conradian Contracts: Exchange and Identity in the Immigrant Imagination*. Plymouth: Lexington Books, 2011. 95–112.

Kaplan, Carola M. Peter Mallios, and Andrea White, eds, *Conrad in the Twenty-First Century: Contemporary Approaches and Perspectives*. New York and London: Routledge, 2005.

Kaplan, Carola M. "Navigating Trauma in Joseph Conrad's *Victory*: A Voyage from Sigmund Freud to Phillip M. Bromberg." In *Psychoanalytic Dialogues,* vol. 20, no. 4 (2010): 441–448.

Kenaan, Hagi. "Touching sculpture." In *Sculpture and Touch*, edited by Peter Dent. Surrey: Ashgate, 2014. 45–59.

Kiernan, V. G. *The Duel in European History: Honour and the Reign of Aristocracy*. Oxford: Oxford University Press, 1989.

Knowles, Owen. "To Make You Hear …': Some Aspects of Conrad's Dialogue," *Polish Review,* vol. 20, no. 2–3 (1975): 164–180.

Knowles, Owen and Gene Moore, eds. *Oxford Reader's Companion to Conrad*. Oxford: Oxford University Press, 2000.

Kozak, Wojciech. "Sharing Gender (?) in 'The Secret Sharer.'" In *Beyond the Roots: The Evolution of Conrad's Ideology and Art*, edited with an Introduction by Wiesław Krajka. Boulder, CO: East European Monographs; Lublin, Poland: Maria Curie-Skłodowska University Press; New York: Colombia University Press, 2005. 319–336. Vol. 14 of *Conrad: Eastern and Western Perspectives*, edited by Wiesław Krajka, 23 vols. to date, 1992–.

Kronegger, Maria Elizabeth. *Literary Impressionism*. New Haven, CN: College and University Press, 1973.

Lang, Adriaan de. "Conrad and Impressionism: Problems and (Possible) Solutions." In *Conrad's Literary Career*, edited by Keith Carabine, Owen Knowles, and Wieslaw Krajka. Boulder, CO: East European Monographs; Lublin, Poland: Maria Curie-Skłodowska University Press; New York: Columbia University Press, 1992.

21–40. Vol. 1 of *Conrad: Eastern and Western Perspectives*, edited by Wiesław Krajka, 23 vols. to date, 1992–.

Leiter, Louis H. "Echo Structures: Conrad's 'The Secret Sharer.'" In *Conrad's Secret Sharer and the Critics*, edited by Bruce Harkness. Belmont, CA: Wadsworth, 1962. 133–150.

Levenson, Michael. *A Genealogy of Modernism: A Study of English Literary Doctrine 1908–1922*. Cambridge: Cambridge University Press, 1984.

Levinas, Emmanuel. *Totality and Infinity: An Essay on Exteriority*, translated by Alphonso Lingis. Pittsburg, PA: Duquesne University Press, 1969.

Lingis, Alphonso. *The Community of Those Who Have Nothing in Common*. Bloomington and Indianapolis: Indiana Unversity Press, 1994.

Lodge, David. *Consciousness and the Novel*. Milan: Rizzoli, 2005.

Lothe, Jakob. *Conrad's Narrative Method*. Oxford: Oxford University Press, 1989.

Lothe, Jakob, Jeremy Hawthorn, and James Phelan, eds. *Joseph Conrad: Voice, Sequence, History, Genre*. Columbus: Ohio State University, 2008.

Macovski, Michael S. *Dialogue and Literature: Apostrophe, Auditors, and the Collapse of Romantic Discourse*. New York and Oxford: Oxford University Press, 1994.

Mansfield, Nick. *Subjectivity: Theories of the Self from Freud to Haraway*. New York: New York University Press, 2000.

Margolin, Uri. "Collective Perspective, Individual Perspective, and the Speaker in Between: On 'We' Literary Narratives." In *New Perspectives on Narrative Perspective*, edited by Willie Van Peer and Seymour Chatman. Albany: State University of New York, 2001. 241–53.

Matz, Jesse. *Literary Impressionism and Modernist Aesthetics*. Cambridge: Cambridge University Press, 2001.

Mayers, Jeffrey. *Joseph Conrad: A Psychoanalytical Biography*. Princeton, NJ: Princeton University Press, 1967.

Middleton, Tim. *Joseph Conrad*. London and New York: Routledge, 2006.

Miller, J. Hillis. "Sharing Secrets." In *"The Secret Sharer": Case Studies in Contemporary Criticism*, by Joseph Conrad, edited by Daniel R. Schwarz. Boston: Bedford, 1993. 232–252.

Miller, J. Hillis. "'Material Interests': Conrad's *Nostromo* as a Critique of Global Capitalism." In *Joseph Conrad: Voice, Sequence, History, Genre*, edited by Jakob Lothe, Jeremy Hawthorn, and James Phelan. Columbus: Ohio State University, 2008. 160–177.

Moore, Gene. "The Sense of Non-Ending: The Suspension of *Suspense*." In vol. III of *Joseph Conrad: Critical Assessments*, edited by Keith Carabine. Robertsbridge, UK: Helm Information, 1992. 678–688.

Moore, Gene. "In Defense of *Suspense*," *Conradiana,* vol. 25, no. 2 (1993): 99–114.

Moore, Gene, ed. Introduction to *Suspense*, by Joseph Conrad, xxvii–li. Cambridge: Cambridge University Press, 2011.

Moore, Gene, ed. *Conrad's Cities: Essays for Hans van Marle.* Amsterdam-Atlanta, GA: Rodopi, 1992.

Moore, Henry. "Notes on Sculpture." In *Henry Moore: Sculpture and Drawings.* London: Lund Humphries, [1944] 1949. xl–xlii.

Morgan, Gerald. "The Book of the Ship *Narcissus*." In *The Nigger of the "Narcissus,"* by Joseph Conrad, edited by Robert Kimbrough. New York: W. W. Norton, 1979.

Morgan, Gerald. "Narcissus Afloat." In *The Nigger of the "Narcissus,"* by Joseph Conrad, edited by Robert Kimbrough. New York: W. W. Norton, 1979

Moser, Thomas. *Joseph Conrad: Achievement and Decline.* Cambridge: Harvard University Press, 1957.

Moyne, Ernest J. "Wamibo in Conrad's *The Nigger of the 'Narcissus,'* " *Conradiana,* vol. 10, no. 1 (1978): 55–61.

Mursia, Ugo. "Notes on Conrad's Italian Novel: *Suspense*." In *Conrad's Cities: Essays for Hans van Marle*, edited by Gene Moore. Amsterdam-Atlanta, GA: Rodopi, 1992. 269–281.

Nadelhaft, Ruth. *Joseph Conrad*. Atlantic Highlands, NJ: Humanities Press International, 1991.

Najder, Zdzisław. *Conrad's Polish Background*. London: Oxford University Press, 1964.

Najder, Zdzisław. "Conrad and Rousseau: Concepts of Man and Society." In *Joseph Conrad: A Commemoration*, edited by Norman Sherry. London: Macmillan, 1976. 77–90.

Najder, Zdzisław. *Joseph Conrad: A Life.* Rochester, NY: Camden House, 2007.

Nancy, Jean-Luc. *Being Singular Plural*, translated by Robert D. Richardson and Anne E. O'Byrne. 1996. Stanford, CA: Stanford University Press, 2000.

Nancy, Jean-Luc. *The Inoperative Community*, edited by Peter Connor, translated by Peter Connor, Lisa Garbus, Michael Holland, and Simona Sawhney, 1991. Minneapolis and London: University of Minnesota Press, 2006.

Nancy, Jean-Luc. *Listening*, translated by Charlotte Mandell. New York: Fordham University Press, 2007.

Nancy, Jean-Luc. *Corpus*, translated by Richard A. Rand. New York: Fordham University Press, 2008.

Niland, Richard. *Conrad and History*. Oxford: Oxford University Press, 2010.

North, Michael. *The Dialect of Modernism: Race, Lnaguage, and Twentieth-Century Literature*. New York and Oxford: Oxford University Press, 1994.

Oka, Mari. *Kioku/Monogatari (Memory/Narrative)*. Tokyo: Iwanami, 2000.

Palmer, John A. *Joseph Conrad's Fiction: A Study in Literary Growth*. Ithaca, NY: Cornell University Press, 1968.

Panichas, George A. *Joseph Conrad: His Moral Vision*. Macon, GA: Mercer University Press, 2005.

Paraskos, Michael. "Bringing into being: vivifying sculpture through touch." In *Sculpture and Touch*, edited by Peter Dent. Surrey: Ashgate, 2014. 61–69.

Pecora, Vincent. "Heart of Darkness and *The Phenomenology of Voice*." *ELH* 52.4 (Winter 1985): 993–1015.

Peters, John G. *Conrad and Impressionism*. Cambridge: Cambridge University Press, 2001.

Peters, John G. *The Cambridge Introduction to Joseph Conrad*. Cambridge: Cambridge University Press, 2006.

Peters, John G., ed. *A Historical Guide to Joseph Conrad*. Oxford: Oxford University Press, 2010.

Phelan, James. "Sharing Secrets." In *"The Secret Sharer": Case Studies in Contemporary Criticism*, by Joseph Conrad, edited by Daniel R. Schwarz. Boston: Bedford, 1993. 128–144.

Read, Herbert. *The Art of Sculpture*. 1956; Princeton, NJ: Princeton University Press, 1977.

Ressler, Steve. *Joseph Conrad: Consciousness and Integrity*. New York and London: New York University Press, 1988.

Richardson, Brian. "Construing Conrad's 'The Secret Sharer': Suppressed Narratives, Subaltern Reception, and the Act of Interpretation." *Studies in the Novel,* vol. 33, no. 3 (Fall 2001): 306–319.

Richardson, Brian. "Conrad and Posthumanist Narration: Fabricating Class and Consciousness onboard the *Narcissus*." In *Conrad in the Twenty-First Century*, edited by Carola M. Kaplan, Peter Mallios, and Andrea White. New York and London: Routledge, 2005. 213–222.

Richardson, Brian. *Unnatural Voices: Extreme Narration in Modern and Contemporary Fiction*. Columbus: Ohio State University Press, 2006.

Roberts, Andrew Michael. *Conrad and Masculinity*. Basingstoke: Macmillan, 2000.

Royle, Nicholas. *Jacques Derrida*. New York and London: Routledge, 2003.

Royle, Nicholas. *The Uncanny*. Manchester: Manchester University Press, 2003.

Ruppel, Richard J. *Homosexuality in the Life and Work of Joseph Conrad: Love Between the Lines*. New York, London: Routledge, 2008.

Sasaki, Ken-ichi. *Nihontekikannsei—Shokkaku to zurashi no kōzō (Japanese Sensibility: Sense of Touch and Shifting Structure)*. Tokyo: Chuokoron, 2010.

Schérer, René. *Utopies nomads: En attendant 2002*. Paris: Séguier, 2000.

Schérer, René. *Zeus hospitalier: Élogue de l'hospitalité*. 1993. Paris: La Table Ronde, 2005.

Schwarz, Daniel R. *Conrad: The Later Fiction*. London: Macmillan, 1982.

Schwarz, Daniel R. "'The Secret Sharer' as an Act of Memory." In *"The Secret Sharer": Case Studies in Contemporary Criticism*, by Joseph Conrad, edited by Daniel R. Schwarz. Boston: Bedford, 1993. 95–111.

Seeber, Hans Ulrich. "Surface as Suggestive Energy: Fascination and Voice in Conrad's 'Heart of Darkness.'" In *Joseph Conrad's Heart of Darkness*. Bloom's Modern Critical Interpretations, edited by Harold Bloom. New York: Infobase, 2008. 79–94.

Shakespeare, William. *King John*, edited by Yoshiko Ueno. Tokyo: Hakusuisha, 1983.

Shakespeare, William. *King John. The Arden Shakespeare*, edited by E. A. J. Honingsmann. London: Bloomsbury, 2007.

Sherry, Norman. *Conrad: The Critical Heritage*. London: Routledge, 1973.

Simmons, Allan H. "Representing 'the Simple and the Voiceless': Story-Telling in 'The Nigger of the 'Narcissus.'" *The Conradian,* vol. 24, no. 1 (Spring 1999): 43–57.

Simmons, Allan H. *Joseph Conrad*. London: Macmillan, 2006.

Simmons, Allan H., ed. *Joseph Conrad in Context*. Cambridge: Cambridge University Press, 2009.

Sparrow, Edward. H. "Conrad's Most Unsuitable Ground for *A Duel*." *L'Epoque Conradienne* 24 (1998): 45–63.

Stallman, R. W. "Conrad and 'The Secret Sharer.'" *Conrad's Secret Sharer and the Critics*, by Joseph Conrad, edited by Bruce Harkness. Belmont, CA: Wadsworth, 1962. 94–109.

Swift, Simon. *Hannah Arendt*. London and New York: Routledge, 2009.

Teets, Bruce F. "Literary Impressionism in Ford Madox Ford, Joseph Conrad and Related Writers." Reprinted in vol. IV of *Joseph Conrad: Critical Assessments*, edited by Keith Carabine. Robertsbridge, UK: Helm Information, 1992. 35–42.

Torchiana, Donald T. "Myth, Mirror, and Metropolis." In Joseph Conrad, *The Nigger of the "Narcissus,"* edited by Robert Kimbrough. New York and London: W. W. Norton, 1979. 275–287.

Ukai, Satoshi. *Otosuruchikara (Responsibility): Kitarubekikotoba tachi e (Towards Words that Are to Come)*. Tokyo: Seidosha, 2003.

Ukai, Satoshi. *Shuken no Kanata de (Beyond the Horizon of Sovereignty)*. Tokyo: Iwanami Shoten, 2008.

Umeki, Tatsuro. "Text wo Shihai shinai tame ni (Against Appropriation of the Text)." In *Gendai Shiso (revue de la pensée d'aujourd'hui): Special Memorial Issue on Jacques Derrida*. Tokyo: Seidosha, 2004. 159–161.

Wake, Paul. *Conrad's Marlow: Narrative and death in "Youth," Heart of Darkness, Lord Jim and Chance*. Manchester and New York: Manchester University Press, 2007.

Washida, Kiyokazu. *"Kiku"koto no Chikara (Power of Hearing): Essays on Clinical Philosophy*. Tokyo: Hankyu Communications, 1999.

Washida, Kiyokazu. *"Matsu" to iu koto (Waiting)*. Tokyo: Kadokawa, 2006.

Watson, Garry. *Opening Doors: Thoughts from (and of) the Outside*. Aurora, CO: The Davies Group, 2008.

Watt, Ian, ed. *Conrad: The Secret Agent. A Casebook*. London: Macmillan, 1973.

Watt, Ian. *Conrad in the Nineteenth Century*. Berkeley and Los Angeles: University of California Press, 1979.

Watt, Ian. *Essays on Conrad*. Cambridge: Cambridge University, 2000.

Watts, Cedric. *The Deceptive Text: An Introduction to Covert Plot*. Brighton, UK: Harvester Press, 1984.

Watts, Cedric. *A Preface to Conrad*. 2nd ed. 1982. London and New York: Longman, 1993

White, Allon. "Conrad and the Rhetoric of Enigma," in *The Uses of Obscurity: The Fiction of Early Modernism*. London, Boston, and Henley, UK: Routledge & Kegan Paul, 1981. 108–129.

White, Andrea. "Conrad and Modernism." In *A Historical Guide to Joseph Conrad*, edited by John G. Peters. Oxford: Oxford University Press, 2010. 163–196.

Whitehead, Anne. *Trauma Fiction*. Edinburgh: Edinburgh University Press, 2004.

Whitehead, Anne. *Memory*. London and New York: Routledge, 2009.

Wiley, Paul L. *Conrad's Measure of Man*. New York: Gordian Press, 1966.

Wordsworth, William. *The Prelude: A Parallel Text*, edited by J. C. Maxwell. Harmondsworth, UK: Penguin, 1971.

Wright, W. F. *Romance and Tragedy in Joseph Conrad*. New York: Russell & Russell, 1966.

Yagi, Shigeki. *"Kantai" no Seishinshi (Intellectual History of "Hospitality": From Scandinavian Mythology to Foucault, Levinas and Beyond)*. Tokyo: Kodansha, 2007.

Yamaguchi, Masao. *Bunka to Ryogisei (Culture and Ambiguity)*. Tokyo: Iwanami, 2000.

Yelton, Donald C. *Mimesis and Metaphor: An Inquiry into the Genesis and Scope of Conrad's Symbolic Imagery*. The Hague and Paris: Mouton, 1967.

Yuasa, Hiroo. *Outousuru Yobikake (Responding Call)*. Tokyo: Miraisha, 2009.

Index